Stephen R. D
the Modern

Stephen R. Donaldson and the Modern Epic Vision

A Critical Study of the "Chronicles of Thomas Covenant" Novels

CHRISTINE BARKLEY

CRITICAL EXPLORATIONS IN
SCIENCE FICTION AND FANTASY, 17

Donald E. Palumbo *and* C.W. Sullivan III, *series editors*

McFarland & Company, Inc., Publishers
Jefferson, North Carolina, and London

LIBRARY OF CONGRESS CATALOGUING-IN-PUBLICATION DATA

Barkley, Christine, 1949–
    Stephen R. Donaldson and the modern epic vision : a critical
study of the "Chronicles of Thomas Covenant" novels /
Christine Barkley.
    [Donald Palumbo and C.W. Sullivan III, series editors]
        p.   cm. — (Critical explorations in science fiction
        and fantasy ; 17)

    Includes bibliographical references and index.

    ISBN 978-0-7864-4288-1
    softcover : 50# alkaline paper ∞

    1. Donaldson, Stephen R.— Criticism and interpretation.
    2. Epic literature, American — History and criticism.
    3. Fantasy fiction, American — History and criticism.
    I. Title.
    PS3554.O469Z56   2009
    813'.54 — dc22   2009005915

British Library cataloguing data are available

Cover images ©2009 Shutterstock

Manufactured in the United States of America

*McFarland & Company, Inc., Publishers
   Box 611, Jefferson, North Carolina 28640
   www.mcfarlandpub.com*

To Laura, Faye, and Kaylee,
who keep the wonder alive

Acknowledgments

My thanks go to Virginia Dall, Laura Lawn, and Judy Cater for their help and support in preparing this book. Diane Lutz and Tom Nelson supplied inspiration and encouragement, without which the book could not have come together as it did. Palomar College granted the sabbatical during which the book was begun. Darla, Jesse, Faye, and Matthew gave valuable insights. But I am especially grateful to Louise Kantro and Sandra Burns for all their supportive, constructive criticism. I also appreciate Steve Donaldson for his encouragement and the valuable time he spent answering my questions.

Table of Contents

Preface

Stephen R. Donaldson is a popular, yet critically under-represented, modern American writer. In scope and imagination, he rivals J.R.R. Tolkien; in complexity, one might argue, only Shakespeare's Hamlet equals Thomas Covenant. Donaldson's fantasy series "The Chronicles of Thomas Covenant, the Unbeliever" juxtaposes the modern, ironic world view of today with the epic, heroic world view of the Land's inhabitants to illustrate his solution to our modern problems; to resolve disparate dialectics, we must, as Western literature uniquely always has, link them in a both/and resolution which Donaldson calls the "eye of the paradox." Far from providing only "escapist" fantasy literature, Donaldson engages the reader in a serious, modern discussion of our need for imagination, responsibility, and acceptance of our limitations and culpabilities to become actualized humans. In re-introducing the epic vision to modern literature, he helps us resolve our paralysis due to today's seemingly insurmountable problems of alienation, pollution, disease, despair, global warming, extinction of entire species, and possible total destruction from nuclear or biological weapons of mass destruction. It is no wonder that most modern writers do not want to tackle the overwhelming problems we face today. They would be impossible to solve without a sense of epic vision.

Donaldson sets enormous goals for himself and then, seemingly effortlessly, achieves them. In his *Epic Fantasy and the Modern World*, he articulates his purpose in writing fantasy literature: "to make epic fantasy relevant to modern literature, to contemporary perceptions of what it means to be human."[1] And despite the fact that our age has wallowed in its ugly wasteland with literature that has forgotten the heroic in man, Donaldson makes of common man — no, not common man but a most uncommon man, a leper — a hero for our age. In doing so he releases us from the stranglehold of our ironic world view. Though he is an enormously popular writer — the books of the "Chronicles" have been on the *New York Times* best seller list for months — few critics have taken him seriously. To date one scholarly book, W.A. Senior's *Stephen R. Donaldson's Chronicles of Thomas Covenant: Varia-*

tions on the Fantasy Tradition, has been published. An unpublished dissertation, Benjamin Laskar's *Suicide and the Absurd: the Influence of Jean-Paul Sartre's and Albert Camus's Existentialism on Stephen R. Donaldson's "The Chronicles of Thomas Covenant, the Unbeliever,"* is available in part online. Only about a dozen critical articles, other than reviews, have been published to date. Most of these works analyze Donaldson's novels either as fantasy or as modern literature; my book illustrates that Donaldson wants his readers to combine the two world views.

In contrast, many critical books and articles have been published on J. R. R. Tolkien, and rightly so as he was the pioneer of the fantasy genre. I myself have published six articles on Tolkien, in the United States and in England, one of which was translated into Spanish for an anthology published in Spain, and into Italian for a critical journal in Italy. Though Tolkien's work is set in another world, nevertheless it has a distinctly modern feel, and Tom Shippey claims that Tolkien spoke for the twentieth century. Tolkien died in 1973. Since then much has changed in our world, and the crises of our day are very different from those of Tolkien's time although we are also still resolving some of the conflicts from the earlier part of last century. Stephen R. Donaldson speaks to the conditions of the latter half of the twentieth century through today: alienation, global warming, the proliferation of weapons of mass destruction, to name a few. In addition, he does so in an imaginative and original way. One purpose of my book is to show how Donaldson carries on the tradition begun by Tolkien and expands on its purpose.

My study of Donaldson's "Chronicles" began for a talk I was asked to give at a Mythopoeic conference, Mythcon, in 1984. Donaldson was the guest artist. The paper I wrote arguing Donaldson's right to be called the heir to Tolkien was published in *Mythlore* and reprinted as part of the edition on Donaldson in *Contemporary Literary Criticism*. The present book, *Stephen R. Donaldson and the Modern Epic Vision: A Critical Study of the "Chronicles of Thomas Covenant" Novels*, is based on a thorough study of Donaldson's work over many years of teaching his fantasy. I began the book during a sabbatical in 2004 and finished over the course of the next three years; however, I have been researching and gathering material for the book for more than twenty years. It is entirely based on Donaldson's "Chronicles" and does not include analysis of either his Mordant's Need books, his Gap science fiction series, his detective fiction written under the pseudonym of Reed Stephens, or any of his short stories.

As I started writing the book, I realized that I could not analyze all aspects of the "Chronicles" under the thesis I chose: to study Donaldson's work as a way to bring an epic vision back to modern literature. Donaldson's stated purpose, articulated in his *Epic Fantasy in the Modern World*, was "I want to reclaim the epic vision as part of our sense of who we are, as part of what it means to be human."[2] I argue that he has accomplished this goal and perhaps even gone beyond his original purpose to include the way that man finds meaning in a world he cannot control. So my planned analysis of the Christian allusions in Donaldson's work and his advances in narrative style in modern literature will have to wait for the next book I write or for another author. I discuss briefly, but not in the detail these subjects deserve, the ecology of the Land, the foiling between characters, and the Land as Covenant's dream and what this reveals of the psychology of modern man.

In this book, however, I illustrate how Donaldson uses the fantasy genre to engage the most important question of our time: how can man recapture a sense of his own importance and the perception that his choices matter? The superstring theory in physics works as a good metaphor for Donaldson's approach to our current ironic world view and its seeming-opposite heroic world view. As the superstring theory unites what had been seen as disparate theories of matter in physics between the quantum theory and Einstein's general relativity theory, as it explores mathematical principles which allow the truths of both conflicting theories to be united in the 10th dimension, so Stephen Donaldson's world view, embodied in Thomas Covenant, which is both epic and ironic, unites our age to the heroic age of the past. Modern literature had relegated the heroic perception of man to our past; Donaldson brings it back into our present. Through Covenant, Donaldson shows how even a modern ironic man can recapture his epic vision through his acceptance of responsibility, by his personal choices, and by his engagement with the crises of the world to create the personal, redemptive meaning of his life. When this transformation occurs within a man (whether through his dream or through his real or imaginary experiences in the Land or only through our reading about and experiencing those experiences vicariously), the barrier to the epic vision is shattered.

Introduction

Stephen R. Donaldson, in his "Chronicles of Thomas Covenant, the Unbeliever" series, stands at the pinnacle of 3,000 years of the best thought in Western civilization, poised to help modern literature out of its paralysis and back into purpose and meaning in the twenty-first century. Too long has the literature of our time wallowed in despair and cynicism, with so-called heroes who cannot act heroically without looking pathetic or cartoonish. Donaldson can help us recover a sense of wonder and passionate engagement with our world, can show us the potential for epic success ordinary man is still capable of achieving even now. In the wisdom of the Western canon's great minds, he finds new, relevant insights and thus leads us away from the narrow-minded restrictions on thought so prevalent in the literature of the last century.

Wisdom is cumulative. Therefore, great literature must be both universal (true and meaningful always) and relevant (true and significant today). Great writers, great literature does not ignore but builds on the foundation of past literature as it evaluates new philosophic perspectives. History and world views keep changing, from peace to wartime, from the focus on reason in the Enlightenment to the emphasis on spirituality in the Romantic era, from the carefree lifestyle of the Roaring Twenties through the long struggles of the Great Depression. Like a pendulum our world situation swings from prosperity and optimism to danger and cynicism. Great literature must find truth in any situation, must be universal, but must also speak to the specific situations of its time and find ways to resolve the challenges never faced before; therefore, it must always be looking for new understanding, new and better solutions to our past issues but also new insights and answers to our unique present concerns. No one answer or world view is valid and relevant for all time periods, but as the pendulum swings back and forth between the focus on mind and heart, we draw closer to the truth which is found only by uniting the two in the center, within what Donaldson calls the eye of the paradox. He means accepting both parts of any dialectic or "the eye of stability

5

within the core of contradictions."[1] Donaldson's main character, Thomas Covenant, acknowledges that he needs both dialectical sides of any contradiction. In *The One Tree*, Covenant claims to have balanced the controversies within himself—his sense of his own culpabilities and his great desire to preserve the beauty and goodness of the Land. This juxtaposition of opposites gives Covenant his power. Among modern American authors, Stephen R. Donaldson is one of the few who understands this need for better answers, for workable solutions to seemingly insurmountable problems, and steers us to find our own answers by confronting and uniting the dialectics of our times. In doing so, we draw closer to ultimate Truth.

New knowledge does not inevitably invalidate the insights of the past. We cannot unlearn what we knew yesterday, nor should we. But best expressed by examining Blake's polarities of innocence and experience, new knowledge/experience which robs us of our innocence is not necessarily "better." However, by a logical, yet as it turns out limiting, series of steps, the writers of the twentieth century came to focus almost exclusively on realism in our literature; from the late eighteenth century to the present, novels have abandoned spirituality and feeling/desire and focused on only what we could validate scientifically. By relying on objective fact, we have ignored the wisdom of Keats from "Ode on a Grecian Urn": "Beauty is Truth, Truth Beauty, that is all ye know on earth and all ye need to know."[2] We can no longer accept or resolve such paradoxes. Many modern writers are guilty of either/or fallacious reasoning. Donaldson brings us back to the same kind of both/and thinking that has resonated throughout the greatest works of Western literature, represented best by Shakespeare, and that is reflected in the paradox of Keats's statement. Donaldson addresses several dialectics and always with the purpose of getting us to conjoin seeming opposites to find the eye of the paradox.

The Western tradition of literature has been a balancing act between rationality/reason and emotionality/spirituality. Jeffrey Hart best explains this in his *Smiling Though the Cultural Catastrophe: Toward the Revival of Higher Education* as the union of Athens and Jerusalem. Briefly to suggest the two ideals, he contrasts the heroic virtues of Homer, as exhibited by Achilles, with the equally demanding adherence to spiritual Law put forth by Moses. These virtues are further refined by the concept of the Ideal Self taught by Socrates in Greece and developed through self-reflection in the teachings of Jesus, who brought spirituality away from mere adherence to religious laws to internalizing goodness (from "thou shalt not commit adultery" to not even lusting in one's own heart). While Western writers have sometimes vacillated between the two views, taken as a whole, Western literature has acknowledged both philosophies, and the uniqueness of Western thought is that we have chosen to try to resolve and juxtapose the dialectics rather than taking the more simplistic, though erroneous, either/or approach. Hart defines the synthesis of Athens and Jerusalem thus: "the mind of the West was born amid tension and contradiction and draws strength from refusing to be either-or but rather both-and, both Greek and Jew."[3]

The creative tension between the world views espoused in Athens and Jerusalem has created the uniquely successful mindset of Western civilization. Jeffrey Hart is a recent advocate of this theory, though he traces it back to Thomas Jefferson and Frederick Nietzsche. He claims that although the beliefs of Athens (from Homer in the heroic age through Socrates in the Golden Age of fifth century B.C. Greece) and Jerusalem (from the laws of Moses to the teachings of Jesus) may appear dialectically opposed, the fact that Western thought can embrace both and, in fact, studies both to discover truths about our world, has resulted in more rapid and greater scientific advancements in the West than under Islam or communism, where either religion or philosophy rules politics and economic concerns. The willingness on our part to move away from a society based entirely on religion to one that embraces science and its resultant technological improvements is, in part, the cause of our economic success when compared to the rest of the world, especially those areas of the world still mired in either/or thinking. Donaldson's two conflicting world views — our modern perspective expressed by Thomas Covenant and the more heroic world view of the inhabitants of the Land — clash at first, but become resolved by the end of each series.

In *Acts of Recovery*, Jeffrey Hart explains that the central Christian concept of Incarnation (spirit becoming matter/flesh) may help to explain our willingness to accept what other faiths see as separate concepts. In Christian doctrine the spiritual deity, the Word became something concrete when Jesus was born as man; both spirit and flesh existed within the same person. "In the beginning was the Word and the Word was with God, and the Word was God. ... And the Word became flesh and dwelt among us."[4] Therefore, we can learn about spiritual truths from concrete examples. Jesus's parables are another good illustration of this material way of looking at spiritual concepts, as are the conceits of the Metaphysical poets of the seventeenth century. Donaldson's own myriad of jarring metaphors works equally well to explain abstractions in concrete form.

A study of the changing view of the hero throughout Western literature from Homer's Achilles and the Bible's Moses and Jesus, through the Greek philosophers, to Dante, Shakespeare, and down to Steven Crane's Henry Fleming (*Red Badge of Courage*), James Joyce's Leopold Bloom (*Ulysses*), and J. R. R. Tolkien's Frodo Baggins (*The Lord of the Rings*) will show that Donaldson's various characters reflect or contrast with changing concepts of the "hero" throughout Western literature. This analysis is well developed by W.A. Senior in his *Variations on a Fantasy Tradition: Stephen R. Donaldson's Chronicles of Thomas Covenant.* Senior posits that Covenant is a uniquely American hero, one who both does and does not fit the traditional role of hero as defined by Joseph Campbell's *The Hero with a Thousand Faces.* Donaldson presents many different kinds of heroes like those from the canon of great Western literature, illustrating how he builds on and combines the wisdom of the past. If we examine just one dialectic as an illustration of our definition of virtue, the cowardice/courage polarity, it can be seen that almost every major author responds in some way to the question of "how can man face his circumstances with courage?" In Donaldson's *Lord Foul's Bane,* the beggar (who is identified as the Land's Creator) in Covenant's "real" world poses a hypothetical situation to Covenant that will parallel his experiences in the Land. He asks Covenant to define the ethics of a man who is transported to another world and told that he must fight to the death as the representative of his own world, and if he loses, then his world will be destroyed. However, the man refuses to engage in single combat for a cause not his own. Also, he thinks he must be dreaming as many things in this new environment are impossible: he can smell sounds, see the colors of smells. So when he is attacked, he does not fight back, and the beggar questions whether the man is brave or cowardly. Covenant does not answer the beggar, but his responses to his experiences in the Land provide Donaldson's answer to this question.

The issue of heroism or courage is such a universal concern that a new exploration of the topic is needed by each new generation because our life situations change so radically. For example, Homer's Odysseus faces the dangers of sailing off beyond the horizon into the unknown or dying by arrow or spear or sword thrust in battle. Down through the ages the unknown has changed from sailing within the Mediterranean Sea, to sailing around the world, to flying to the moon, Jupiter, or somewhere beyond our solar system; and battles now cause shell shock and the possibility of civilians, even children with bombs strapped to them, committing suicide in order to destroy others. We must defend against biological weapons as well as bullets now. The post–Vietnam War era, the late twentieth century to now, seems mired in the depressing view that heroism is futile or impossible because "winning" is impossible. Though we can strive to be courageous, we appear naïve for trying. No matter how we react to dangers, we are inevitably left with madness or guilt or rage rather than a sense of accomplishment or pride. Donaldson, by showing many different kinds of courage, incorporates many views already explored in Western literature, including what seems to be the modern view, to show how limited our options have become and, hopefully, to help us recapture the potential for courage and success, despite our circumstances, by presenting a new approach.

The heroic stand of fighting against overwhelming odds is represented in the Western canon through, among others, Achilles, Beowulf, or Henry V: sometimes the hero fights bravely and loses his life but his side wins, in part based on his effort; sometimes the hero wins at first but eventually faces a foe greater than himself; sometimes the battle is won even against overwhelming odds. In each situation, great writers who analyze the heroism of their protagonists do not simplistically portray the hero choosing to be brave without qualms or fears. In *The Iliad* Achilles at first refuses to fight due to a petty argument with Agamemnon; then in *The Odyssey*, his spirit in Hades claims that he would rather have lived a long, obscure life than the short, heroic life he did live, effectively undercutting the classical heroic concept of *kleos* (reputation for prowess in battle) as the ultimate achievement. Henry V is afraid that the sins of his father and Henry IV's questionable claim to the throne and to his title of king might affect God's judgment about the outcome of the Battle of Agincourt, yet his tired, outnumbered men find inspiration and win the day. On the Jerusalem side of the dialectic, Moses exhibits physical bravery standing almost alone within easy reach by Pharoah's guards to demand the release of the Jewish slaves of Egypt. The concept of heroism, of what is admirable, of what calls forth the greatest amount of courage from willing participants that comes from Achilles's and Moses's actions and the ultimate sacrifice of Beowulf or those at the Battle of Agincourt, is still often revived in modern fantasy as well. In the mid-twentieth century, such heroism is rare in mainstream fiction and found mostly in fantasy fiction: in Tolkien's *The Lord of the Rings*, the ride of the Rohirrim, the last march of the Ents, Dernhelm/Eowyn's challenge of the Nazgul, Frodo's trek across Mordor all have the feel of futility, of imminent defeat, yet the effort is still made, and because it is attempted, success is possible.

Many of Donaldson's characters reflect this same attitude toward heroic courage. The Lords all fight bravely, sometimes sacrificing themselves for the success of the overall battle, like Mhoram's parents, Variol and Tamarantha, at the battle of Soaring Woodhelven; Verement standing alone against the Giant Raver Fleshharrower at Doom's Retreat; or Mhoram heroically charging against the Giant Raver Satansfist. The Bloodguard and Foamfollower fight for the Company at Soaring Woodhelven as does the First of the Search for those of Starfare's Gem when they escape from Bhrathairealm. The long, forced march of the Waymark and the heroic stand of the few at Doriendor Corishev to allow the rest of the army to escape toward Garroting Deep are other good examples of the stamina and determination that are part of our standard idea of courage. Hamako with the help of the Waynhim sacrifices himself to destroy the *croyel* of the one Arghule so that Covenant can escape. In each situation, their motivations, hopes for success, the complications of their own individual sense of guilt or self-worth are also explored by Donaldson. Since courage is considered a universal virtue or concept, great authors have and will always be analyzing it.

Often at stake when courage is called for is physical survival, life or death. However, physical bravery against one's enemies is only one kind of courage. Another kind of courage takes into consideration the willingness to look inside ourselves, to evaluate our strengths and weaknesses honestly and to strive to improve ourselves. This self-evaluation, the Greek philosophers would have us do to improve our minds and our reasoning ability. Jesus would also want this but for spiritual growth. And, indeed, the traditional kind of heroism in battle is not the only kind of heroism/courage Donaldson explores. The conquest of fear within one's self is sometimes more important than the winning of battles. When courage is internalized, when the battle takes place within the character himself, it is often not apparent that it is courageous unless there is a narrator (omniscient or first person) to document the struggle. Of course, if the "Chronicles" are all part of Covenant's dream, then all the conflicts are internal.

Again the differing interpretations of inward courage are a reflection of the major tenets of great Western literature. The movement from 1200 B.C. to 500 B.C. in Athens and to the time of Jesus in Jerusalem in both world views was to take the prevailing concept of heroism (Achilles or Moses) and internalize the philosophy. Thus, virtue in Greek heroes becomes the quest for self-knowledge to Socrates. Moses's commandments and focus on law evolve into Jesus's sense of personal holiness in the Sermon on the Mount. Socrates wanted cognition/understanding and strove to discover his Ideal Self; Jesus wanted not just adherence to law ("thou shalt not kill") but purity of spirit (do not even harbor anger in your heart). The uniqueness of Western belief is that somehow these two views can converge or at least co-exist, can be compatible, can lead to a better understanding of truth and to greater self-awareness. The inner struggle for perfection is the focus, not some outward battle; the classic conflict of one vs. self rather than one vs. another can best exemplify inner courage. Therefore, Jesus's battle is fought when he is alone in the garden of Gethsemane and he resolves to accept his fate. And the real battle in a novel like Steven Crane's *Red Badge of Courage* is more universal than the story of actual fighting at a battle like Gettysburg during the Civil War in America; it reveals the inner conflict of Henry Fleming, who first runs from battle but then finds his courage and returns. In J.R.R. Tolkien's *The Hobbit*, Bilbo discovers that his greatest battle is fought in the tunnel leading to the dragon Smaug's lair: "It was at this point that Bilbo stopped. Going on from there was the bravest thing he ever did. The tremendous things that happened afterward were as nothing compared to it. He fought the real battle in the tunnel alone, before he ever saw the vast danger that lay in wait."[5] He first had to conquer his own fear.

In Donaldson's works, many characters, including Covenant, Linden, Mhoram, Trell and Triock, Seadreamer, Hollinscrave, and even to some extent Findail, face and overcome their own personal fears. Donaldson illustrates many kinds of inner courage, including the personal judgment between right and wrong even in the face of cultural indoctrination to the contrary: Mhoram shows courage in sharing with the other Lords the knowledge that allowed Kevin to call up the Ritual of Desecration; Memla rebels against the Clave and what she has believed all her life (as do Sunder and Hollian); Lady Alif is willing to help the Search escape the Kasreyn. Even the *jheherrin*, who have no physical prowess, nevertheless overcome their own fear to aid Covenant in defiance of Lord Foul on the chance that by doing so they can be freed.

Covenant's own courage is very complex, contradictory, and paradoxical. Twentieth century literature complicated any exploration of heroism and courage when Joseph Conrad forced us to acknowledge our own heart of darkness, our own potential for evil. Once we admit we are flawed, it is hard to attempt to be courageous. For centuries our literary tradition taught us that God protects the righteous (hence, the tournaments of knights in the Medieval period), and if we have to admit we have culpabilities, we wonder how our weaknesses will affect our potential success in courageous endeavors. For Covenant to go on despite guilt over the rape of Lena, despite ignorance over how to use wild magic, despite feeling powerless and not wanting to become involved, shows a special kind of courage, one which seems to paralyze most others in the modern age. At the end of each series, Donaldson forces us into the eye of the paradox, as Covenant faces Foul but does not fight him. The pacifism of Donaldson, the concept that we cannot win wars by fighting battles, is here given its strongest test. In the first series, all the passion that has kept Covenant going even on a broken ankle, in spite of dehydration, cold, and hunger, is directed in anger against Foul; Covenant wants nothing more than to destroy Foul physically through force, and the only, or at least most common, means of accomplishing that task is to kill, imprison, or otherwise physically constrain Foul according to the prevailing wisdom of the literature of our time. Covenant says, "'I'm going to bring Foul's Creche down around his ears.'"[6] But Covenant's experiences give him wisdom to try new techniques, knowing the old ones never ultimately worked. Through Covenant's ultimate choices, Donaldson gives us two new approaches — first, either Foamfollower's and the Lords' laughter at the personification of despair and hatred until it is diminished (*The Power That Preserves*), or second, Covenant's surrender and sacrifice of himself in order to be able to fight from beyond the border of death (*White Gold Wielder*). Hence

Donaldson's solution — that the most important battle takes place within a character and that the greatest expression of courage and strength is to refrain from fighting — follows the best wisdom of Jesus ("turn the other cheek") and more recently Gandhi and Martin Luther King, Jr.

Following the Western tradition down through the ages, Hart claims that Dante added to the both/and union between logic and spirituality the value of emotion, probably introduced to Western thought by the Troubadour poets of Medieval France. Dante's importance within this dialectic was to bring passion/love/emotion to the intellectual debate regarding truth. Thus, the both/and eye of the paradox of Western thought is not just a combination of reason and spiritual inspiration (which could be explored entirely dispassionately), but also includes human passion as a positive trait as well. Again, Donaldson is embracing the best of the Western canon as Covenant's passions (anger and guilt, but also love and loyalty) are his strongest motivators; even unbelief and acceptance-of-the-Land-as-real are battling passions within him. Indeed, twentieth century critics have criticized Donaldson for his writing style, saying that he exaggerates Covenant's and his other characters' emotional responses. Actually, what critics call exaggeration is simply Donaldson's emphasis on integrating emotional response into his eye of the paradox solution.

T.S. Eliot places Dante on par with Shakespeare in importance to Western thought, but for very different reasons: Shakespeare understands human nature, but Dante comprehends the extremes of emotion better. Dante's two guides, Virgil and Beatrice, represent reason and love, with reason here meaning both rationality and spirituality. Dante establishes the dialectic, not between two sources of insight (reason and spiritual revelation or intuition), but between thought and emotion. Shakespeare comprehends the both/and resolution to dialectics but his preference for the golden mean, control of one's emotions rather than allowing the lows of depression or the highs of joy, represents a "neither" approach to passion. Donaldson favors Dante's acceptance of the extremes of emotion over control exercised rationally. In this sense Donaldson takes a both/and stance on questions of reason/spirituality and stoicism/passion.

Since the Renaissance, Shakespeare has been considered by most to be the greatest writer in the Western canon because he presents a clash of ideas in the guise of normal personal conflicts and thus explores not only interpersonal relationships, often of those in power, but also illustrates how the conflict between dominant world views could play out. In addition, he represents the clash of Athens and Jerusalem so central to Western thought as best exemplified by his most complex and enduring character: Hamlet. Hamlet is caught in seemingly unbridgeable contradictions: "thou shalt not kill," "revenge [Old Hamlet's] foul and most unnatural murder," and "taint not thy mind." Hamlet cannot resolve his contradictions and live. Covenant does resolve his dialectics; he fuses venom and leprosy with wild magic and passion in the Banefire. By unifying the opposites within himself and recognizing the lesson of Caer-Caveral, Covenant learns how best to defeat Lord Foul's purpose to break the Arch of Time.

In Donaldson's "Chronicles" this clash of world views plays out several ways. Like the conflict between the Renaissance Christian Humanist view and the Machiavellian view that Shakespeare explored, Donaldson contrasts our modern world view with the old world beliefs of the old Lords, Berek and Kevin, which are like the Renaissance Christian Humanist world view. Berek is able to call forth lava from a volcano, the Fire Lions. The arras in Covenant's room in Revelstone depicts this scene: the earth itself chooses sides between Berek and the King, and nature actively supports Berek's cause, reinforcing the idea that the earth has power and can/will act. The combination of Prothall's knowledge and power along with the recovered Staff of Law and Covenant's wild magic ring defy rational explanation to do the same thing in *Lord Foul's Bane*. In Shakespeare's *Richard II*, Richard calls on God's angels to fight for him.

> For every man that Bolingbroke [Henry IV] hath press'd
> To lift shrewd steel against our golden crown,
> God for his Richard hath in heavenly pay
> A glorious angel: then, if angels fight,
> Weak men must fall, for heaven still guards the right [3.2.59–63].

These examples illustrate the Renaissance Christian Humanist view of divine intervention as part of an overarching plan. In our modern world we say that we have discarded such superstitions, as part of our either/or response to the world (either there is science or there are miracles). Here the eye of the paradox is very complex. Does Divinity (in the form of a god or nature itself) support Good or are individuals alone responsible for a righteous outcome? In Donaldson's "Chronicles," the people of the Land do not rely on the Creator to intervene on their behalf. In fact, they acknowledge that he is powerless to help them without destroying the Arch of Time that keeps Foul imprisoned. But the people of the Land do accept the "divine" intervention on the part of the Earth itself and accept that the Lords can master some Earthpower and that places such as Andelain can resist Foul's corruptions, which would represent divine intervention if the Earth itself were considered sentient. In our real world, do we not do the same thing when we harness the power of the waterfall or wind, or the atom? The difference is that now we acknowledge "science" for that power, where Richard II would have credited God, and the Lords of the Land, Earthpower. Donaldson's paradoxical view does not let the question end with the repudiation of the unrealistic view that earth can and will rise up to protect "the right." At the end of *Lord Foul's Bane*, Covenant unconsciously and unwittingly calls on the Fire Lions, as an aspect of the natural world of the Land, to defend the Lords and Company, and he later also calls the Ranyhyn to rescue them. In fact, the Lords' entire study of Earthpower is precisely to acknowledge, not deny, the power of nature and to learn how to control it. Another world view, closer to the Machiavellian view of the Renaissance which Shakespeare so often contrasted to the Humanist view, is our modern "realistic" view of scientific objectivism, which will be more fully explored later. Through the character of Covenant, Donaldson is constantly contrasting these two world views, much as Shakespeare does.

In Shakespeare's *Hamlet*, the ghost's command to Hamlet to "taint not thy mind" with anger or blood lust could apply to Covenant, and Donaldson states in the conclusions of each of the first two "Chronicles" that Evil/Despite (Lord Foul) cannot be conquered the wrong way. As Shakespeare brought a Christian understanding to the pagan Revenge tradition, Donaldson advocates a pacifist view to the resolution of conflicts. Hart claims, "The Ghost now supplements the heroic demand for justice and revenge with the interior command of the Sermon on the Mount. This is surely one of the contradictions that tear at the heart of the prince, indeed perhaps the most powerful one."[7] Heroes must combine the outward heroics of Achilles or other Greek heroes with the adherence to Law demanded by Moses, while also embodying the inner perfection, awareness of logic/reason of Socrates and the purity of spirit of Jesus. Hamlet must live up to the "heroic ideal of Justice urged by the Ghost, and also the interiority of Christianity."[8] Hamlet's attempt to resolve these dialectics makes him the quintessential Western Hero. Donaldson adds to this concept of heroism the power of passion — the ability to understand and embrace the depths of despair and the heights of joy and glory as explored by Dante, going beyond the Golden Mean of the Sophists and Shakespeare, and even attempting to go beyond Homer and Virgil in epic scale, not the either/or world of good and evil in conflict from Dante, but the both/and of Shakespeare with the union of passion to reason and spirituality (what Hamlet attempts to reach but does not achieve). Donaldson not only shows Covenant juxtaposing the both/and of logic and conscience, but he also includes emotional engagement rather than objective evaluation (not the dispassionate intellectual debate of "to be or not to be" alone but also the high passion of a Wagnerian opera).

Covenant is definitely on par with Hamlet for complexity in Covenant's insistence on a rational universe (the Land as a dream), his struggles with worthiness, his assumption of responsibility for Justice single-handedly, and in the 2nd "Chronicles" his willingness to take on the corruption of the state (the Clave). The contradictions of Hamlet could be said of Covenant:

> He also has fully engaged most or even all of the contradicting possibilities of the Renaissance, from the lofty aspirations of Pico della Mirandola ["what a piece of work is man. How noble in reason!"] to bottomless skepticism, from the ideals of humanism to recurrent thoughts of suicide, from the intellectual reaches of Wittenberg to mocking cynicism and an awareness of the yawning grave.[9]

The greatness of Western thought is shown by how we combine these beliefs. "Because Hamlet was everything, he ran the risk of being nothing."[10] One of the central defining characteristics of Covenant is that he is both everything and nothing, powerful and helpless.

> And he who wields white wild magic gold
> is a paradox.[11]

Hart cites Paul A. Canter's critical work *Hamlet* to explain the paradox further: "'the conflict between the classical and Christian traditions has been central to Western Civilization, and has provided the basis for its profoundest cultural achievements and its most deeply problematic moments. That Hamlet reflects these tensions, which reached their peak during the Renaissance, is one reason for the enduring power of the play.'"[12] Covenant wrestles with the same issues that Hamlet tackles: appearance vs. reality, predestination vs. free will, the way of force vs. the way of peace, good vs. evil (but in Donaldson as external combatants reflecting man's inner conflict).

In this last emendation of the eternal struggle, Donaldson illustrates the idea that "society" can be seen as an external entity to the individuals who make up society and that "society" can be manipulated/changed, like the Clave's manipulation of truth. When their perception of their world changes with their eating of the supposedly-poisonous aliantha, Sunder and Hollian view the Sunbane differently; they come to see it as being sustained, not fought, by the human sacrifices of the Clave. What they have accepted as good is revealed to be evil. Modern philosophy illustrated the power of changing a whole people's world view when Marx influenced our view of "society" by lessening the importance of the individual and magnifying the supremacy of group dynamics. Donaldson reacts against such abrogating of individual responsibility or individual potential. The ability to perceive truth, despite the dominance of statements to the contrary, is an essential personal virtue. Thus the internal struggles of Hamlet and Covenant to understand the realities of the worlds around them may be the most important question of their lives.

Donaldson writes throughout the "Chronicles" about the conflicts between different interpretations of reality. He argues that contradictory understandings of what is real must be accepted even if we find those contradictions within ourselves. Certainly, at first, Covenant perceives the Land and his role in solving its difficulties very differently than its inhabitants do, but eventually Covenant must accept both views. Donaldson's "Chronicles" suggest that we need to be on our guard against depictions of our world which minimize man or nature and try to redefine the good. And this modern exploration of truth is one area in which the twentieth century's either/or preference for realism has failed us, but Donaldson's eye of the paradox provides a better answer.

Like Shakespeare's both/and view of the world, another dialectic that Donaldson delineates was first explored by the Metaphysical poets of the seventeenth century: the union of abstract and concrete thought, similar to the union of spirit and matter represented by the Incarnation. Poets such as John Donne and George Herbert use metaphysical conceits to create unusual comparisons which often juxtapose seemingly disparate ideas/images. Rather than using the Petrarchan convention of comparing love to positive images only — "my love is like a red, red, rose"[13] — Donne compares the necessary parting of two lovers to a mathematical compass used to draw a perfect circle in "A Valediction: Forbidding Mourning." He also likens inviting God into his heart to a conqueror breaking down the defenses of a town in ["Batter My Heart, Three-Person God"] and provides the dialectic "for I, / Except You enthrall me never shall be free, / nor ever chaste, except You ravish me."[14] The eye of the paradox expressed here joins abstract thought (such as Keats's truth or Donne's faith) with the concrete (such as Keats's beauty or Donne's defeated city) and with high passion and idealistic moral/religious fervor. Many of Donaldson's metaphors, though not expressed in poetic form, do exactly the same thing: "Darkness murmured in his ears like the distant rumor of an avalanche"[15]; "their earlier elation ran out of them like water leaking into parched sand"[16]; "a blaze like a melody of flame sang out over the elfmound."[17] These examples are only a few of literally thousands of such metaphors in Donaldson's works.

The history of Western literature has taught us that as a culture we tend to embrace new ideas and take them to their logical extreme, find their limitations, and then explore a contrary idea which is not limited in the same way. Thus, we have vacillated between reason and imagination throughout Western literature, from the rationalism of the seventeenth century to the romanticism of the early eighteenth century, to realism, then determinism, and finally deconstructionism. But modern mainstream literature is stuck in nihilism, nothingness, existentialism, meaninglessness, and needs to find again possibility, imagination, epic vision, and hope. In his *Epic Fantasy in the Modern World*, Donaldson traces the diminution of the grandeur of man from

Beowulf (in which man is heroic, though doomed) to *Paradise Lost* (in which man is insignificant to the conflict between God and Satan), to *Idylls of the King* (in which modern man brings down the heroic Arthur), to *The Lord of the Rings* (in which Tolkien restores the epic but only by setting his tale in another time and place). Donaldson claims that his goal is to bring the epic vision back to modern literature, that our sense of ourselves as powerful, capable people, the part that strives for excellence and epic possibilities, needs to be re-embraced as part of our human potential. To understand the enormity of this task, we need to see how literature has changed to and through the twentieth century.

The modern focus on scientific objectivity began in what became known as the Enlightenment Era. Perhaps in an attempt to limit religious differences which had led to bloody wars, John Locke advocated restricting man's discourse to what could be known objectively and excluded whatever was beyond our capacity to prove scientifically, including what Plato would call Ideal Love or Ideal Self or what Jesus would have described as evil or pure good in a person. Focusing on "reality" created a scorn for superstition (and probably helped put a stop to witch burnings), and governments developed rationally. So the change produced good outcomes. But such a limited view does not validate both Athens and Jerusalem. Our modern concentration on realism in literature is a direct result of our reliance on objective truth. Hart claims that Ian Watt's concept from *The Rise of the Novel*—the "'primacy of fact as the reality of the world'"[18]—has been the defining characteristic of the modern novel. However, this view does not acknowledge the part of Western culture that developed through a desire for spiritual intuition or passion or imagination. It effectively ignores Jerusalem and Dante in exchange for a purely rational interpretation of and a demand for scientific proof for truth.

The seventeenth century Enlightenment era embraced the philosophies of rationalism, the supremacy of reason and the sophists' Golden Mean, which found the extremes of emotion abhorrent, preferring the philosophies of Athens. In "An Essay on Man," Alexander Pope says, "the proper study of mankind is man,"[19] but he means intellectually, analytically only. Donaldson claims that he chooses to write fantasy literature because one of its accepted purposes is that it explains what it means to be human, but he, of course, refers to exploring both humans' intellectual and intuitive capacities and limitations as well as revealing the extremes of emotions humans feel.

The eighteenth century Romantics in Britain and the Transcendentalists in America reacted against total reliance on rational analysis and looked for insight. The Romantics, probably in reaction to the failure of rationalists to explain all of human existence, embraced the Jerusalem focus on spiritual insight and development of the individual through inspiration, semi-religious experiences, or expression of deep emotions. However, great Western literature, though it may lean one way or the other, cannot totally dismiss the opposing view; in fact, it must maintain the tension of the dialectic and be firmly set in the both/and resolution of the supposed conflict. Friedrich Nietzsche posits that the "Ubermench" or ideal man is "'meant to unite Jerusalem and Athens at the highest level,'"[20] but we have yet to see this paragon in literature or real life. Nietzsche also recognizes the limitations of modern thinking and reliance on science to the exclusion of religion (illustrated by Matthew Arnold's "melancholy, long, retreating roar"[21] of the allegorical Sea of Faith in "Dover Beach") and argues that we need both Apollonian intellectuality (Athens) as well as Dionysian passion or religious fervor (Jerusalem).

The Romantics attacked the writers of the Enlightenment as unheroic, narrow, not concerned with morality, ignoring the depths and heights of human experience, having no ideal of self, and merely satirizing the vices and foibles of man. The focus in the Enlightenment Era on the common man allowed no sense of heroism or the extraordinary in man.

> The Romantic individualism of Wordsworth, Blake, and Goethe celebrates the vital importance of the intuitive, the irreproducible moment of insight and of direct access to truth in its unmediated essence. Each [poet] accuses science, especially in its schematic, mathematicized form, of blindness, or worse, stubborn refusal to see. Each fears a world in which scientific thought has become the sovereign mode, and recoils from the spiritual degradation and servility that, in his opinion, must inevitably come to characterize such a world.[22]

In our modern world James Joyce illustrates a similar concept he calls an epiphany. "The belief in direct, revelatory, intuitive truth to be had from communion with nature is the obverse of a deep epistemological skepticism about the kind of 'systematic' truth that is the core of scientific knowledge."[23] In Donaldson's "Chronicles" this intuitive awareness plays out in many ways: Mhoram's understanding of the key to the Ritual of Desecration, Covenant's ambiguous decision to step into the Banefire which effectively fuses the venom and wild magic in him, Covenant's change of purpose both times when he actually confronts Foul.

Novels in the nineteenth century, while still focusing on realism, took us away from the mannered drawing rooms of Jane Austen's Pemberley to the dirty streets of London populated by Charles Dickens's Fagan and the Artful Dodger. The twentieth century, as we faced the shock of world wars and a heightened awareness of man's heart of darkness, took us down what looked to be the logical progression from realism (Charles Dickens) to determinism (Thomas Hardy, Theodore Dreiser) to skepticism (Joseph Heller). In rare instances imagination crept into twentieth century "mainstream" literature, in such works as Kurt Vonnegut's *Slaughterhouse 5* or Ken Kesey's *One Flew over the Cuckoo's Nest*, but only as madness or an "unreal" or dreamlike reality. Covenant in Donaldson's "Chronicles" at first represents the extreme view that any belief in the imaginary would inevitably lead to madness and danger for he could forget the self-protection so necessary to any leper; that only the reality of his "real" world matters; that his capacity for imagination could kill him; that there could not possibly be a role in a heroic struggle for such a flawed creature as himself. Thus the ironic world view is restricting because it represses imagination and denies the tension between Athens and Jerusalem that has always been the foundation for answers to how we choose to live our lives, based on both thought/reason/analysis and faith/insight/spirituality. Our modern age has relied almost exclusively on reason/logic, and unfortunately, as we face more and more difficult obstacles to overcome and more awareness of our own individual limitations, weaknesses, and even culpabilities and thus our inability to resolve today's problems, we are left with nothing but despair. Of course, Lord Foul, the antagonist of the "Chronicles," personifies Despair/Despite. Donaldson's "Chronicles" directly attack the limitations on thought brought on by our either/or reasoning; thus Donaldson provides a symbolic solution for the paralysis of twentieth century literature in his eye of the paradox.

Donaldson builds on and reflects the major ideas from Western literature but with a distinctly modern awareness; he isn't writing just escapist literature that hearkens back to the good old days before we knew about our own heart of darkness. Nor is his message that we've fallen from a Golden World (as Tolkien believed) and the best we can hope for is a sentimental, nostalgic sense of loss in this world. Donaldson is, above all, a writer of our times. However, he is a very optimistic one. He knows all the depressing truths we've discovered, and certainly doesn't sugar-coat any ugly aspects of our truth. Donaldson chooses instead to point the way to the twenty-first century when the epic can once again be viable. Thus, he is fulfilling Northrup Frye's contention, developed in his *Anatomy of Criticism*, that the cycles of literature change from the epic to romantic to high mimetic to low mimetic to ironic and back to epic mode.[24] Whether Frye's view is a valid interpretation of literature will become apparent only if literature matches his prediction — Donaldson has stated as his goal his desire to make epic literature believable again, so he is leading the movement. Twentieth century literature wallowed in the ironic to the point where deconstructionists called it absurd even to analyze literature any more. Donaldson, on the other hand, says that he wants to refute Jean-Paul Sartre's claim that futility is the hallmark of man. He wants to turn our attention away from the depressing view of our unimportance and futility and emphasize more what makes us heroic. In fact, he proposes, our need is greater because as cultural, political, or technological change comes faster and is more jarring, mainstream literature does not provide enough examples of how we can cope. So his characters acknowledge the conditions which might frustrate and paralyze us but consciously fight to remind us that "'Man is an effective passion.'"[25] Earlier literature reinforced the importance of man, the significance of his choices, and the potential influence he can have on his own fate and on the world, though current wisdom recognizes that success must often be a collective effort relying on several individuals' participation. Donaldson, by emphasizing the both/and resolution in his eye of the paradox, is a most necessary and influential writer in the twenty-first century.

T.S. Eliot's concept of the objective correlative shows that modern literature expects literacy on the part of the reader and that modern authors rely on comparison and contrast to other authors' points and depiction of character, action, and theme to express their own ideas and world views. The most obvious example is James Joyce's deliberate patterning of Leopold Bloom's experiences in the modern world in *Ulysses* (the Roman name for Odysseus) on Homer's of Odysseus's feats in *The Odyssey*. Joyce's purpose in making the comparison is to claim that modern man can no longer act heroically. Donaldson uses the best ideas from the entire Western canon to illustrate with his characters that exactly the opposite conclusion is more valid and reasonable.

All of Western literature tries to answer the questions "What are the ideal characteristics of man? What makes us virtuous? How can we become better people?" The earliest writers, Homer and Moses, focused on man's outward actions. Achilles and Odysseus, the heroes of Homer's epics, are physically courageous, fight bravely, and do not back down from danger, even against overwhelming odds. Moses and Jesus stand up to absolute power. These admirable traits are reinforced throughout Western literature, from Beowulf and Lancelot, to Aragorn in *The Lord of the Rings*, Paul Atreides in *Dune*, or Mhoram in the "Chronicles." Once we have established that we admire a certain virtue, it becomes part of our identification of a hero, though the kinds of battles may change and the potential outcomes of the battles may change. Western literature has also explored how man can better himself, reaching for an ideal in the Socratic or Christian mode, based on an inward attitude or awareness. Again, critical self-reflection is evident throughout Western literature, from Sophocles's Oedipus to Shakespeare's Hamlet, to Austen's Elizabeth Bennett, to Conrad's Kurtz, to Donaldson's Covenant and Linden Avery.

Our modern perception of our world focuses on what we've lost, our alienation, the wasteland we've made of our world, our inability to believe in our own capacities, our sense of impotence to solve the many and overwhelming problems of our times. For Donaldson to show us how to deal with our current situation, he must fully acknowledge the dilemma we are in and the solutions that have not worked and do not work. No matter how limited the modern world view is, Donaldson does not reject it; he embraces it. This, too, is a manifestation of the eye of the paradox, the both/and rather than the either/or view of the world, for sorrow and suffering and guilt can teach us as much as wonder and recovery and heroic action, though neither view alone can lead us to Truth. When the Giants of the Search first see Revelstone, built by the Unhomed Giants of the 1st "Chronicles," the First tries to put into words the wonder they feel at the message of Revelstone. She can see that built into the stone fortress is both the Giants' great love of the Land and tremendous grief at their own loss. They have captured and combined both emotions. She is proud and pained and humbled at their perception. The twentieth century has reflected our despair; we have many more physical challenges than have ever beset the world before, more rapid changes, more potential for destruction and extinction, not the least of which was the great revelation of our own heart of darkness. According to the both/and wisdom of Donaldson, embracing that truth is our only way to go beyond it to greater insights and wisdom. We need to find our balance in the eye of the paradox.

Covenant has seen his own heart of darkness in recognizing his rape of Lena and the larger parallel significance of Foul's rape of the Land as a reflection of his own guilt (especially if all the "Chronicles" books are part of Covenant's dream and Lord Foul is actually a part of Covenant's inner personality). Covenant has learned to diminish the power of despair through perspective/laughter, has learned to fuse his constructive and destructive forces, to sacrifice self for the betterment of the larger community, but he has not yet learned exactly what to do with his shadow self; he has not learned to embrace his shadow self as Ged did at the climax of Ursula LeGuin's Earth-Sea trilogy or Captain Kirk did his violent darker half or Luke Skywalker did when he accepted his dark side in Darth Vader. The "Last Chronicles" should give us a way out of the paralysis that Conrad forced us to acknowledge but we haven't yet resolved.

Twentieth century writers wore the blinders of realism; what they perceived and presented to us may have been "true" in a scientific sense, but it was certainly not all there is to Truth. Our senses help us to explore our world, but there is more to human consciousness than our five senses. We do have imagination; we can picture that which is impossible and even react to it — imagination has the power to scare us or force us to react in awe to the wonder of it (as dreams sometimes do). Literature through the ages has known the importance of imagination; the Renaissance called it Fancy, Tolkien refers to our ability to subcreate and then, as Coleridge advises, to suspend our disbelief to experience what we have imagined.

W.A. Senior argues well the importance of imagination/fantasy in modern literature and explains away the reluctance of some critics to accept as serious any literature that includes the fantastic, successfully placing Donaldson within the more well-known authors of fantasy and comparing him to other mainstream writers such as John Fowles, Anthony Burgess, and Gabriel Garcia Marquez. Senior also acknowledges the limitations of the twentieth century against which Donaldson and other fantasy authors are often judged. He explores the fallacy that reflecting reality is the only acceptable purpose for literature, recognizing that Donaldson chooses the fantasy genre because hopefulness or the eucatastrophe Tolkien mentions of the great joy possible is more prevalent in fantasy works. Our attraction to Donaldson is that his fantasy characters find answers and learn to be effective. Donaldson posits that throughout literature, "epics articulated the best religious and cultural, the best social and psychological sub-perceptions of their times."[26]

One purpose of fantasy heroes from Tolkien's Bilbo and Frodo to Donaldson's Covenant is to face the great perils of their own day and find an imaginative solution for those seemingly insurmountable troubles. Thus, Bilbo represents the world view of the early twentieth century with its desire to share wealth and knowledge with third-world countries through the Commonwealth; Frodo and other characters from *The Lord of the Rings* represent allegorically a solution to the problems of the mid-twentieth century concerning the possible extermination of entire peoples (the Jews) and dominance by a "Master Race" as well as our fear of atomic weapons. But Covenant must provide at least allegorical solutions to these same problems and others that have arisen since the middle of the twentieth century (pollution, extinction of whole species, global warming, depletion of our natural resources) that cannot be solved through physical might or through the destruction of ultimate weapons (as Frodo does the Ring), because the knowledge of how to build nuclear weapons still exists on the Internet and even individual terrorists can make bombs using common ingredients. Since the problems that plague our world cannot be solved as conflicts have been resolved in the past, literature needs new, imaginative approaches, and heroes need new, heroic qualities to fight the wasteland, our sense of alienation, our potential for total destruction. Fighting our own capacity for evil requires more than the physical prowess and bravery of a hero such as Bilbo, or even the endurance and perseverance of a hero such as Frodo. We now need the self-control/restraint and acceptance/integration of a hero such as Covenant. We must accept our limitations, our impotence to solve all problems, and still strive for non-violent, inclusive solutions to the world's problems.

Donaldson's "Chronicles" illustrate both the microcosm of the conflicts of the Land and the macrocosm of how we can contend with the limitations of twentieth century thought. While he acknowledges our alienation, our awareness of our heart of darkness, our reliance on realism, and our limitation of believing only what we can perceive with our senses, he also provides symbolic, allegorical ways out of the abyss we have dug for ourselves. He suggests in the "Chronicles" that when Covenant loses one sense, he can learn to value the other senses more (through the Giant's proclivity to rely on hearing rather than sight) or by suggesting that there may be other, more intuitive, senses for us to cultivate, such as the ability to see health, to sense murder.

The concept of Despair in the "Chronicles" has layers of meaning, again a microcosm and a macrocosm. For Covenant the individual, despair represents his natural reaction to the way his wife and society have shunned him due to his disease. For modern society and for the literature of our age, Lord Foul as Despair/Despite can also symbolize the brick wall of limitations we have run into in following realism to its logical extreme, into determinism, nihilism, nothingness. Donaldson provides answers for both the microcosm and macrocosm of despair and angst that has so dominated our world view on the macrocosm level since the two world wars, the Vietnam conflict, Watergate, 9/11, and other incidents that have worn away at our optimism, our sense of value in ourselves, our hopefulness for the world. He allows us to confront the causes for our despair, not by denying or ignoring the realities we face, but by translating our conflicts into the psychological realism of the Land and facing them there. The result for us is a sense that we can regain our imaginative qualities, our hope, and our sense of purpose and community. Tolkien was the first to suggest that even with a modern ironic world view, heroism was still possible. Roger Sale in *Tolkien and the Critics* claims that the seriousness of the Ring shows

> Tolkien (almost against his will, it sometimes seems) that the heroism about which he writes best and therefore most cares about is of a distinctively modern cast — a heroism based upon the refusal to yield to despair rather than on any clear sense of goal or achievement, a heroism that accepts the facts of history and yet refuses to give in to the tempting despair that those facts offer.[27]

Tolkien deliberately sets his fantasy in another world, Middle-earth; Donaldson chooses to include a character from our real world in his fantasy world to show a bridge between a fantasy world and our modern world. Donaldson redefines fantasy as the playing out of our inner conflicts as battles with external antagonists within the fantasy world. Thus, Covenant's battle with despair is a life-and-death struggle with an external evil character, Lord Foul, who represents despair. Whether the characters of the Land are actual beings or representatives of Covenant's inner conflicts, either way, the story and the modern world connect. Donaldson uses the Land to analyze the twentieth century character. The heart-of-darkness awareness fits Donaldson's and other modern writers' view that both good and evil are inside of everyone. The chapter titles in this book are designed to illustrate Donaldson's engagement with (not denial of) modern literature and the inclusion of modern themes. Donaldson is influenced by all of great Western literature, but he reflects his own time by including the insights articulated by great modern writers as he joins the debate on the role of the artist, the power of memory, the multiplicity of identity, the nature of evil and of power, and the exploration of time and space so often explored in modern literature.

Modern literature seems to be more interested in the depravity of man than in his heroic potential, in his helplessness rather than in his capacity for resistance, perseverance, loyalty, or goodness of spirit. The either/or of the modern world view admits weakness and evil but not virtue or strength of character. Donaldson challenges assumptions about epic quests as did Tolkien, but Tolkien changed the expectations of quest literature from seeking something (the dragon's treasure in *The Hobbit*) to taking the journey to lose or destroy something (the One Ring in *The Lord of the Rings*). For Tolkien, physical combat does not determine the outcome of the important conflicts. Donaldson's pacifism functions in a similar way to limit choices about action; he will not allow a physical battle to determine Truth. Power is not the answer. His second book, *The Illearth War*, explores the viability of the muscle solution, ironically proposed by the once-blind Hile Troy, another representative of the modern world, but Donaldson shows how the expectation of using strategy or power or force is unrealistic and cannot overcome the kinds of evils we face. Donaldson's "Chronicles" also clearly reinforce the common modern view that battle/war is not glorious. In addition, Donaldson challenges traditional quest motivations by providing different purposes for different members of the group. Whereas Prothall's desires may conform to the more traditional quest as he seeks the Staff of Law, Covenant's need for answers, for a way out of his dream, sends him along on the same quest.

Modern man is on a quest for self-actualization, and we need to be as productive, inclusive, and positive as possible. It is not enough to acknowledge our own capacity for evil; we must find a way to control or redirect it toward productive ends. The peoples of the Land are prevented from unlocking the secrets of Kevin's Seven Wards of power by the Oath of Peace they have taken, by their decision to embrace stoicism and reject destructive emotions. Covenant is similarly restricted at first by his own desire to find solutions that do not involve coercion or physical combat, a reflection of Donaldson's need to take a philosophical stand as a conscientious objector to war (his own Oath of Peace, so to speak). Covenant is also hampered by his acceptance of the scientific rationalism of the twentieth century and his fear and unwillingness to release his unbelief in order to embrace imagination. However, like Mhoram who learns to both honor Peace and use the knowledge he gains when he understands the secret to the Ritual of Desecration, Donaldson shows how to find the eye of the paradox and to fight without battling, to resolve conflict by refusing to fight, even to win by surrendering.

The Romantic poet Blake discusses innocence and experience and assumes both are good (the Lamb is as important as the Tiger); Tolkien values the innocence of the Shire and desires to preserve its innocence even if some hobbits need to learn about the hard experiences of life to protect it. The modern world would say that once we have passed from innocence to experience as individuals or as a society, we cannot then recapture innocence but must learn to live with our depressing new knowledge and awareness about man's inhumanity toward his fellow man, our exploitation of the earth's resources, the frightening forces which can be used for coercion, and especially our own capacity for evil and destruction. Donaldson's eye of the paradox shows us how to find ways to recapture and embrace innocence or redemption after we have gained experience. Foamfollower's baptism of fire in Hotash Slay purifies him so that he can laugh at Lord Foul. Before Linden can heal the Land of the Sunbane, she must discover "there is also love in the world"[28] and heal herself of her helplessness, guilt, and paralysis. Even the weaknesses and limitations of Covenant's personality are burned away by Lord Foul's violent attack on the Arch of Time, which Covenant prevents by accepting the power and pain himself.

Throughout the "Chronicles" Donaldson evaluates many dialectics: Stone and Sea in connection to the Giants, the pull toward life and death in Linden Avery, disease and health (leprosy and the Sunbane vs. Linden's health sense and ability to heal), fire and ice (Hamako vs. the Arghule with a *croyel*), the Vow of the Bloodguard and Corruption, hope and despair, power and impotence, good and evil, madness and sanity, preservation and destruction, choice and possession, joy and pain, strength and weakness, reality and dream, peace and grief, laughter and tears, pity and loathing, judgment and mercy, weakness and strength, love and hate. Donaldson raises discussion of these many dialectics, always with the same purpose: to show us that we need to understand and accept both extremes and that we need to maintain our both/and view of the world by embracing not only what we might call our positive traits but also our negative ones. Only by doing so can we escape from the paralysis of the twentieth century, which showed us our heart of darkness but didn't tell us how to overcome or control it. Donaldson doesn't solve all our problems, but he does tell us to accept the seeming contradictions and go on living in hope, that guilt and anger and despair are inevitable human reactions but are not the only answers to the realities of our world. To illustrate how positive and negative traits can coexist, he presents another important paradox, the contrast between the ironic world view and the heroic world view. In the 1st "Chronicles," Covenant represents our modern ironic world view within the heroic landscape of the Land; in the 2nd, when the Land is under the control of the Sunbane and thus the imaginary world is even more ironic, Covenant strives to act more heroically. Eventually, he joins the Search of the Giants, and their courage reinforces the potential for heroic action, which was almost lost in the ironic world of the Sunbane and in Covenant's powerlessness since he is too powerful to use his wild magic power safely.

Donaldson leaves several dialectics unresolved, such as Linden's yearning for both life and death. Like the characters in *Star Wars* who fight their own dark side ("Anger, fear, passion, the dark side are they"[29]), Linden must resolve the paralysis she felt as a child having to watch her father die and aid her mother in dying and her chosen passion for healing. She is conflicted in her attitudes both for and against death. Donaldson also explores two different perspectives about suicide: Linden's father's self-loathing and Hamako's, Seadreamer's, the First's father's, Caer-Caveral's, and Covenant's self-sacrifice. Linden must also face the paradox of her need to heal and her own desire for power, which she can have only through the evil of possession. She is conflicted about how to rescue Covenant from his *Elohim*-imposed blankness. The only way she can think of to help him is to possess him, but the idea of possession is absolutely abhorrent to her. And she doubts her own motivations since she also craves Covenant's power. Her inability to resolve her conflicts paralyzes her. She believes that she must make an either/or decision and has not learned to find the eye of the paradox. Yet she has models in Covenant himself and also from her "real" world. Western thought, rather than arguing that systematic deductive reasoning or intuitive insight is the only possible road to Truth, can embrace both. Ironically, even the most ardent rationalists must acknowledge that the scientific method itself begins with a hypothesis, a reasonable, though intuitive, guess at the outcome of the experiment.

Another dialectic that Donaldson has not yet resolved but that has plagued the twentieth century is the "them/us" conflict: black/white, gay/straight, Christian/Jew/Muslim, Pakistani/ Indian, Serbian/Croatian, Israeli/ Palestinian, North/South Korean or Vietnamese. We still think we have to choose sides, and we become passionate about our allegiances. We identify these factions as "good" vs. "evil." Whether they are based on national pride, religion, old rivalries, or philosophical ideals about governments and power, we become polarized. Among science fiction/fantasy writers, Orson Scott Card has resolved this paradox well in his *Ender's Game* series. Young Ender becomes the guardian and savior of his enemy, the buggers' Hive Queen, and even speaks for tolerance toward a sentient descolada virus, reflecting Card's overall theme of acceptance of all aspects of life and coexistence and interdependence. But in the Land there are clearly good folk and evil creatures. While Donaldson has not yet confronted the paradox of acceptance of all, the 1st "Chronicles" focuses mostly on Covenant's individual responsibilities; the 2nd on partnerships and love. If in the planned "Last Chronicles," Covenant does become Lord Foul, as Donaldson has announced is his plan, then the line between "them" and "us" will be blurred and some kind of resolution that involves the acceptance of both good and evil will be part of the paradox. In *The Power That Preserves*, Donaldson already suggests that when the Waynhim, who in appearance are like ur-viles, attack the Giant Raver Satansfist, they provide encouragement for the Lords. Also, Lady Alif's and Rire Grist's change of allegiance signals that the "them/us" delineations are not absolute. The gift of Vain, made for Covenant by the ur-viles (who had been the enemy), is essential in the creation of the new Staff of Law and therefore also of the healing of the Land from the Sunbane. Although some in our world still try to resolve conflicts with armed confrontation, as television and the Internet make the world smaller, as our interdependence grows, and as national borders and philosophical/religious differences become less important, we should be better able to find the eye of the paradox in acceptance, union, inclusion, and peaceful coexistence with "others" (and even those aspects of ourselves we are hesitant to admit to having) as the next great challenge for our time.

Modern literature acknowledges and sometimes tries to resolve its several paradoxes. And it should take a lesson from science. Michio Kaku, in his *Hyperspace*, explains the two most prevalent theories of physics which have battled for supremacy in the twentieth century: "Einstein's general relativity is a theory of the cosmos, a theory of stars and galaxies held together via the smooth fabric of space and time. Quantum theory, by contrast, is a theory of the microcosm, where sub-atomic particles are held together by particle-like forces dancing on the sterile stage of space-time."[30] Twentieth century scientists took sides in this either-or conflict to prove which theory more completely explained the Truth of our universe. And for many years the proponents of the more recent quantum revolution (similar to the realist writers of twentieth century literature) seemed to be "winning." But finally, scientists figured out how to unite the two disparate theories into one both/and concept of the superstring theory: "String theory can explain not only the nature of particles, but that of space-time as well.... String theory can derive the particles of matter as resonances vibrating on the string. And string theory can also derive Einstein's equations by demanding that the string move self-consistently in space-time. In this way, we have a comprehensive theory of both matter-energy and space-time."[31]

It's time for literature to follow science's lead. Donaldson has begun. Writers such as Donaldson are willing to face the abyss which the twentieth century created, by acknowledging it and jumping into the void to find out what can be learned. We can find our way back to the unity found in the Western canon by joining Athens and Jerusalem again with the emotion of Dante. Stephen R. Donaldson is an important modern writer because he encompasses and unites many dialectics within his "Chronicles of Thomas Covenant, the Unbeliever" series. He does not try to place modern society on any one side of the faith/science, madness/sanity, power/impotence, hope/despair, dream/reality continuums, but places us squarely in the eye of the paradox, challenging us to find our balance and purpose, to resolve the contradictions as Western society uniquely always has, not with an either/or, but rather with a both/and world view.

CHAPTER 1

Ur-Lord of the (White Gold) Ring

Donaldson admittedly owes his major literary debt to J.R.R. Tolkien whose *The Lord of the Rings* (published in 1954) created a market for fantasy. Tolkien also articulates the need for imagination and fantasy in modern literature in his 1938–39 speech "On Fairy Stories," which was later published as part of "Tree and Leaf" in *The Tolkien Reader*. Of course, the idea is not new to Tolkien. Harold Goddard states the Renaissance view of imagination: "the imagination is not a faculty for the creation of illusion; it is the faculty by which alone man apprehends reality."[1] Both Tolkien and Donaldson believe fantasy can reveal truths more significant than mere facts, truths about what it means to be human. Donaldson is a natural heir to Tolkien not only because they both explore similar themes but because while Tolkien acknowledges and deals with twentieth century concerns through the Second World War (during which he was writing *The Lord of the Rings*), Donaldson's awareness goes beyond Tolkien's. Especially in his later books, Donaldson tackles symbolically/allegorically many of the ills that have plagued us since the last half of the twentieth century: pollution, the real and potential extinction of entire species, global weather pattern changes, the capacity for total destruction in the hands of many different countries and even individuals, the proliferation of false doctrines designed to create hatred and prejudice. But Donaldson's work is more than an updated version of *The Lord of the Rings*. He takes a different perspective on fantasy than Tolkien did and provides a better answer.

When Tolkien identifies the setting of fantasy as a Secondary World, he differentiates it from the Primary World. But he also acknowledges that modern man has great need for the elements of fairy tales: fantasy, recovery, escape, and consolation. Since Covenant's power exists only in the Land and Covenant himself must disavow the reality of the Land, a great paradox is created for him. This dilemma is similar to the either/or thinking of the modern world which has decided that science and miracles (or magic) are contradictory and cannot both exist. Tolkien in his "On Fairy Stories" claims that fantasy cannot be seen as the mere slight of hand of the magician but must be taken seriously. Fantasy is the power of the imagination to envision other than realistic actions/solutions. Donaldson says that the power manifested by his characters is actually just an expression of their inner beings, their personalities, their deep desires, fears, and potential. Mhoram confirms this concept when he tells Covenant that no actual white gold ring is necessary since its power comes from within Covenant himself. Whenever either Covenant or Linden accesses the wild magic, it may seem to spring forth as lightning from the ring, but each has to find the trigger within to initiate the power. Tolkien also says that fairy tale solutions must depend on the virtues of the characters and not a cheap magic trick or device. Since Tolkien is wary of any kind of power — one of the main themes of *The Lord of the Rings* is that power corrupts the user — for him heroics cannot be connected to power or magic but must come from strengths of personality and not physical prowess or magical accoutrements.

In "On Fairy Stories" Tolkien speaks of the limitations of modern man, steeped in scientific objectivism, in appreciating what he calls fantasy. He admits to the poor reputation of fantasy and understands that fantasy writing has the same reputation today that the novel had in the Renaissance: it was not to be taken seriously because it was a false art form. Ironically, drama was relegated to the same position, and now the Renaissance dramatist William Shakespeare is considered the greatest writer ever, more for his plays than for his poetry (supposedly the only true art form his time period recognized). Modern critics prefer writers to reflect only the familiar world of realism and not deviate from this Primary World as they create and people their Secondary Worlds. Anything supernatural or magical in literature is suspect and relegated to dream, hallucination, or delusion/madness. Obviously, Covenant in *Lord Foul's Bane* at first represents this kind of modern thinking and rationalizes his rejection of fantasy, of the Secondary World of the Land, by his need for awareness of and constant vigilance to monitor his disease of leprosy and the danger his willing suspension of disbelief could create in his "real" world. But Tolkien argues, we needn't take an either/or approach to fantasy. Fantasy has no quarrel with reason and does not negate the desire for scientific validation in the real world. Donaldson goes a step farther when he claims that both belief and disbelief are necessary, that we need to include imagination into the realism of the world.

Tolkien allows his Secondary World to be located in another place at another time, but Donaldson has stated that his goal is to bring the "real" world and the imaginary world into co-existence. Both writers, however, want the reader to recover the wonder of the entire world, not just of the fantastic characters: "*Faerie* contains many things besides elves and fays, and besides dwarfs, witches, trolls, giants, or dragons: it holds the seas, the sun, the moon, the sky; and the earth, and all things that are in it: tree and bird, water and stone, wine and bread, and ourselves, mortal men, when we are enchanted."[2] Donaldson expands on the idea of understanding mortal men to mean beyond their words or actions or even motivations, to the deep psychological level of their being where their fears and inadequacies, their commitment and strength of personality can be acted out symbolically through character interactions in the Secondary World.

Recovery of wonder is another important purpose of fantasy literature for Tolkien: both Tolkien and Donaldson provide the shock of new wonder, a new vision even of familiar things like trees or stone. For both authors recovery consists mainly of a new view of nature, more reverence for, care for, and notice taken of the natural world: for Tolkien, primarily trees and light; for Donaldson, stone, wood, horses, the sun and moon, the cycles of life, the power within the earth. Tolkien's elves enhance our love of living trees, especially because they brought the Ents to life. In Donaldson's works both the *rhadhamaerl* and the Giant Pitchwife can heal stone, Gravelingas and Hirebrands can use stone or wood for heat or light without consuming the natural resource, and a natural phenomenon like the Fire Lions can be called from the earth to help save the Company at the end of the quest for the Staff of Law. In addition, the Land also grants to Covenant on his first trip the ability to see health, to perceive the goodness of natural places such as Andelain. Tolkien allows Frodo a similar glimpse of the beauty of the life of the forest of Lothlorien, but not to the extent that Donaldson not only reawakens our sense of the beauty of nature but also makes us aware of the fragility of such beauty. In *The Lord of the Rings*, the "Road Song"[3] which begins "The road goes ever on and on," encapsulates the essence of Tolkien's theme: that fate may lay out one's path, but the individual must still choose to follow it, finding help from others along the way. Donaldson also includes a defining poem that perhaps sums up the beauty and power and vulnerability of the Land (possibly even of fantasy itself):

> Something there is in beauty
> which grows in the soul of the beholder
> like a flower.[4]

In *The Power That Preserves* Mhoram agrees to release Covenant from the first summoning in order for Covenant to be able to save the life of a child in his "real" world, claiming that because Covenant has known and appreciated the Land, even if the Lords should fail, Covenant will still retain the memory of the beauty he has seen. Here is an excellent example of the "immortality through art" theme of much of Western literature: through a poem or a novel, described beauty remains ever fresh and vibrant. In recovering the beauty of our world, we must also learn to protect it from the blights that would destroy it, to heal it, to help it flourish, to emulate the profound purpose of the Lords of the Land. Nevertheless, just by visiting the Land in reality or in a dream (Covenant) or through the imagination of literature (we the readers), the seeds of the beauty of the Land, and by extension of our own world as well, are planted in our souls and make us yearn for such beauty and willing to work to recreate our own world in that image. Thus both authors encourage us to recover our love of nature.

For Tolkien escape implies not only the undesirability of the present circumstance but a vision of a better place and time, an improvement to present reality. He defends the man who, looking around his real world, sees only ugliness and evil and attempts to find a better reality. Donaldson is not quite so judgmental to call the modern world evil (since obviously it will be included in the eye of the paradox), but in the few times Covenant directly compares the two places/times, our modern world suffers in the comparison. When told of the marriage of Trell and Atiaran in which, through their particular knowledge and skills, they are able to end a drought which plagued the people of Mithil Stonedown, Covenant feels acutely embarrassed that the only gift he had thought to give his wife Joan at his own wedding was a pair of riding boots. Later in the tale, Covenant's story of the man who committed suicide in the bathroom of an airplane by slitting his wrists to explain the term culture shock is compared to the Giants' story of Bahgoon the Unbearable and Thelma Two-Fist, a tale so long that by its telling a war was averted because no one could remember why he had wanted to fight in the first place. In each case Covenant's "real" world seems more petty, self-indulgent, and tawdry in comparison to the Land. But where Tolkien lists the realities of today from which we might wish to escape — "hunger, thirst, poverty, pain, sorrow, injustice, death"[5] — Donaldson adds these: disease, alienation, irresponsibility, futility, despair — particular characteristics of the late twentieth century.

Tolkien identifies specific purposes for fantasy writing. Wonder isn't created for itself, so the reader will say "how unusual and imaginative this is" but for the way it satisfies our desire to understand ourselves and our world better. Tolkien lists two primary purposes: "One of these desires is to survey the depths of space and time. Another is ... to hold communion with other living things."[6] Later he also identifies escaping the finality of death as a third desire. Tolkien explores time through the contrast of men with his long-lived or immortal characters. Tolkien also introduces his readers to many marvelous beings: elves, dwarves, wizards, Ents. In Donaldson's work one aspect of time is explored through the different rates of the passage of time in the Land and in Covenant's "real" world. Whereas for Covenant only ten years pass between the time of the 1st and 2nd "Chronicles," within the Land 3,500 years have gone by. The Bloodguard perceive that only a few seconds have passed between when they are sent out of the *clachan* of the *Elohim* and when the rest of the Search joins them, yet the entire individual questioning of the Giants, Linden, and Covenant, and the *Elohimfest* have taken place. For Donaldson there are layers of meaning in the interactions Covenant has with other beings in the Land. Covenant obviously meets many marvelous other living things, including Giants, Ranyhyn, *Elohim*, a sandgorgon, Waynhim, and *jheherrin* as well as many other men from *rhadhamaerl, lillianrill,* Ramen to Lords, Bloodguard, and Bhrathair. But in Donaldson the dual view of the story, that the characters are outward manifestations of inner characteristics of Covenant, adds another layer of meaning to these interactions. He is communicating with other living beings and exploring psychological insights about himself at the same time. The escape from death that Tolkien explores through the immortality of the elves and the Valar, Donaldson also explores through the *Elohim*, the Forestals, Foul and his Ravers, and the breaking of the laws of Death and Life.

Tolkien disavows dream tales, such as *Alice in Wonderland*, as true fantasy stories. He claims the author negates the reality of the Secondary World by allowing it to be seen as merely a dream. He believes that the interior laws of logic must allow for belief in the Subcreated World or the author cheats the reader of imagined wonder. So if the fantasy author dismisses his tale as just a dream, he is not honoring his own world. Donaldson obviously disagrees. Not only does Covenant eventually find the eye of the paradox in which Unbelief and the Land can co-exist, but Donaldson must have both to make his point that both are necessary. Donaldson's "Chronicles" must be both a dream and actual reality for Covenant. In his "real" world Covenant is obviously affected by his experiences in the Land; one of the books he writes in the ten years between the 1st and 2nd "Chronicles" deals with guilt, a major emotion he has to understand and resolve within the Land during the time of the 1st "Chronicles" because of his rape of Lena. Also, Covenant is the only character in the Land who does disbelieve; to all other inhabitants, the Land is their truth, their reality, their world. Even Hile Troy and Linden Avery do not need to wrestle with the fundamental question of whether the Land is real. And its reality is obviously more attractive to most readers, who are not therefore deprived of imagined wonder.

If the Land is "real," then as Covenant meets Giants, Waynhim, *jheherrin,* a sandgorgon, and *Elohim* and even other human cultures (*rhadhamaerl, lillianrill,* Ramen, Lords, the Bhrathair), he is interacting with the "Other." He is breaking down (or in the case of ur-viles, cavewights, and Ravers, reinforcing) the "them/us" dialectic. He is exploring what it means to be human. But if the Land is a dream, or a psychological working out of Covenant's real life problems, it can still be truth. Donaldson claims that the fantasy genre allows him to show individuals as external character aspects or personality traits so that as the events work out, the protagonist is actually analyzing and resolving parts of himself— his weaknesses, inadequacies, fears, and even potential evil. It is not by accident that the antagonist in the "Chronicles" represents exactly the kind of despair and self-hatred that Covenant himself is susceptible to once he contracts leprosy and is shunned and abandoned by his family and neighbors. Therefore, self-awareness rather than global peace could be the overall goal of Donaldson's fantasy story. However, again the eye of the paradox, the need for the Land to be real and to be a dream, makes both goals significant and interconnected.

For Tolkien consolation is a sudden joy, unexpected but profound and as powerful as any sense of loss or grief. Tolkien also suggests that passion needs to be part of human experience in direct contradiction to the concept of the golden mean of control over emotions and in support of the notion that we can experience joy only to the extent that we open ourselves to experience its opposites of sorrow and pain. If we protect ourselves from the negative emotions, we will be denied the blessings of ultimate joy. This balance, in essence, epitomizes the eye of the paradox: we must embrace both to have either, even knowing that one is desirable and the other will cause grief. In *Shadowlands*, the film about C.S. Lewis' relationship with Joy Gresham, their moment of greatest happiness is experienced with the knowledge that she is dying of cancer. She says, "The pain then is part of the happiness now. That's the deal."[7] Donaldson, like Tolkien, ends his tales with a juxtaposition of emotions, both sorrow and joy. Middle-earth is saved, but Frodo can no longer enjoy the Shire. The Land is saved but at the cost of Saltheart Foamfollower's life, or of Covenant's sacrifice. The joy of the happy ending balances an awareness of its cost.

Even Tolkien admits that fairy tales should reflect/connect with the real world. The creator of a Secondary World wants it to provoke wonder but also seem as real as our own reality. It must be a believable place, one the reader could suppose exists and would want to visit. Donaldson, of course, deals separately with the "real" world of Haven Farm and the Secondary World of the Land, but they are undeniably connected through the consciousness of his "real" world characters, Covenant and Linden. It is easier, of course, to bring a modern awareness to a fantasy realm (Mark Twain did so in *A Connecticut Yankee in King Arthur's Court*), and much harder to introduce the heroic world view to our jaded modern sensibilities. Donaldson says his desire is to bring the epic back as a viable literary form for modern literature and to bring together the real world and the imaginary world. As will be illustrated later, Donaldson exposes his fantasy characters to modern awareness and only then do they reach their full potential.

The modern critic can interpret Donaldson's 1st "Chronicles" on many levels: within the Land, within Covenant's "real" world, within Donaldson's real world (the late twentieth century to the present), and within the world of Western literature across time (from Homer and Moses to the present). The different layers of possible interpretation of Donaldson's works are best illustrated by concentric circles, but Donaldson's metaphor of the peeling of an onion works also. Layers of an onion both works and does not work as an analogy — it is good for visualizing the levels of reality in Donaldson, but it could imply that the central portion of the onion, or the center circle, in this case the reality of the Land, has the most significant meaning, like peeling back the layers of reality to find truth. Donaldson uses the metaphor of the onion this way in his interview with Senior in reference to his Gap science fiction series. But I claim that all these layers interact with each other to produce the richness of Donaldson's works and make him a great writer. Contrasting the idea that the central level holds the most meaning, actually the meaning on the outer layers is more insightful and profound. For this reason Donaldson is superior to most other fantasy writers, on par with Tolkien and Dante, who give us as outer layers the real world and the world of myth coexistent.

Most readers, if asked to summarize the plot of any of Donaldson's "Chronicles of Thomas Covenant, the Unbeliever" novels, might include a short introduction, such as "a leper from our world finds himself translated into the Land," but most of what would be related would involve the actions and characters from the Land. However, because Covenant is always aware of his own perceptions of reality and his memories, his knowledge of his "real" world, we cannot simply experience the Land, the 1st level, the 1st circle, without the modern perspective from the 2nd level. For this reason I have represented the division between the two as

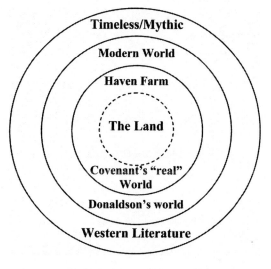

Figure 1. Concentric circles illustrating several layers of reality in Donaldson's 1st "Chronicles."

a dashed circle. An excellent analogy for this is the way William Shakespeare introduces *Taming of the Shrew* with a short scene of a Lord tricking Christopher Sly into believing that he is a Lord being entertained by the play we see as well. But since Sly's "wife" is a boy in a dress playing a role, we cannot forget that in Shakespeare's day, all the women's roles were played by young boys and the audience was being entertained as well. So we have a dual view of the play, as "real events" happening to Sly and as a play. Similarly, the "Chronicles" are both an adventure for Thomas Covenant and his dream.

Donaldson creates ambiguity in the 1st "Chronicles" by focusing on Covenant's point of view and his conviction that his experiences within the Land must be part of a dream, thus continuously juxtaposing the first two concentric circles and forcing the reader to consider both possible interpretations at once. Herein lies the paradox. For pure modernists it is on the 2nd level, Covenant's "real" world, that this novel is truly modern. The character of Covenant in his world is alienated, impotent, riddled with disease. An obvious parallel is to Vonnegut's *Slaughterhouse 5* where Billy Pilgrim escapes his memory of the horrors of the bombing of Dresden during World War II by "being transported" at times to his own imaginary place, Trafalmadore. One could read Thomas Covenant in the same way. But Donaldson does not allow Covenant to forget his "real" world while in the Land or to interpret the Land totally as a dream.

An analysis of the style of writing in the frame tale about Covenant in his "real" world with the style of his adventures in the Land shows Donaldson's command of the tone or style conventions we accept for mainstream and fantasy writing and reiterates his insistence that the two world views must be understood separately but conjoined. Following mythic fantasy conventions, Covenant's quests in the Land are presented chronologically with narrative details about the terrain and the actions and dialogue of other characters. The first few chapters before each of Covenant's translations to the Land, or his "real" world experiences, use associative logic to present information through the kind of manipulation of time often found in the novels of William Faulkner. Here the action is less important — Covenant's walking to town to pay his phone bill or wandering around the woods near his home — whereas his interior monologue, the memories triggered by chance encounters with young girls or his analysis of his own changing view of the world, are reminiscent of James Joyce. To illustrate Donaldson's modern manipulation of time, the following chronology of events is also labeled numerically to show the order of presentation of that information within the frame tale.

These actions and thoughts are presented in the order that the reader learns of them at the beginning of *Lord Foul's Bane*. A similar analysis could be constructed of any of Covenant's experiences in his "real" world, but these three chapters are the best example to illustrate Donaldson's use of associative logic, a staple of modern literature. The numbers will be used on the graphic of the chronology of events by time presented below:

1. A woman comes out of a store and gets her son out of Covenant's way
2. Covenant remembers the leprosarium, does a VSE (visual surveillance of extremities)
3. Covenant notices the telephone company is two blocks away
4. Covenant thinks about Joan's leaving him
5. Covenant rationalizes why he is walking to town
6. Covenant walks past the Courthouse, noticing the giant heads atop the building
7. Covenant sees girls shopping in the store and thinks about Joan's nightgown
8. Covenant runs into the beggar
9. Covenant remembers that his electric company bill was paid by someone else
10. Covenant thinks about the Golden boy tune
11. Covenant thinks about the success of his first novel
12. Covenant remembers writing his first novel
13. Covenant remembers marrying Joan
14. Covenant remembers Joan's working before his book was accepted
15. Covenant remembers when his book was accepted for publication
16. Covenant recounts Joan's decision to get pregnant
17. Covenant recounts Joan's quitting her job
18. Covenant remembers when his son Roger was born
19. A boy gives Covenant a note from the beggar
20. Covenant thinks he sees eyes when he looks at the beggar's "Beware" sign
21. Covenant almost bumps into Joan's lawyer in front of the phone company
22. Covenant composes/recalls "pale deaths" poem
23. Covenant remembers laughing
24. Covenant thinks about writing his 2nd book
25. Covenant thinks about Joan's discovery of his leprosy
26. Covenant remembers the leprosarium, dreaming of lectures about leprosy
27. Covenant remembers returning home and burning his manuscripts
28. Covenant remembers trying to pay his electric bill
29. Covenant reads the ethics problem as he waits for the receptionist
30. Covenant leaves the phone company
31. Covenant runs into the beggar again, tries to give away his wedding ring
32. Covenant decides to see his lawyer
33. Covenant steps off the curb and is almost hit by a police car

The chronology of events by time with the corresponding detail number above can be pictured thus:

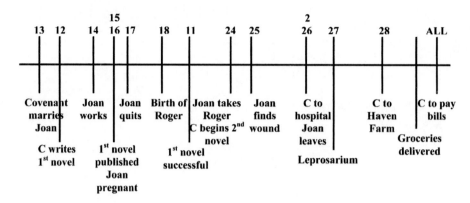

Figure 2. Chronological events of Covenant's experiences in the "real" world in *Lord Foul's Bane.*

In another form, the spatial layout of Covenant's town can illustrate again Donaldson's use of associative logic. The numbers on top correspond to Covenant's actions or thoughts as he goes to pay his phone bill. The woman's reaction is typical of the reaction of others to his leprosy. The Courthouse reminds Covenant of his divorce; the high school girls stimulate him sexually and remind him of his conjugal life with Joan. These thoughts remind him of his writing, his best seller and the second novel, and he is reminded of Joan's discovery of his leprosy. As he is noticing his current time and surroundings, he must pass the electric company to get to the phone company,

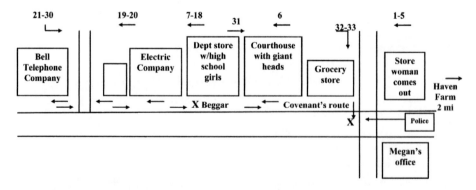

Figure 3. Spatial diagram of Covenant's "real" world town illustrating the associative logic in his thinking.

so he is reminded of trying to pay his bill there. Meeting the beggar and getting the note from the beggar cause him to react to the ethics question.

The 3rd level, that of Donaldson's real world (the 3rd of the concentric circles), exemplifies my own theory of the relevance of how a good author illustrates concerns of his own time. Here the fact that Donaldson deals with modern world issues — alienation, the wasteland, the role of the artist, our heart of darkness — illustrates that he is not using fantasy to escape the modern perspective but to engage with it. Thus, Donaldson is a modern novelist. However, on the 4th level Donaldson becomes a truly great author, for he also reflects issues and concerns of all Western literature from Homer through the present day and reveals universal truths. And as experience is cumulative, the fact that he responds to major literary movements again makes him a modern novelist. Most important, Donaldson's main theme is universal: no matter what particular dialectic we try to use as a filter through which to understand our world, Donaldson's message remains the same — for ultimate truth, we should not argue for one side against the other but find a way to embrace both. The eye of the paradox is the both/and view of the world which allows us to move forward out of paralysis and into an appreciation and acceptance of all of life.

Another way to evaluate the several levels of interpretation for Donaldson's work is to show the concentric circles in a slightly different way, showing how Donaldson insists on presenting both the ironic and the heroic modes simultaneously, by juxtaposing both world views for his readers at the same time, forcing us to accept both and find a way to unite them. For him this unity is the eye of the paradox. Another important juxtaposition is that of universal truth applied to relevant issues of today. This additional concurrence broadens our world view from the limiting modern world reliance on realism and scientific objectivism, to acknowledging timeless truths as they have been presented over the years, from the time of Homer and Moses to the present.

This juxtaposition of

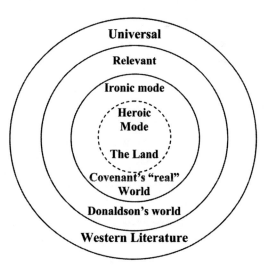

Figure 4. Concentric circles illustrating contrasting world views in Donaldson's 1st "Chronicles."

world views is presented slightly differently in the 2nd "Chronicles," since at that time the Land is even more ironic than Covenant's "real" world. Today we do not still accept superstitious beliefs that require human sacrifice, in the form of human blood to be mixed with the soil to ensure a bountiful harvest. The Clave's doctrine is similar to pagan human sacrifice beliefs, which have been satirized in short stories such as "The Lottery" by Shirley Jackson and films such as *Children of the Corn* or *Wicker Man*. The Sunbane represents one extreme in man's inability to control his environment (or even predict it more than a few days ahead), the classic definition of Northrup Frye's ironic mode. Today in our ironic real world, we feel overwhelmed by many areas of concern over which we don't seem to be able to exert any control, such as terrorism or global warming; nevertheless, there is also much that we can control, such as electricity, solar power, the dwarf wheat that has virtually saved India from starvation. So we are not as impotent as those under the Sunbane.

The dream motif, or the dialectic between the Land-as-real and the Land-as-a-dream, is only briefly touched on in the 2nd "Chronicles," showing that the inner psyche of Covenant is not as important; he has worked out his personal fascination with despair/death and must work on other relationships through this adventure. The world of the Land expands as well as the kinds of confrontations the group faces. There is an additional layer to the circles illustrating the several layers of reality in the 2nd "Chronicles." In this additional space, Covenant can interact with very different other beings, the *Elohim*, the Sandgorgon, the *merewives*, the One Tree (The Worm of the World's End). But Donaldson needs to have Covenant leave the Land for another important reason. Because the Land has become extremely ironic, and Covenant's own world is ironic, he needs another world to provide the heroic perspective and contrast. Covenant strives to act heroically in the 2nd "Chronicles," but he is continuously hampered by the venom that the Ravers introduce and keep triggering with their several attacks.

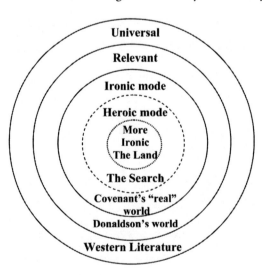

Figure 5. Concentric circles illustrating contrasting world views in Donaldson's 2nd "Chronicles."

So the Giants and their willingness to undertake the Search for the One Tree help provide that heroic viewpoint, without which we would not still have to juxtapose both ways of looking at the world and would be robbed of the eye of the paradox.

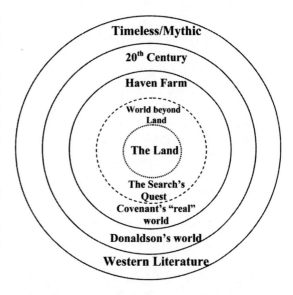

The argument that Covenant is a modern hero becomes even more apparent in contrasting the 1st and 2nd "Chronicles." In the 1st, the antagonists are other powerful, physical beings. This conflict is not unlike our fighting against a ruthless leader today, such as

Figure 6. Concentric circles illustrating several layers of reality in Donaldson's 2nd "Chronicles."

Hitler or Saddam Hussein, who must be confronted by physical means, or by the use of what Donaldson calls the muscle solution. The conflicts in the 1st "Chronicles" are mostly physical: Drool Rockworm and Foul against the Company, Foul's armies against the armies of the Lords, Covenant against the elements, Covenant against his own limitations and his unwillingness to be engaged fully in the affairs of the Land. Covenant's inner battles against despair, anger, guilt, and shame culminate in the laughter which diminishes Lord Foul. But in the 2nd "Chronicles" he cannot win against the ravishment of the Land through strength/battles/physical confrontation, even if the entire peoples of the Land united with him, any more than our modern world can defeat its problems — pollution, global warming, terrorism, extinction of endangered species — through wars or by confronting our own inner psychological demons.

One question in the 1st "Chronicles" is that of power; in the 2nd, it is that of restraint and endurance. To use a martial arts analogy, it is the difference between attacking and waiting for the enemy to attack in order to use his power and momentum against him to protect oneself and redirect and thus thwart the enemy's desire for dominance. I'm predicting that the major question of the "Last Chronicles" will be acceptance/union, where the two combatants no longer fight at all but work toward wholeness. But as we have discovered through modern literature, this task is hard to accomplish. Yes,

Kurtz in Joseph Conrad's *Heart of Darkness* recognizes his darker self, but he doesn't really admit this epiphany until he is on his death bed and we never see him functioning as an effective person with his new knowledge.

Most modern writers (in fact, writers across the ages) reflect just two of these concentric circles of reality — the world of their characters and, through inference, their own real world. Great writers are also universal and can be read and interpreted on that level as well. Few authors are as complex as Donaldson in which the juxtaposed view of Covenant's "real" world and the Land is forced on the reader. It is synonymous with Shakespeare's play-within-a-play complexity in *Hamlet,* that compels the viewer/reader to enjoy the play and be aware of the fact that it is a play at the same time. The fact that Covenant is a character from what purports to be our world transported to the Land and he does not lose his awareness of our world views mandates that we readers maintain that same dual awareness, to suspend our disbelief and believe in the people and the actions in the Land as we would for any fantasy and to see the Land as a work of imagination, possibly as Covenant's dream designed to help him heal himself of the psychological hurts that our world has inflicted upon him since he became a leper.

Part of Shakespeare's greatness is that his most profound, significant characters can simultaneously act in the world and analyze their own actions and thus grow in awareness (Richard II in the prison soliloquy, Lear on the heath, Hamlet throughout). Covenant, too, has that dual vision (part of the eye of the paradox of life) of himself as participant in the reality of the Land and as "real" person in his own "real" world. By extension we place him within the author's and our own real world (the 1970s to the present). In addition, self-analysis of what it means to be human also involves transcending our limitations. Donaldson says that he, as a writer of epics, wants to transcend our understanding of ourselves and to show the quest for true self-knowledge itself can be the means by which we become more than we were, more than we thought we could be. Epics not only analyze transcendence but help us to grow and transcend also. So he reflects timeless themes and approaches to universal problems. But it is the multiple view that reflects Donaldson's genius, the eye of the paradox.

Ur-Lord, rather than Lord, is an important title for Thomas Covenant. It connects him to the side of the Lords but also differentiates him from them. Foul is also referred to as Lord Foul. "Ur" as a prefix often refers to something which came before, as in an "ur-Hamlet" manuscript that was supposedly a source for Shakespeare's major work but has been lost and cannot be proved to have previously existed. Thus, Covenant is associated with older power, and his connection with the great heroes of the Land's past, especially Berek, is strengthened. He is given the title Ur-Lord by High Lord Prothall when he reveals at the Council of Lords his white gold wedding ring that he had concealed with *clingor* to his chest to avoid being mistaken for a Berek-like hero since he does not understand how to use the wild magic of the ring. Covenant is different from the Lords also in that his power does not come from lore, from any awareness of Kevin's Wards, or from any knowledge of Earthpower. But at the same time he is not limited by the Oath of Peace that hampers the Lords from comprehending all of Kevin's Wards. He is limited only by his own ignorance of how to use his power, and his own miscomprehension at first of what power really is.

Mhoram tells Covenant, "'*You* are the Wild Magic.'"[8] The wild magic is a manifestation of himself, his character, his emotions, his passionate desires. Covenant's white gold wedding ring is connected to his self-identity and reminds him of his Golden boy life with Joan as well as the loss of that marriage and that life. So it is simultaneously a representation of his own promise and of what he does not have. The wild magic white gold ring is the most powerful force within the Land but is unpredictable because Covenant does not know how to trigger or control its/his power. Here also Donaldson's ring, which is the centerpiece of his fantasy trilogies, is like Tolkien's, except that the One Ring of Sauron is evil and cannot be used for good, whereas the wild magic is ambiguous. Covenant could save or damn the Land. His ring makes him both powerful and helpless. For Covenant it is a symbol of his love for Joan, his fidelity, the covenant of his marriage vows, which were legally negated by their divorce. It is intrinsically connected to his memories, which are all he has left of the happiness and self-fulfillment that he possessed in his Golden boy days. Since he rejects as "supercilious trash"[9] his previous world view when he burns his first novel and what he has written on his second, the ring also symbolizes his naiveté. Thus, it embodies both the innocence and experience of his world view that Covenant must learn to unite through the eye of the paradox. Therefore, Donaldson's story of a ring of power is much more complex than Tolkien's.

CHAPTER 2

Portrait of the Artist
as a Young Leper

It is no accident that Thomas Covenant is an artist/writer in "The Chronicles of Thomas Covenant, the Unbeliever." Thus, Stephen R. Donaldson can evaluate the process of creating artistic works — as have many modern writers, most notably James Joyce in his *Portrait of the Artist as a Young Man* (published in 1916). But this self-reflexive quality also adds several layers of possible interpretation to the character of Thomas Covenant, for even as a writer in his "real" world, Covenant changes many times. Covenant reflects the twentieth century focus away from acknowledging our imagination/fantasy to allowing only scientific realism and from trying to act heroically to being restricted by our sense of culpability to inevitable failure. When Covenant contracts leprosy, he believes that he cannot afford imagination, the faculty that can imagine happiness, health, and he is thus typical of twentieth century man who feels overwhelmed by these realities: pollution, the extinction of whole species, terrorism, the nuclear capability for total destruction. Modern man has become paralyzed by his own awareness of his heart of darkness and disbelieves in his ability to act heroically to solve his own problems.

Covenant, as a writer in his "real" world, can comment in part on the writing/creating process. Before Covenant is diagnosed with leprosy, his writing is imaginative. At first, Covenant writes in a frenzy as if inspired by some divine muse. He sees the landscapes and people of his subcreated world as if they were formed fully realized on his drafts, and he cannot write fast enough to capture their entire essence. He likens this instant creativity to a flash of lightning. There is both force and startlement in his creative power. As the "Chronicles" may represent a dream or a psychological working out of his "real" world problems for Covenant, the power of his creativity is thereby connected to the power of the white gold wild magic, which operates like lightning within the Land, intensely powerful, uncontrollable, and unpredictable.

Mhoram tells Covenant "*You* are the White Gold."[1] Thus, the wild magic in the Land is equated to the creative force of imagination in our world.

For Covenant, at first his creativity comes from joy. After his first book is a success and he begins work on a second, his excitement gives him energy and his creativity provides joy in a building self-feeding spiral of productivity and satisfaction. He likens the relief of finishing a segment of his book to a sexual climax. Creative output is thus likened to sexual satisfaction. And if the leper represents modern man, then writing/creativity is the highest form of orgasm possible in an ironic world.

Clearly, also, Donaldson's description of Covenant's writing process is self-reflexive. The reading, as well undoubtedly as the writing, of the "Chronicles" is emotionally draining. The overwhelming force of the opposition, the impossible antagonists to overcome, the self-acknowledged limitations of the heroes provide little rest from fear, doubt, guilt over inadequacies, potential despair in the characters. Most frustrating is Covenant's refusal to get involved or take responsibility. For the reader as well, the story of Thomas Covenant is "a peculiar work that repels even as it attracts."[2] We are angered by Covenant as much as we associate with him for his fears and inadequacies, and yet we want him to act heroically. Donaldson claims his interest is in the moments of intense emotions. In comparing his own style to Tolkien's, he says that Tolkien focuses more on the settings, especially the Shire, where Donaldson wants to know more about Frodo's and Sam's struggles through Mordor, not just the physical challenges, but how they face the deep emotional toll of the weight of the responsibility and the uncertain outcome. How man faces battle — against others or within himself — is more psychologically interesting to Donaldson than scenes of the idyllic Shire. Peter Jackson, in interpreting *The Lord of the Rings* on film, seems to agree with Donaldson. The battle of Helm's Deep encompasses about 10 pages out of the over 1000 pages of *The Lord of the Rings*, or about 1 percent of Tolkien's work. Yet it takes Jackson about 30 minutes out of a slightly over 10-hour trilogy of films, or closer to 5 percent to depict it. To be fair, though, Jackson may have wanted more action and Donaldson would want more emphasis on the internal thought processes or emotions of the characters involved, but such are the various strengths of films and novels. By Donaldson's language we are drawn into the emotions of the tale, the depths of the degradations of Foul's warped beings to the panic and fear of the people of the land. Donaldson spares neither his characters nor his readers. He pushes us to the extreme edge of emotion, forces us to peer over that edge no matter how much we are afraid of heights and thus keeps us as off balance as his characters are. Donaldson heightens the "pitch of intensity"[3] to push us beyond our limits again and again before he finally reestablishes order. So the physical relief of the reader is as intense as it was for the writer.

As Covenant works on his second book before becoming aware of his growing leprosy, his production becomes more erratic, and he is not able to maintain the fever-pitch pace of creativity. He fumbles with the words and cannot keep up with his imagination. Obviously, Covenant's growing leprosy hampers his ability to type. But Donaldson could also be commenting on the process of creation: the end result never comes out quite as it was imagined or thought out by the author. Words are never quite adequate, nor are they precise enough — or perhaps they are too precise, too limited — to convey everything an author wants to say, or at least everything he wants his reader to understand from what he says. The real work of art lies somewhere in the imagination of the author and can never completely be given spatial/temporal form. In addition, discerning readers will allow the work to reside in their own imaginations, making the proper connections, juxtapositions, leaps of logic and intuition to put the work together as a whole; they will also not let contradictory information confuse them but will allow all that is said to make up their understanding. Only then is the process of creation complete. But this idea is a Romantic or Renaissance view of the purpose of creativity: to appeal to our imaginations to find out what could be rather than what is, to strive for perfection which is only possible in the imagination. It is also the opposite of the deconstructionists' view which seeks out contradictions but cannot resolve them and then claims that they invalidate the author's whole purpose. Donaldson would say that these critics completely miss the point of contradictions. However, to resolve the major dialectics of our age, Donaldson must acknowledge the realities of this world and show how imagination is still valid, perhaps even more necessary today. Therefore, Covenant the writer of the best seller has understood a fundamental insight that Covenant the leper who later rejects imagination loses.

We never really know what Covenant's first book is about; we know only that it becomes a best seller. We are aware that his perception of his own first book changes after he is diagnosed with leprosy and has spent time in the leprosarium, and we know that Dr. Berenford, who later calls the best seller "'fluff—self-indulgent melodrama,'"[4] agrees with Covenant. But Covenant's whole world view has changed by then; he has accepted the twentieth century view of the futility of man, the impossibility of heroic or even meaningful action. He tells the beggar that futility is the normal state of affairs for man. When he returns from the leprosarium, he rereads what he had written on his second book and reacts as many modern critics react to fantasy literature today: that his work is naïve, unrealistic, "supercilious trash."[5] Now he has a different view of imagination. He sees it as dangerous for it would seduce him into believing the impossible; it would make him despair to be able to imagine what he could never be or have again. That very faculty which was originally a blessing because it could allow man to envision perfect joy, health, peace now is seen as a curse for the same reasons.

In the first "real" world section of *Lord Foul's Bane*, Donaldson has already evaluated two views of imagination possible in our own modern, ironic world. Imagination can be seen as exhilarating or nothing but lies. And Donaldson is always reminding us that a leper can never afford to forget the "lethal reality of facts."[6] When Covenant burns both his second manuscript and his first published book, he denounces his own imagination. He becomes an either/or modern man, denying an important part of his potential for the sake of self-preservation. He decides that he cannot afford imagination. Here again Covenant reflects the dominant world view of the twentieth century toward prose writing.

The new, despairing Covenant, when he creates poetry, reveals the cynicism and fatalism of his beliefs. The first poem which comes to him is remembered or created to a tune:

> Golden boy with feet of clay,
> Let me help you on your way,
> A proper push will take you far —
> But what a clumsy lad you are![7]

Since he has already called himself a Golden boy, he now sees himself as being pushed/manipulated by his clumsiness, his leprosy which robs his feet and hands of feeling and thus makes it harder for him to control them or to control the insensitivity and malignancy of fate. When Lena seems to be humming some music similar to the Golden boy tune while the hurtloam is working to cure Covenant the first time, he and we are reminded of his modern "real" world perspective, successfully juxtaposing the dialectic of health/disease just as Covenant is regaining his health in the land.

Covenant's second poem is reminiscent of T.S. Eliot's "The Hollow Men" (published in 1925), in which he likens men to "hollow men," strawmen. Actually, in Eliot's poem there is a kind of hope in the possibility of "death's other Kingdom," if only for empty men, that is matched only by Donaldson's breath-in which brings the "scent of green things growing" but ends as the breath-out of "an exhalation of the grave." Covenant's poem deals with the futile lives of men who have lost purpose and the perception of beauty of the world.

> These are the pale deaths
> which men miscall their lives:
> for all the scent of green things growing,
> each breath is but an exhalation of the grave.[8]

Donaldson's poem also robs man of volition, making him a puppet to some other force, perhaps evil as hell laughs (whether in hysterical glee or sadistic anger we don't know). Man is even less than a "paltry thing, a tattered coat upon a stick"[9] since he is already a corpse. Covenant's poem reeks of despair. However, if Donaldson is to redeem modern man and modern writing, he must first demonstrate that he understands the despair that moved us to abandon imagination.

Covenant may have felt that his first book was "supercilious trash"[10] because it lacked any acknowledgment of the truths his leprosy taught him, but Donaldson makes no such error. He writes fantasy to explore the man-vs.-self-dynamic of self-realization, but he chooses a "real" character to confront, not avoid, the truths that the twentieth century has learned about itself. According to interviews with Donaldson, his own creative process must be similar to Covenant's. The entire Covenant story came to him in a flash as he listened in church to his father speaking on the psychology of lepers and realized that the disbelieving hero of a vivid dream he'd had must have been a leper. And though a realist writer usually chooses familiar worlds as settings, Donaldson does not want to be limited by the twentieth century world view and chooses to create a new world out of nothingness to give us the opposite world view as well. What results is, of course, the Land. He does confront the critical twentieth century questions of the purpose of the writer, what kind of heroism is possible in our ironic/cynical world. And he makes Covenant a modern man so that his work cannot be judged "escapist." He doesn't allow Covenant to forget the realities of his disease or any of the hard lessons man has learned about himself in this age. Covenant faces his own sins, his rape of Lena, and his inadequacies, and therefore he must be taken seriously as he is analyzed as a representative of the modern era. Donaldson wants to elevate the intellectual discussion of fantasy novels, so he does not gloss over any part of our modern awareness. As Covenant faces his experiences without ignoring what has prevented modern characters from becoming heroic, Donaldson can make his point that fantasy literature can deal with serious issues and themes.

In one of the seven published novels he has written in the "real" world between the time of the 1st and 2nd "Chronicles," *Or I Will Sell my Soul for Guilt*, Covenant implies that guilt is the most powerful and effective human emotion. Donaldson's main theme in the 1st "Chronicles" has to do with overcoming or learning to use the negative emotions of anger, guilt, and shame about our own evil deeds. But Covenant, though he feels helpless, is sometimes rather effective in the Land. So his experiences in the Land (whether real or a dream) teach him important lessons in the "real" world. In the 2nd "Chronicles" Covenant needs to learn to accept himself and be willing to sacrifice that self that is now needed (by Joan) and loved (by Linden). Donaldson, therefore, is a more mature writer than Covenant, who is still struggling with the limitations of the ironic world view. Interestingly, Dr. Berenford tells Linden that Covenant also has three or four unpublished manuscripts, which logical deduction might suggest could be the 1st "Chronicles." Both his published and unpublished writings would suggest that his first journey to the Land helps him to confront, at least psychologically, the despair he feels after losing everything due to his leprosy and to become productive/creative again. In the 2nd "Chronicles" both Covenant and Linden must learn that love and joy are equally important emotions that cannot/should not be repressed, even out of self-protection. Here is another level of paradox. Even combining the emotions of anger and shame seems contradictory — yet Donaldson forces this juxtaposition on us in *Lord Foul's Bane*: "Shame and rage were inextricably bound together in him."[11] How much more difficult is combining the dialectic of anger and love or shame and joy? Yet to get to the eye of the paradox, we must learn to unite these dialectics as well.

The emotions of shame and guilt are quite understandable in an era which has had to face its own heart of darkness and then go on living. In Joseph Conrad's *Heart of Darkness*, Kurtz does not share his awareness of his heart of darkness with Marlowe until the end of his life. Tolkien also acknowledges a similar self-awareness in Thorin's admission to Bilbo at the end of *The Hobbit* and in Frodo's inability to accomplish his stated purpose and destroy the Ring at the end of *The Lord of the Rings*. Both Marlowe and Bilbo can go on living in relative naiveté because it is not their own guilt that is revealed; Frodo cannot fit back into the carefree life of the Shire and within a few years chooses to take the ship to the Undying Lands. Covenant, on the other hand, has first to acknowledge his own guilt over Lena's rape, then realize that it is similar to Foul's devastation of the Land which he is fighting against, but still go on living and trying to expiate his guilt and find purpose for his actions. What both Tolkien and Donaldson reveal is that the best way to cope with guilt is to learn mercy and (self) forgiveness. Gandalf shows mercy toward Saruman as does Frodo, even after the Scouring of the Shire. Frodo's understanding of Gollum shows how much he acknowledges his own temptations and weaknesses. Covenant's guilt over his own killing at the battle of Soaring Woodhelven, not just the actual killing ("thou shalt not kill") but his feelings of anger, at first causes him to be sarcastic toward his friend Foamfollower, accusing the Giant as he would want to accuse himself inside. Then Covenant fore-swears violence entirely and tries fasting to find wisdom to expiate his sense of guilt, and eventually both he and Foamfollower learn that such killing affects them, cheapens them, encourages them to become what they hate. But Covenant does not really learn mercy until *The Power That Preserves* when he accepts old, mad Lena as his companion and treats her as his "Queen." He doesn't learn to make sacrifices for love rather than for guilt until the end of the 2nd "Chronicles." Covenant's reactions to his own writing in his "real" world is worked out and refined/changed by his experiences in the Land.

Donaldson uses Covenant's role as an artist in his "real" world to join the twentieth century's debate on what that role should be. Is the artist unaffected by his own creation? Donaldson would say that emersion in the Secondary World changes both writer and reader. Does the artist merely reflect his world or does he use his creative abilities to try to change the world for the better? Donaldson claims that artists must confront and resolve chaos, whether the danger is real and external or psychological and internal. From the beggar's questions of ethics, we can infer that Donaldson values engagement as a clear prerequisite for transcendent growth. James Baldwin in his short story "Sonny's Blues" about an artist who expresses himself through jazz also talks about the purpose of the artist (be he musician or writer):

> All I really know about music is that not many people ever really hear it. And, then, on the rare occasions when something opens within, and the music enters, what we mainly hear, or hear corroborated, are personal, private, vanishing evocations. But the man who creates the music is hearing something else, is dealing with the roar rising from the void and imposing order on it as it hits the air. What is evoked in him, then, is of another order, more terrible because it has no words, and triumphant, too, for that same reason.[12]

Greek philosophers and the Renaissance Christian Humanists would have avowed that we always need to be striving to improve ourselves, individually and socially. But the focus on realism in modern literature allows simply portraying the world in all its ugly detail without taking responsibility for suggesting ways to solve the problems of the world. Donaldson summarizes the modern world view as the juxtaposition of undesirable conditions: alienation, a nightmare quality to experience, an inability to fulfill the promise of our character, and our comical and cynical view of our potential; these traits seem to characterize modern American fiction. Donaldson proposes a resolution to the question of what the role of the artist should be, a solution which brings us back to the both/and thinking of the best of Western literature and places us squarely in the eye of the paradox. Though the Land and our real world are still separate through the end of the 2nd "Chronicles," few readers could react to the beauty and then the devastation of the Land without comprehending the relevance of such revelations to our situation today. Donaldson's statement about the purpose of writing is to present the human condition in un-cynical, not just comic terms. He wants us to find as models in our literature those who will show us how to love our world and feel proud of our potential, not be prevented from even trying by our self-fulfilling prophecy of failure and defeat. The role of the artist is not just to present a realistic view of the world but to engage the reader to want to find ways to improve it.

Thomas Covenant is also significantly a leper from the very beginning of the story. And this, too, is no accident. Dr. Berenford perceptively reveals to Linden, "'He doesn't think of himself as Thomas Covenant the writer — the man — the human being. He thinks of himself as Thomas Covenant the leper.'"[13] As a leper he is alienated from his society, divorced from his family, unable to sense his world through touch, impotent, and hence lonely, angry, sorry for himself. Donaldson uses leprosy symbolically because it so clearly expresses our view of our modern world. Leprosy doesn't kill the afflicted physically but merely blunts his ability to feel pain and thus protect himself from common cuts and scrapes which could become infected. It does not affect other ways in which the person can perceive or interact with the world. It creates deformities that are unsightly but not debilitating, though eventually as the nerves die, blindness may occur. But having leprosy is irreversible and incurable. Donaldson makes it clear that leprosy is not contagious nor is it a death sentence. Covenant's reaction to his leprosy is despair which he gets from the refrain at the leprosarium: there is no hope for a cure. He learns to control the spread of his disease with constant VSE (visual surveillance of extremities) to make sure he has suffered no harm that he did not feel but which could fester and become infected. Also, there is medication that can help — DDS or diamino-diphenyl-sulfone and synthetic antibiotics. As a leper, Thomas Covenant represents modern man as many twentieth century writers have depicted him, as alienated from others and stuck in nightmare scenarios in which he is helpless. Through Thomas Covenant, Donaldson depicts a typically twentieth century view based on total reliance on scientific objectivism. Objectively, there is no hope for a leper. Covenant's leprosy creates another paradox: since his disease is repugnant to others, no one wants to be near him, so he loses whatever potential support system family or society could have provided. His own self-repugnance reinforces the view of others. No wonder the twentieth century ended in paralysis, unable to move beyond the awareness that depresses us so much.

Covenant's reaction to the "real" world is sorrow at his loss of feeling. If he touches a tree, he feels nothing. Feeling is an integral aspect of the way we perceive the world, the way wonder is inspired in us. Those who love fantasy cannot help but notice the contrast with Frodo's first experience in Lothlorien in *The Lord of the Rings*: when Frodo touches a tree, he feels appreciation for the life of the tree, not what it could be made into or how it could provide heat if it were burned. The twentieth century looked to fantasy literature for such recovery of wonder. So when Covenant reaches the Land, he finds a world which could be possible, his realistic mind tells him, only within his imagination or subconscious mind. In the Land, Covenant gains the ability to perceive more than just the outward feel of a tree, without even touching one. The health sense that Lena's hurtloam awakens in him allows him to perceive the world more acutely. He can observe a tree and experience its life, the spread of its branches and leaves, the way its sap flows. He can contrast this life with the stillness of the rock around it. Such awareness, which is clearly beyond the perceptive ability of the average man, startles, enchants, and frightens Covenant with its depth of discernment. Either Covenant is going mad (in other words, that the quality of imagination makes modern man insane because it seduces him into believing impossible things) or he might be able to find some psychological solace through his imagination (that fantasy can help modern man cope with a cold, stressful world). Covenant chooses to believe the latter (though he fears the former). His reawakened senses that had been lost to leprosy make him want to believe in the Land, even as his survival instinct warns against belief. The resolution for the conflict between the desire for belief and the need for unbelief begins when Covenant admits that if his experiences in the Land are only part of his dream, it might not be a completely negative situation, as "his dreams might heal other afflictions."[14]

To explain why she is leaving and taking Covenant's son Roger with her, Joan rationalizes her abandonment as protection for their young son Roger since she believes that children are more likely to "catch" leprosy than adults. But she may be reacting precipitously out of unrealistic fear since this dire consequence usually occurs only if those children are living in poverty conditions. Undoubtedly this false belief contributes to the guilt Joan later feels. What do we know of leprosy? For most of us our only exposure is the hopelessness of lepers in the Bible and the fact that it takes a miracle to cure them, or movies such as *Ben Hur* and *Papillon*, depicting lepers as deformed outcasts. But we also have faced, especially since the 1980s, an equally devastating (more so because more deadly) disease in AIDS. Like leprosy, AIDS cannot be romanticized as leukemia is today or tuberculosis was in the past. Those afflicted with AIDS suffer the same kind of outcasting, suspicion, and in some cases prejudice and hatred as lepers of old. Thus, we get a new view of the quality of imagination, one which is not in conflict with reality, and a new purpose for creativity. Imagination cannot change reality, but it can make the real-but-undesirable aspects of life more understandable and bearable. Whatever lessons Covenant learns about his acceptance of his leprosy in the "real" world through his experiences in the Land might help others to cope with their AIDS or cancer or any other debilitating disease in our real world. By putting Covenant's consciousness from his realistic world view into the fantasy setting of the Land, Donaldson can force us to combine the two views, to find the eye of the paradox. As Covenant finds acceptance and purpose in the Land, we can look to our own outcasts (those afflicted with AIDS) and see them in a new way and find a better way to accept them, include them and thus counter alienation in the modern world.

Another paradox Covenant must resolve, perhaps the central question of the "Chronicles," involves his inability to believe the Land true: the conflict between his Unbelief and his need for his experiences in the Land to have meaning, to teach him important lessons about life (even if the Land is merely a dream). Donaldson makes Covenant an Unbeliever to connect reality with fantasy, to show how a modern man who decries the importance of imagination can survive and thrive in a world which demands epic heroism. The problem for many readers is that Covenant's "real" world is so stark, the people in it so extreme in their abhorrence for him, and our initial perception of the changed Covenant himself so negative that we find the Land more "real," the people in it more genuine, and we get frustrated at Covenant for his unbelief. Supporting our view of the unreality of Covenant's "real" world is the dream he has of all the townspeople pointing at him when he has fallen in front of the police car. That dream seems more unreal than the Land.

At the end of the 1st "Chronicles," before Covenant can confront Lord Foul, the personification of his own despair, Covenant must resolve the question of his unbelief. He must choose to engage with his enemy and, therefore, must believe such a contest will have significance. It is the ethics problem posed by the beggar in his "real" world. At the end of *The Power That Preserves*, Lord Foul states his own either/or perspective of the dialectic of belief in the Land and Unbelief. Foul derides Covenant for thinking he can accept both perspectives as true. But Covenant knows that his sanity and wholeness demand that he affirm both sides of the contradiction — that the Land is real and that it is only his dream. Only his ability to combine both contradictory dialectics, to find the eye of the paradox, gives meaning to his experiences in the Land and to his dream of the Land and to his existence in his "real" world.

Toward the end of the 2nd "Chronicles," when Covenant has become so powerful that he is effectively powerless because he dares not use his power for fear of the consequences (not unlike a world leader today sitting firmly atop the lid to his arsenal of nuclear weapons capable of destroying the earth ten times over), he engages in a conversation with the First about the need for doubt. She claims that she is following him and does not doubt him because of the goodness and purity of his purpose, to fight Lord Foul. Covenant warns her to retain her doubt, to avoid the either/or of certainty, because when certainty fails, despair is close behind. This truth, that certainty is dangerous, is so often illustrated by Donaldson; it is definitely one of his main themes. Absolute conviction is the cause for the downfall of both the Giants of the Grieve and the Bloodguard when they break their Vow. The Giants do not believe any Raver can ever take over a Giant, and they have such pride in the omen of the three triplet Giant-children, that when a Raver is able to control Kinslaughterer, the shock of learning they are wrong so stuns them that they simply accept death at the hands of the Giant-Raver. The *Haruchai* also do not doubt their own ability to be faithful; they see themselves as the epitome of fidelity. So when Korik, Sill, and Doar break faith with the Lords as they break their Vow, again the impossible happens and in an either/or world, when one side is lost, all that is left is the other. So if the dialectic is the Vow or Corruption, and then the Vow is broken, the only conclusion for the *Haruchai* is that they have become Corruption. Donaldson does not tolerate that kind of narrow conclusion. However, rather than condemnation, he encourages toleration and waiting for insight. So he encourages doubt rather than certainty. Covenant himself doubts and believes. But by the end of the 2nd "Chronicles," Covenant's perception of himself has changed. He no longer sees himself defined by his disease. Leprosy is real, but his awareness of the wonders of the Land and his desire to preserve its beauty motivate his actions much more than his fears do. And he is effective in fighting despair, Lord Foul, surprising himself as much as anyone else. Even though he doubts that the Land can be true, he must act as if it is true to remain faithful to his essential self, and then when he tries to act, he can act.

To Donaldson the belief/doubt and reality/illusion dialectics are more complicated than the necessity to choose one and disavow the other; one must choose both and accept the disparity. Neither alone will suffice. For Covenant, belief in the Land is like succumbing to the power of the Sirens or remaining behind on Lotus Land. There he is healthy, more than just physically healthy himself, but able to perceive health in others and in the Land itself. And he regains his sexual desire and potency, which his disease should have made impossible. Andelain especially has the power to seduce him into forgetfulness, and soon his life-preserving habits — his VSE, his anger, his recognition of the reality of his disease — are forgotten. The danger comes from the wonder it inspires in him, which seduces him into forgetting his life-saving rituals. On the other hand, Covenant's recitation of the ills of his "real" world — his culture shock story of despair and suicide, his view of the townspeople all hating him — is an equally one-sided picture of reality. To be believable, to be relevant, literature should be a combination of both reality and imagination. Modern works rely too much on the former and not enough on the latter. Much of fantasy is the opposite. Donaldson's kind of fantasy, though, combines both. For us, then, there is a need, as Donaldson has said, to be aware of the bed even in the midst of the dream. Hence, the "real" world frame tale — which so many readers find disconcerting — is essential to provide the touchstone for all the fantasy adventures, and we must be unbelievers and doubters even as we suspend our disbelief.

Covenant reveals another purpose of fantasy, of imagination: its power to "heal other afflictions."[15] Imagination cannot change the reality of any world, the Land or our real world. But it can help us learn to cope with our fears, our inadequacies, our impotence. It concerns more our psychological responses to the world. Therefore, it is appropriate that Donaldson creates ambiguity about whether Covenant's adventures in the Land are actual or part of a dream. Both world views, that within the fantasy and that within the "real" world, are essential for us to confront the paradox. As a dream, Covenant's experiences can be seen as a healthy working out of conflicts/problems he has within himself in his "real" world. His impotence and desire for sensory experience, his feelings of helplessness and inadequacy and desire for a place of importance within his society are handled openly in the Land. Donaldson claims that fantasy is always the working out of internal conflicts by externalizing them. This solution, however, works only for the character himself. What benefits do we the readers gain from Covenant's sojourn in the Land, whether it is his report of a real happening or his reconstruction of his dream? Again, the question involves the purpose of fantasy, this time not on those who experience it but on those who only hear tell of imaginary happenings or read fantasies.

Therefore, a fuller exploration of the question of the importance or purpose of fantasy (of creativity) also involves the significance of story-telling itself. The power of songs or stories to inspire, to cheer, to touch, to strengthen is often reiterated with the "Chronicles." The Giants, especially, but all the free peoples in the Land, gain solace and psychological relief from the telling of and listening to stories. Only Covenant at the beginning feels threatened by the telling of tales. He runs away after the tale of Berek Halfhand is sung by Atiaran at the Gathering because he thinks too much will be expected of him due to his physical resemblance to Berek. In our modern age, we also seem to shun tales of heroism in our mainstream literature (though interestingly not in films), perhaps because they make us feel cowardly or make our world seem tawdry by comparison.

The culture shock story Covenant tells Foamfollower does not have the same power to heal, to strengthen, but actually has the opposite effect. Using this story as a self-reflective statement about the purpose of writing, Donaldson could be commenting on how various writers have used or could use their creativity. Covenant, the modern storyteller, draws attention to a serious problem such as culture shock but gives no constructive way to resolve it. He tells of a man who slits his wrists and dies slowly in the lavatory of an airplane simply because the man does not understand how his action will kill him as finally as the more familiar ways his culture knows of to commit suicide, for example, by drinking Belladonna tea. Covenant's story reads like many realistic novels; Foamfollower's tale of Bahgoon the Unbearable and Thelma Twofist follows the fantasy mode. One drains the hearer and causes despair to the teller; the other is a tale that produces laughter.

Stories (and thus fantasy/imagination) are not limited to the formal tales we tell each other. Covenant's language shows that at first he is stuck in the modern realism/determinism mode. In his first interaction with the beggar in his home town, Covenant's responses can be read as depressing tales; when the beggar asks him why he does not just commit suicide, Covenant replies that giving up is the easy solution, and he will fight to survive as long as he can. In the Land Foamfollower also comments on how Covenant's responses are sad stories: Giants love tales, and especially long stories. All Covenant's stories are short and depressing. When asked if he enjoys telling stories, Covenant says that he once did, when he was a writer of the best seller. Foamfollower recognizes that Covenant has given up this joy and presses him for how he can survive without the solace of stories, to which Covenant replies, "'I live.'"[16] Foamfollower finds this answer even more depressing than Covenant's previous response and begs him to say no more because all his tales are sad.

Covenant becomes the embodiment of modern realism within Donaldson's fantasy tale. He forces us to juxtapose the two world views, never to lose sight of reality, even of the mundane, the petty, the undesirable or painful in our world, no matter how much we desire the escape that fantasy provides. But we should also never forget the healing possible through imagination. Donaldson states his overall purpose in his short paper *Epic Fantasy in the Modern World*. He wants to force an alienated, cynical modern man to interact with heroic characters in the fantasy world, not as he might interact with people of similarly limited expectations in our ironic world, but as he could in a world of epic possibilities. And the wondrous creatures of the Land — the Giants, the Lords, the Ranyhyn, the *Haruchai*— call forth from Covenant not the despair which threatens to overwhelm him but the love and devotion he is capable of when he is able to engage in conflicts larger than his own self-concern. Today our imaginations are held tightly under control and only allowed free reign in our dreams, but dreams force inspiration/ imagination on us and rob us of control at the same time. This kind of imagination is like tapping into one's muse but being unable to steer or direct the course of the story. Perhaps because we have lost the technique of using our imaginations freely, we feel, like Covenant, victimized by our capacity for imagining that which we think we cannot have or achieve. Thus, imagination might bring us only frustration and sorrow.

Story telling, on the other hand, is a controlled use of imagination. The Giants especially see the purpose and power of stories: as Foamfollower tells Covenant, stories can sustain and rejuvenate the listeners. In the Land, stories can create a sense of communion, shared experience, as when Atiaran tells the tale of Berek Half-Hand. The story also results in an uplifting of spirits, and the Stonedowners spontaneously want to hug her to share the elation the story inspired. To pass the time and keep his mind off his soreness, Covenant asks Atiaran to tell stories of the history of the Land as they travel toward Revelstone. When Elena discovers that her boat will not move across Earthroot without the sound of her voice, she tells Covenant the tale of her childhood interaction with the Ranyhyn.

Story telling has other purposes more connected with the healing of afflictions. Linden tells Covenant about her mother to help explain why she tried to kill Ceer when she hadn't quite come back to full consciousness after taking on the darkness the *Elohim* had imposed on Covenant. She is appalled by her actions and feels compelled to explain the blackness of the memory of her mother's death and her desire to give her mother some relief from the pain of the cancer and the connection Linden sees between her mother and Ceer, who was mortally wounded in Bhrathairealm. When Linden can connect her epiphanies in the Land to her experiences in her past in the "real" world, she can finally let go of the memories that haunt her. As a result of admitting her guilt over her killing of her own mother which had held her paralyzed, Linden can make personal choices and find "'there is also love in the world,'"[17] and she takes an important step to overcoming the paralysis or inability to make or act on her decisions that is one of her greatest challenges. On the other hand, it is not enough that she realize within herself this connection, as Covenant had finally recognized that what Foul was doing to the Land was so much like his own rape of Lena. For the cleansing effect, Linden must also share the previously hidden shameful truth about herself with someone else. Covenant tells Linden that whether the Land is real or a dream, her experiences can alter her basic personality and her view of herself. In addition, Hollinscrave admits to Covenant that he was responsible for the scar his brother Seadreamer has, which may have precipitated the EarthSight and Seadreamer's resultant muteness. These examples illustrate how stories can help to expiate a sense of guilt over actions that have affected someone else. Like James Baldwin's Sonny, the storyteller in Donaldson's tale is trying to create order out of chaos, but not until his point is understood by his audience is his purpose accomplished.

Another purpose of storytelling is to give honor to the subjects of the story. Hollinscrave tells the tale of the events in Bhrathairealm, concentrating on the roles of Hergrom and Ceer, who died there. "This he did as an homage to the dead and a condolence for the living."[18] Pitchwife tells of the heroic death of the First's father, Brow Gnarlfist, when he sacrificed himself to allow Pitchwife to wive the stone hole in the *dromond's* hull. Though Pitchwife had felt guilty that in setting the stone, he had also caught Gnarlfist's chest, together they saved the ship, and the ultimate result was a new relationship between Gossamer Glowlimn (the First) and the crippled Giant who had given meaning to her father's death. In both these cases the story is both happy and sad, another manifestation of the eye of the paradox. Also the tales provide a new view of death by focusing on the purpose of the life that was lost, what was accomplished by that death, not on the sense of loss felt by those who must cope with this death. Pitchwife's tale is especially significant because without his role in the death of her father, the First might not have noticed him especially or gotten to know his personality and grown to love him. Foamfollower tells Covenant not to worry about whether he can escape from Foul's Creche, telling him "'I have beheld a marvelous story.'"[19] Being part of significant events gives purpose and meaning to both the life and the death of the participants.

Sometimes stories make comment on the events of the quest. Pitchwife tells Covenant how Linden saved Starfare's Gem by taming the Nicor. Galewrath's tale of two contrary Giants who constantly fight with each other, mistaking their love for each other for conflict, reflects the other Giants' perception of how long it takes Covenant and Linden to openly acknowledge their love for each other. Findail tells a tale of some other *Elohim,* each of them chosen to serve as an Appointed, like the Colossus of the Fall, who was bound to stone to keep the Ravers from destroying the Forest, and Kastenessen who, because of his love of a mortal woman, tried to refuse the burden of being Appointed to cap a fire which threatened the foundation of the North. Findail states as his purpose, "'I desire to be understood.'"[20] Covenant tells the Giants of the Search about Berek, which interestingly had been the story he had run away from in Mithil Stonedown when Atiaran first told it, to help explain his desire/need to find the One Tree and to create a new Staff of Law. Covenant's willingness to honor Berek with his story shows his changed attitude toward the Land during the 2nd "Chronicles."

Another insight into the purpose of story telling can be seen by examining the creation myths of the various peoples of the Land for these are the tales cultures tell themselves to explain their worlds and their places in those worlds. Myths are a special kind of long-tested story — creation myths especially — but in Donaldson these stories aren't presented as dogma, as a religious belief, but as a way to explain origins and differences between cultures. Donaldson provides several examples to drive this point home and to illustrate that the tales reveal more truths about the people who tell them than they do about the world itself. Foamfollower tells the Unhomed's version, the legend of the Wounded Rainbow.[21] This creation story begins with a world without stars. The people of the land are separated from the Creator by a void. The Creator is happy in his relationships with others and the children who brightened his life with their play and their song. But the Creator desires to make something new to please his children, so in his forges, using both his power and his theurgy, he creates a rainbow. He throws the rainbow into the sky, creating an arch between his world and the Land. At first the Creator is pleased, but then he notices a flaw in the rainbow. According to Foamfollower, the Creator is unaware that his Enemy has sabotaged his great creation and created a wound which mars the rainbow. So the Creator returns to his workshop to devise a way to repair his beautiful rainbow. And while he is distracted, his children discover the rainbow, and finding it wonderful, they run and play and dance their way up the arch. When they come to the wound, they do not understand it and go through it into the sky of the Land. They marvel at the darkness and continue to play, casting their light on the Land below. Not realizing his children have discovered the rainbow, the Creator thinks he has found the cause of the wound, and he tears the rainbow from the sky. Therefore, he traps his own children in the sky of the Land until he can defeat his Enemy and perfect the rainbow to get them back. But in the meantime, the Creator's happy children remain as stars in the sky and are used by the Giants as guides on their journeys.

Interestingly, this story shows that even the original Creator is flawed and cannot create perfectly. His Enemy is able to mar his creation. But also, clearly his Enemy is someone outside of himself and not related to him in any way. Donaldson reinforces the idea of creations being flawed when Kasreyn must include a blemish in everything he does unless he can harness the power of the white gold which is already an alloy. Thus Donaldson suggests that creation is ongoing, and no work of art is ever complete or perfect. This idea of continuous creation becomes his addition to the dialogue the twentieth century found so fascinating about the creative process and whether the deconstructionists were right that each work also includes something that unravels its purpose. On the other hand, the same concept also supports the Lords' position that their purpose and that of others in the Land is to participate in the perfecting of the Land, and it reinforces Donaldson's view that often the connection between dialectics cannot be rationally understood, yet we must still be willing to embrace both.

Not only does this creation myth provide a sense of security from the overarching universe, the idea of a creator who is still trying to undo what evil has done to his creation — as do most of the creation myths given — but this one also has special meaning for the Giants of Seareach in the Land.

Foamfollower makes this connection himself when he tells Covenant, "'So it was with us, the Unhomed.'"[22] They, too, like the Creator's children are cut off from home and trying to find a way back. The Giants come to the Land because of the same kind of curiosity and joy of exploring which prompt the Creator's children to venture up the rainbow. As sailors, the Giants rely on the stars to direct them, so personifying the stars as celestial beings is logical for the Giants. Both groups seem to be stuck where they are until the Enemy is defeated. The major difference is that the Creator's children wait for him to clear the way, while the Giants, because of Damelon's promised omens, attempt to find the way themselves. Furthermore, just as the Creator puts rainbows in the sky after a rain as omens of hope for his children, the Giants see portents of hope in the birth of children, especially in the birth of the triplets.

Though Mhoram at first states that the Lords do not really know of an origin story, his mother Tamarantha gives a different version of creation to Covenant.[23] She reports the oral tradition of the Lords in which again there is a single Creator who works with his hands to create an arch in the sky, this time the Arch of Time. Tamarantha claims that the Creator is striving for perfection when he creates the arch that provides a place for his new Land. He uses white gold as the wild magic of his forgery because it does not exist in the Land so that the Arch of Time will be unbreakable and long-lasting. The process of creation is trial and error, not one flash of insight as Foamfollower had suggested in the Giants' creation myth. Tamarantha says the Creator tested and perfected his creation so that "'when he was done his creation would have no cause to reproach him.'"[24] Then he creates the people of his new world to help him continue to make the Land more perfect. In addition, he gives them Earthpower so they are able to participate in the creation process. And, at first, he is pleased.

Nevertheless, either he has forgotten his enemy, Lord Foul, or has underestimated him. As the Creator gazes in pride on his creation, he sees that Foul has been at work as well creating "banes of destruction"[25] inside the earth that are powerful enough to destroy his creation. At this point in Tamarantha's version of the creation story, she introduces ambiguity. As the Creator tries to figure out how the flaw came about, he thinks that another being, Despite/Lord Foul, might have influenced his creation, but he also recognizes in himself the potential for destruction. To the Lords, it does not matter if Despite is part of the Creator or not, for he banishes his enemy, or the destructive part of himself, into the world he has created. Because the Arch of Time is strong, Despite is caught and imprisoned in the Land, and Lord Foul, as the people of the Land come to call him, resents being trapped and makes it his goal to destroy the Arch of Time and if he cannot, then to destroy what the Creator has made in the Land. Whereas the Creator regrets his hasty action of banishing Despite to the Land, he cannot undo his action, nor can Foul now leave the Land. So the Creator attempts to aid the peoples of the Land to resist the destructive power of Lord Foul. He responds to Berek's cry for help and teaches him the uses of Earthpower and leads him to create the Staff of Law. But the Creator is locked out of the Land as Foul is locked in by the Arch of Time, and if he were to intervene more directly to help the people of the Land, he would break his own Arch which would free Lord Foul to destroy the rest of the universe. Lord Tamarantha implies that the Lords are fighting Lord Foul within the Land with only the indirect aid of the Creator through lore and Earthpower.

As with the Giants' version of the creation myth, the Lords envision a creator who tries to create perfection, but is hampered either by some outside force (the Despiser) or by some flaw or destructive side of his own that mars the perfection. Both include an arch or rainbow that contains and isolates the created world. In Tamarantha's version the emphasis is on the harm Lord Foul is free to do to the Land because the Creator cannot directly intervene, and on how the creatures of the Land must fight against the Despiser with whatever aid they are given indirectly — Earthpower and the Staff of Law, for instance. The purpose of the Lords becomes to survive and heal as best they can the desecration that is inevitable because of the banes of destruction built in at the creation of the Land. Again, the focus of the myth is on the hope, but not the promise, that the Lords will be able to accomplish a task that seems impossible. The Lords' version of the creation myth also provides for a much less oppositional vision of the role of the creation. Whereas for the Giants, the Creator is good and his Enemy creates the wound in the Rainbow, for the Lords there is ambiguity created: the Creator may have wrested with an external Despiser or may have recognized the fault in himself. So the possibility of good and evil residing in the same person in internal conflict is suggested, and more responsibility is placed on the inhabitants of the Land to save and protect its beauty.

The contribution this story makes to the twentieth century debate about the creative process might reinforce the position of the deconstructionists — that inevitably there are flaws within every created work. Conversely, it also supports the concept of continual improvement as the Creator "'formed and reformed, trialed and tested and rejected and trialed and tested again'"[26] as a writer might revise a manuscript. Also, to this version is added that the purpose for wanting to create perfection is not simply for itself but to please the beings he is creating. Since he is not able to create perfectly, by implication the people of the Land have cause to reproach the Creator for leaving them to deal with Despite. Also, we certainly have cause to wonder why a loving God allows poverty, wars, disasters, and disease today. Of course, this view of creativity also implies that, once imagined/created, his beings are real.

It is interesting that, although the Search visits the land of the *Elohim* and Covenant and Linden do interact with them, the report of their origin story comes instead from the Giants. Pitchwife narrates the story.[27] The *Elohim* begin their creation story not with the Land but with the cosmos. At that time the universe is populated by many more stars. The stars dance in the heavens in great joy. They are self-contained but not lonely because of the multitude of bright beings that exist. Then from some other place in the universe comes the Worm, the personification of destruction, the polar opposite of the essence of the stars. As it awakens from its great sleep, it begins to roam the universe, consuming all the stars in its path. Though the Worm is not big at first, it has an insatiable appetite and is able to devour large numbers of stars, greatly diminishing the population of the stars in the heavens. However, the stars do not die even after being devoured; rather they exert their power to put the Worm to sleep. Since the time of its great sleep is not come yet, when it curls around its own tail, it is to rest only briefly. Time obviously has a different meaning when it is being measured in eons by the immortal *Elohim*.

While the Worm slumbers, the stars within it cause the world to be created on the surface of the Worm. The stars are credited by the *Elohim* for creating all aspects of the Land, its mountains, rivers, and oceans. The *Elohim* then say that, at one point in time, the life of the Land is "born," but the story does not explain how life is created. The *Elohim* are not referring just to the peoples of the Land, but also to the animals and the forests, all life.

The pattern of creation to destruction to new creation appears to be the neverending cycle of the world, and the *Elohim* believe that the Land will one day be sloughed off the exterior of the Worm when it reawakens to continue its destruction in the cosmos. The *Elohim*, therefore, see their purpose in the life of the Land as merely to be, for as long as the Land exists. They contemplate their own existence and share such joy as they find with each other as they can. However, their view of time is different than that of other beings of the Land. They see the Land as temporary, for eventually the Worm of the World's End will awaken.

The *Elohim's* version of creation is vastly different than either the Giants' or the Lords', as different as are the *Elohim* from any other peoples. There is no talk of good and evil, an Enemy or a Despiser which must somehow be fought and overcome, but only of creation and destruction as two forces opposite yet united in a natural order. The Worm destroys because that is its nature. Equally naturally, the stars create the Earth when the Worm rests. The stars are beings, god-like in the *Elohim's* version, the Creator's children in the

Giants' myth. But there is no focus on hope since the eventual awakening of the Worm is inevitable, and what is known as the Earth will be shrugged off. Instead, the focus is on the loneliness of the stars which have been significantly reduced in number by the Worm, and on their difference from any other beings. The sense of purpose in this myth is much more positive, though, for instead of having to redress wrongs, to fight to heal destruction, the *Elohim* and also the Giants of the 2nd "Chronicles" in interpreting the *Elohim's* creation story, see their purpose as to live, to strive, to seek to define the essence of their being. This interpretation is much more positive than merely the repairing of wrongs.

This version of a creation myth is closer to Tolkien's creation story as presented in *The Silmarillion*, in that the Ainur, "the offspring of [Eru's] thought,"[28] create Middle-earth first through song and then eventually, as god-like personifications of natural forces (like the Sea or vegetation), work as the Valar to bring about the reality of the vision of the creation of the world that they were given by Eru as a visual perception of the song they sang. In the *Elohim's* story the stars, who in Foamfollower's version are identified as the Children of the Creator trapped in our world, become the creators of the physical Land when they have been eaten and are trapped in the Worm.

In terms of the modern debate about the creative process, the *Elohim* take a distinctly different view of the way to define purpose. Whereas for the Lords purpose consists of meaningful actions to resist and defeat Lord Foul, for the *Elohim* no action is needed. No conscious choice is made by the stars to create the world; they merely express their nature. The *Elohim* also do not define purpose as "to do" something, but rather as "to be." The *Elohim* occasionally feel compelled to prevent or redress some wrong or create something valuable, but they relegate that responsibility to an Appointed. Most of the time they spend trying to understand their own natures. Perhaps this broader focus is connected to their immortal perspective, since if they are right, then they will see the eon's end or the time when the Worm awakens, while many individual generations of men will not.

Creation stories are especially interesting because they are often passed orally from one generation to the next and may change in the retelling, possibly based on new insights or a change in circumstances of the younger generation. Therefore, it is especially interesting to see how Covenant retells the Lords' creation myth to Linden in *The Wounded Land* with slight but significant changes.[29] Covenant tells of a Creator who is one of many immortals or gods. This Creator desires to please his children by creating something beautiful for them. For the Creator (as for Covenant himself when he was writing his best seller), the process of creation is exhilarating. At this point Covenant's retelling of the story parallels the original. The Creator makes the

Arch of Time and then forms the earth. His desire is to create something that will engender joy in the beholder. He makes creatures to inhabit his new Land who can appreciate its beauty, and he gives the inhabitants the power to create their own beauty.

When he pauses to examine his creation, he is surprised to discover flaws and evils, for these he has not intended. Obviously, as Covenant reports the story, another being, either a son or brother to the Creator, has been interfering in the creative process and spoiling it for some malignant reason. In this version, there is no admission that the Despiser might be an aspect of the Creator's own personality. The Creator then grapples with his brother or son and throws him to the Land, catching him within the Arch of Time. Covenant judges the Creator and blames him for harming his own beloved creation and thus teaching the inhabitants of the Land self-blame. The son or brother of the Creator, trapped in the Land, takes out his frustration on the Land and its inhabitants, and the Creator can do nothing to stop him without breaking his own Arch of Time. Therefore, the people of the Land must now contest with despair.

The significant difference is that the Despiser is related to, a son or brother, but not necessarily the same as the Creator, whereas the Lords' tale allowed for the ambiguity of the Creator and Despiser being the same person. Even by the end of the 2nd "Chronicles," Covenant is still seeing himself and Foul, good and evil, as an either/or opposition. But his other significant additions are that he suggests that the Creator's purpose is to create beauty and to give joy to his created beings and that he makes those beings also capable of creation and love. These additions support Tolkien's concept that writers subcreate in imitation of God's creation and that the beings of Covenant's dream can become real. Covenant also importantly brings in the emotions of joy and love, whereas the Lords focused on sorrow and humility and the ability to strive for perfection (but without the pride of accomplishment because of the flaws inherent in the created work).

Sunder's father knows the story that Covenant tells, but it is contradicted by the Rede of the na-Mhoram, the Clave, which is led by Gibbon-Raver and is part of the superstition that reinforces the need for human sacrifice to "fight" (but really to sustain) the Sunbane. Sunder recounts that version.[30] The Clave, of course, wants to keep the people of the Land subjugated and to reinforce their sense of guilt. So its text states that the Land is a jail for all its inhabitants, not just the figure of Despite who has tried to destroy the Creator's work. The Clave also avows that all men and women deserve this punishment because they do not fight hard enough against Lord Foul. It declares that men conspire with Foul, aid him. And it especially blames men like Berek, half-handed men. The Clave says that the Creator abandoned the people of the Land and, in displeasure, inflicted them with the Sunbane. Of course, the na-Mhoram claims to help the people of the Land, supposedly by fighting against the Sunbane through human sacrifices.

This particular creation myth is especially instructive, since it is a deliberate corruption, designed to bolster the authority and power of the Clave and to create a sense of futility and guilt in men. It also creates distrust and suspicion directed toward Covenant because of his lost fingers. It further suggests that storytelling can manipulate politics and people's emotions. To the dialogue about the purpose of the artist in the modern world, Donaldson is creating distrust of didactic purposes. Truth must still be judged by individuals, as Sunder and Hollian learn to do when they choose to trust Covenant rather than the stories they have heard all their lives from the Clave.

Overall, Donaldson, through the creation stories especially, affirms that the stories one tells reflect more his own view of the world than any objective reality. After contracting leprosy, Covenant tells no happy tales until he records his adventures in the Land. On the other hand, Foamfollower can see his own story of becoming what he hates most, of excruciating pain and inevitable death in Kiril Threndor as a tale of salvation. Donaldson himself, though he relates the prejudice and despair in Covenant's "real" world, also tells of the epic journeys and heroic actions of those in the Land.

Thomas Covenant's most significant roles are those of writer, leper, and unbeliever, but his personality also determines his actions and the outcomes of the stories. He is a man of high principle, who wants to extract justice for the Land, even while he doubts whether it is a real place or an aspect of his imagination. He has also learned that how one accomplishes tasks is as or more important than whether the result is success. He has learned how he feels if he personally causes death, even to "evil" creatures intent on killing him. Further, because of his own ignorance in how to call up and use the white gold, supposedly the most powerful force in the Land, he has learned of the limitations of power, so he searches for other means to fight against Foul. Perhaps because he is a writer, he trusts his own intuition, even as he seems to accept the modern view that only facts matter, and he is willing to change his mind about his purposes if he thinks of a better way to resist Despite.

Among the reasons that the old beggar, the Creator, may have chosen Covenant are his stubbornness, his determination to stay alive and go forward, the discipline he learns from his VSE, and also for character traits which we may consider negative but which are also necessary: his perception of himself as flawed, his extreme need for community, even his bitterness and his abhorrence of his own weakness. Some of these characteristics keep us from appreciating Covenant at first, but as we get to know him better, we realize how much he is like us, and how, by learning to love him, we are also learning to accept even the negative aspects of ourselves. By seeing how he can be effective, even with and eventually because of his culpabilities and inability to understand all that is going on around him, we can have hope that we can be effective also. Similarly, when we are able to unite our disparate personality traits in a healthy both/and world view, we, too, can find the eye of our own paradox.

CHAPTER 3

Remembrance of
Some Things Past

Marcel Proust in his seven-volume work *Remembrance of Things Past* (published between 1912 and 1930, eight years after his death in 1922) illustrates the significance of memories. Proust demonstrates the potency of memories of joyful occurrences in one's past that he can relive by remembering them, like Charles Swann's memory of Odette's passionate first kiss. Donaldson takes the idea of the power of memory a step further than Proust by suggesting that the power of imagination can have the same effect whether what we are remembering is an actual incident from our own past, or we are re-experiencing something we simply dreamed or imagined, or we are reacting to something we read about and experienced vicariously. Similarly, Keats refers to this kind of experience in his "Ode on a Grecian Urn" when, simply by viewing the vase that pictures two lovers about to kiss, he imagines that first-love, infatuation feeling, and we the readers can also by reading his poem. Once the beauty of the Land is experienced by Covenant (and Linden), written about by Donaldson, and read by readers, it becomes immortalized through art and will not fade or die. For this reason the "Something there is in Beauty" poem is as emblematic of one of Donaldson's themes (beauty is immortal) as the "Road Song" was for Tolkien. When Linden has healed the Land and is about to be transported back to her "real" world, she holds a short conversation with the now-dead Covenant, and though she doesn't want to lose him and tries to say farewell, he replies, "'There's no need for that. I'm part of you now. You'll always remember.'"[1] And so will we.

Memory can have a negative effect on a person's ability to cope with the world as well. Today many psychologists and psychiatrists make a living treating patients who are controlled by powerful fears, guilts, pains, or sorrows from their pasts. Personal history is part of the sum of who each of us is. In our world, history helps define the character of a nation or region of the world. Mythic stories such as Tolkien's and Donaldson's are enhanced by a sense of the history of the world they are exploring, which includes a rich record of creation stories, legends, and tales of historical figures. This history gives us insights into the motivating factors influencing the characters, their sense of what makes someone a hero, the important events of their past which shape them as a society. In the "Chronicles," Donaldson analyzes both Covenant's "real" world and the personal history of the characters who come from that world, and the Land and its great historical figures to explore another modern literary theme: the potency of memory.

Covenant has already decided that even if his experiences in the Land are a dream, they can still "heal other afflictions"[2] for him. Previously, I explored his personal challenge of coping with his leprosy and how it alienated him from his community and robbed him of the human support system so needed to cope with such a life-changing situation. The Land's demand that he act heroically even if he doesn't feel heroic in any way helps him past his own personal sense of inadequacy and impotence. When he finds himself back in his "real" world after his first adventure in the Land, he has more self-confidence and self-pride at accomplishing something important, though admittedly he is also plagued with guilt still over his inadequacies and especially his culpability over the rape of Lena. Covenant has experienced both his own success as part of the quest for the Staff of Law and his aid in calling the Fire Lions, and also his failure to save Elena when he is faced with the task of saving the little girl bitten by a snake in his "real" world. The leper Covenant of the first part of *Lord Foul's Bane* might not have felt himself capable nor had the overwhelming desire to save the child. But Covenant, because of his experiences in the Land, is changing.

His character is not only informed by his career as a writer, his leprosy, and even his disbelief in the Land; his own personal history in his "real" world affects his decisions and actions within the Land. From the 1st "Chronicles" we learn nothing about his childhood and very little of his marriage with Joan. He was happy; he was optimistic; he believed himself creative; he recognized and respected Joan's strengths. He was in awe of her that she could tame horses even though she seemed small and vulnerable. She had a surety about her, knew when they could afford to try to conceive a child, knew when it was time for her to stop working to protect that child in her womb, knew exactly what she wanted to name her son when he was born. Covenant didn't always agree with her decisions (in fact, he didn't particularly like his son's name Roger), but he respected her decisiveness. However, this same ability of hers to make difficult decisions finally and quickly causes him to lose her. When he is diagnosed with leprosy, she believes that she had to leave him, divorce him, to protect their son Roger, since children are supposedly more susceptible to the disease than adults. Covenant sees her only once before he is sent to the leprosarium, and he is still groggy after the amputation of his two fingers, is just learning about his diagnosis of leprosy, and has had no time to process the information or deliberate about its repercussions or how it will impact his life and his family. Although he agrees with Joan, he does not understand the finality of her decision to divorce him or how it will make him feel until later. Her abandonment of Covenant, perhaps even more than the physical changes caused by his leprosy, shapes his attitude and actions thereafter.

The reaction of the townspeople to Covenant when he walks into town to pay his phone bill is a typical reaction to the feared unknown — avoidance and revulsion. Later when Covenant believes he must interact with other people again, he catches a ride into a neighboring town to visit a nightclub, the Door. The truck driver who drives Covenant and joins him for a drink represents the kind of barrier of exclusion modern man places between himself and anyone else he doesn't understand, doesn't approve of, or fears. The truck driver tells Covenant that lepers ought to keep to themselves and leave others alone. Many of his assumptions and conclusions about Covenant the leper have sometimes been voiced, equally unfairly, in our world against those with AIDS — that he tries to hide his disease, that he deliberately goes around people to spread it, that he would be gleeful if others were similarly afflicted. What is especially significant about this insight of Donaldson's is that the 1st "Chronicles" were published in the late 1970s, the 2nd in the early 1980s, and it wasn't until the mid–1980s that AIDS was discussed openly when it became epidemic. Donaldson's perceptions of modern man and our reactions to our fear of disease was as prophetic as it was insightful regarding leprosy.

On the macrocosm level of interpretation where Covenant represents modern man, Joan's abandonment, as well as that of his neighbors, is an exaggerated form of our feelings of being disassociated from others. Families move away from each other, often to other states or even across the country. We live in neighborhoods that really aren't communities. Rarely does anyone know the names of most of his neighbors on the same block. We have acquaintances at work but rarely true friends. Unlike the Council of Elders or the Heers in the Land, in America our government is representative and most of us have never even met, much less exchanged ideas with, our elected officials. The divorce rate is close to 50 percent now, so at least half of the couples who marry will experience the kind of separation that Covenant experiences when Joan leaves him. Though we may not be shunned as Thomas Covenant is, we are not connected within close communities either. Some people find a sense of belonging in community service/volunteer work, through religious organizations, or via family, friends, neighborhood, school, or work associations, but not all.

Donaldson also does not allow any kind of close, communal connection for Covenant in his "real" world. When Covenant goes in search of connection, Donaldson points up the insincerity of some preachers through his depiction of Dr. B. Sam Johnson, revivalist and "healer." The scripture that is chosen for the Sunday night tent meeting is more a threat of punishment for disobedience than an invitation and promise of peace. Johnson perpetuates the old superstition that illness is caused by wickedness and represents a judgment from God. His compassion is artificial, and he lies to the congregation when he implies that Covenant will be cared for when he is dragged away by Matthew Logan, whose main concern is for the evening's offering. Covenant finds no blessed assurance in organized religion.

Cults are exaggerated and condemned by Donaldson, who suggests that Lord Foul could gain some influence over cult followers, enough to influence them to kidnap and prepare to sacrifice Joan. However, in keeping with Donaldson's sense of the eye of the paradox, he does not just condemn but also tries to understand and explain the poverty and hopelessness of the conditions that move a woman to try to purify herself with fire and to encourage even her own children to voluntarily submit to the pain of the burns. The human sacrifice, the arcane symbols of the ritual — the triangle, the knife, the blood — in the frame tale of *The Wounded Land* prepare us for the overly ironic world that Covenant finds when he arrives back in the Land. Or if this is all Covenant's dream, perhaps they subtly suggest the pagan world that the Sunbane has made of the Land. In terms of Covenant as a representative of modern man, the wasteland of the Land under the Clave is an exaggerated form of Covenant's perception of his own "real" world. While our own world is not as beautiful or healthy as the Land when Covenant first journeys there, it is also not as desecrated and artificially controlled as the Land of the 2nd "Chronicles."

Despite her absence Joan continues to influence Covenant. When he visits a nightclub to find a place of acceptance and a way to go among other people, he absent-mindedly orders a gin and tonic, Joan's drink. When he returns home, he readjusts Joan's picture to face him. When she calls after midnight wanting to talk with him, he cannot speak and then is furious that Elena has chosen this particular time to call him back to the Land. After he returns again from the Land and has suffered rejection by his community to the extent that someone hid a tarnished razor blade within a bun to cut him, he again turns to Joan through the picture he has of her, but his condition is so desperate that all he can do is laugh hysterically, splattering the picture with his blood, the opposite kind of laughter that will eventually be used at the end of *The Power That Preserves* to diminish Lord Foul, the personification of despair.

In the 2nd "Chronicles," Joan returns to Covenant to play a significant role. Covenant tells Linden that Joan suffers a sense of guilt for leaving him and taking Roger back to live with her parents. Covenant claims that she has become a kind of moral leper; he equates Joan's sense of guilt and loss of self-respect and the way both are eroding her sense of self to the way leprosy robs him of the ability to feel with his fingers. Joan's affliction is psychological whereas Covenant's is physical. She has tried popular psychotherapy fads to alleviate her pain; she goes through a period of time of trying to punish herself; then she becomes extremely involved in her church. When nothing helps, she seeks out a commune, where the members undergo humiliation to expiate their "sins." Covenant claims that she is possessed by Lord Foul when she breaks into his house to claw at him and put his blood in her mouth. So she becomes the bait to make Covenant voluntarily sacrifice himself. Covenant eventually learns to sacrifice himself, not through coercion but completely voluntarily, to thwart Lord Foul.

Donaldson uses Joan to introduce one of the main themes of the 2nd "Chronicles": possession. Joan is possessed as is Linden, but with Linden he gives the reader the point of view of a victim invaded by a Raver. As usual Donaldson explores all aspects of the concept of possession, including its most negative attribute of robbing the possessed of volition and power over herself, over what she says or does to what she is consciously aware of, since the Raver tries to force the personality of the victim into a catatonic state to escape the psychological torture of the Raver. However, Donaldson also illustrates how Linden can use her health sense to probe and examine Mistweave's and her own injuries (even internal ones) and thus diagnose the healing necessary. She is able to thrust her awareness into Covenant's mind to try to steady him and get him to pull back the wild magic if he has gone into a venom relapse and his power could threaten the *dromond* or his friends. She uses this same ability to find the essence of Covenant's spirit deep inside him almost completely hidden by the silence imposed on him by the *Elohim* to bring him back to awareness. These initial trials are necessary to teach Linden how to use this Land-given ability and when to withdraw and allow the other person to make his own choices.

Linden herself is conflicted about possession. She craves Covenant's wild magic power, but her experiences with Gibbon-Raver have convinced her that evil is a real force in the world, and that one of its worst manifestations is possession. She doesn't learn until the end of the 2nd "Chronicles" that power itself is ineffective without the driving forces of motivation, intent, and passion that control the power. And, therefore, any form of power, even the while gold or possession or the secret to the Ritual of Desecration, can be utilized for good given the right purpose and character of the user. The ability to see power, so often denigrated as a corrupting influence, as both good and bad, is another manifestation of the eye of the paradox.

Donaldson uses Linden's past to reiterate the power of past negative emotions — helplessness, guilt, shame, fear — on someone's present ability to act constructively, a universal theme in modern literature. Though Linden is not coping with leprosy or any other physical disease, her sojourn to the Land heals some of Linden's other afflictions as well. Through Linden, Donaldson teaches us that we don't have to have leprosy or AIDS to benefit from the healing power of fantasy/imagination. She confesses to Covenant about the helplessness she felt being locked in the attic with her father as he committed suicide and accused her of never loving him. She later also recounts her sense of guilt over her role in the death/mercy killing of her mother and the anger she felt toward a selfish mother who didn't even try to comfort a grieving daughter but rather joined the father in placing unfair blame on the child. These powerful past experiences influence Linden's choice of career, her decision to seek out a small town like the one near Haven Farm, her self-imposed alienation, and even her need to deny the reality of deliberate evil perhaps so that she will not have to look too closely at herself. Her father's vicious suicide and her mother's pathetic desire for death confound Linden's ability to find an eye of the paradox solution for her own questions regarding life and death. Though she has dedicated herself to saving lives, she becomes paralyzed when she has to admit moral responsibility and judgment into what for her is an automatic, objective response based on her scientific knowledge of wounds and diseases. She immediately and instinctively reacts when the old beggar seemingly suffers from a heart attack near Haven Farm, and she works to save his life almost to the end of her strength and endurance. When faced with the reality of evil, however, she retreats into herself, becomes the child-victim she was, and cannot act. Only eventually admitting the power of her memories and trusting another with her own most vulnerable moments and private truths about herself allow her to discover several important insights: that nothing is purely good or evil and even possession can be undertaken with good motivations; that she needn't repress or be controlled by her memories even if they bring on a sense of guilt or shame but can accept them, integrate them into who she knows herself to be and what she knows of her own motivations, intentions, and desire to do good. But most important she learns that power isn't what she (and the world) have always considered it — the ability to coerce others — but is the power of personal choice, so everyone's power is part of the self and not dependent on weapons or symbols of power such as the white gold ring.

Linden's importance to the "Chronicles" is not limited to the dialectics she needs to resolve, like the pull toward life and toward death. Donaldson has indicated that the 2nd "Chronicles" focuses more on Covenant's relationships with others, his ability to open himself to friendship, partnerships, even love, and obviously the Creator in the guise of the beggar who supposedly has a heart attack right in front of Linden believes that she, too, needs to learn that "'there is also love in the world.'"[3] Covenant is shut off emotionally from others because he has been shunned by others, ostracized by his community, and divorced by his wife. Linden has imposed her own alienation on herself out of a sense of unworthiness, powerlessness, and guilt. Only her medical knowledge and abilities make her feel useful and needed.

As they open up to each other and finally admit their love for each other, each is changed. They both learn how to escape from the hold of their pasts. Still, as Proust suggests, the defining memories of the past are re-remembered at significant moments in the present, but both Covenant and Linden learn the power of choice, of deciding not to be controlled by those memories. Linden's part in her mother's death — the conflicting emotions of pity for a dying woman, anger at the role the mother wanted her daughter to play in her own death, and guilt over the relief Linden felt when she'd done what her mother begged and smothered her mother — controls her half-conscious actions to spare Ceer's pain by attempting to take his life as she struggles out of the darkness which she'd taken on to release Covenant from his *Elohim*-imposed stupor. She is caught and cannot find her way to the eye of the paradox because she cannot resolve the conflicting emotions of pity, anger, guilt, relief, vindictiveness, pain, and loss she had felt at that moment of her child-self's life when she killed her mother. The power of those remembered feelings and past decisions threatens once again to send Linden into a paralysis of indecision and inability to act. One reason for her paralysis is the absence of the one emotion — love (for herself, for her mother, for Ceer) — which would have allowed her to conjoin the other emotions productively. Finding the connection between Ceer and her mother and admitting to Covenant her secrets from her past allow her to face and resolve that controlling moment in her memory.

Hile Troy, another character transported from Covenant's "real" world to the Land, provides the point of view and the direction for much of the conflict depicted in *The Illearth War*. The tales of the Bloodguard Runnik and Tull are told through Hile Troy as the point of view character. Donaldson eventually chose to take the material in *Gilden Fire* out of *The Illearth War* because it would have been yet another point of view, and especially a point of view of a character of the Land. With the exception of Mhoram in *The Power That Preserves*, Donaldson mostly sticks with the point of view of characters from Covenant's "real" world (Covenant, Linden, Hile Troy).

Again if all the characters of the Land are reflections or manifestations of parts of Covenant's personality, Troy is especially interesting. Troy is brought to the Land by Atiaran who returned to the Loresraat to learn more of the knowledge contained in Kevin's 1st and 2nd Wards. Apparently she is trying to call Covenant back, whether to aid the Land or to extract her own personal vengeance on him isn't clear. Somehow, instead, she brings Hile Troy to the Land from certain death in the "real" world as he is hanging out the window of his burning, ninth-floor apartment, and, in doing so, she dies in the fire that accompanies him. Troy is blind and has been from birth. He is another character whose illness or handicap is healed by the Land. Just as Covenant regained, through the use of hurtloam, the feeling his leprosy took from him, Troy also gains a kind of sight.

With his natural ability to hold complex spatial units, movements, and placements in his head, due in part to his blindness, he becomes a natural leader to organize coordinated attacks by the Lords, riders, and foot soldiers of the Waymark against Foul's army. As an inner part of Covenant's character, he represents the overcoming of limitations, but unlike Covenant, who is a reluctant hero, Hile Troy seems all too willing to take on the ultimate responsibility for the defense of the Land. He also represents modern man in his reliance on superior fire power, numbers of soldiers, or strategy to win wars. His blindness could suggest a kind of ignorance, and certainly Troy feels overwhelmed and inadequate when he finally sees the vastness of the Raver Fleshharrower's army; Troy has not imagined such overwhelming odds. But he is also resourceful and can redesign his defense to find a possibility of success even in the face of almost certain defeat. He never hesitates to take upon himself the entire responsibility, the potential blame, and the ultimate cost of his desperate bargain with Caerroil Wildwood for safe passage for his army through Garroting Deep. Perhaps these traits of Troy's represent the part of Covenant that would like to accept the Land as real and strive for the kind of heroism in which he no longer believes.

Hile Troy's history in the "real" world contrasts Covenant's in several ways. He has coped with his lack of sight since birth and has never known the sense of vision until he gains his Landborn sight, so for him the Land does not miraculously give back something he'd lost and his mind tells him can never be regained, as Covenant feels about his ability to feel in his fingers and toes once he has accepted that his leprosy is irreversible. For Hile Troy sight is a great gift, and one that makes him prefer to remain in the Land. When he is brought to the Land five years before Covenant's second sojourn, the Lords heal the burns on his hands with hurtloam and apply the healing mud to his eyes as well. Troy begins to see with his mind; Elena teaches him to believe what he perceives because it can be verified by touch and it matches the spatial organization in his mind. Hile Troy pledges his life to use his strategic abilities, learned and perfected in his job with the Department of Defense in the "real" world, to fight for the Land against Foul. Troy makes this vow to repay what he considers a much bigger gift — the gift of sight (and also his love for Elena). Hile Troy is "a man so overwhelmed by the power of sight that he could not perceive the blindness of his desire to assume responsibility for the Land."[4] In this action he is like the Bloodguard who swear their Vow to serve the Lords because they have no better answer to Kevin's largess. In both cases it is an extravagant promise that costs years of unquestioning dedication, years without choice or personal purpose. Since Donaldson believes all personal power and character come from choice, both the Bloodguard and Hile Troy are cautionary tales. There is no gift so great that it requires even one lifetime of service to repay it, much less many thousands of years. The either/or thinking of both the Bloodguard (either the Vow or Corruption) and Hile Troy (either sight and complete dedication, including paying any price for the rescue of his army, or ingratitude and unworthiness and failure) becomes the limiting world view which robs them of a life of personal choices.

Yet Elena, Covenant's daughter, is as much a gift to Covenant as sight is to Troy; she inspires love, protection, loyalty in Covenant for Lena's sacrifice, for the Land which restored the potency his leprosy had taken from him, for Elena's own love and acceptance of him, and even in some small way she takes the place of his son Roger who was taken from him as a baby. Yet Covenant still retains his power of choice, makes no elaborate vow of service to the Lords or to Elena or to the Land and thus preserves his own freedom of choice, his ability to change his mind based on new circumstances, which he later explains to Linden as the necessity of freedom of choice.

Hile Troy takes on too much, and Donaldson warns that expecting too much of one's self can lead to a sense of failure and despair. Covenant wonders if Troy is doomed to be inadequate because he is summoned by Atiaran and her motives are ambiguous. But Troy fills another purpose for Donaldson. In the 1st "Chronicles" Covenant is wrestling with the dialectic of his Unbelief in the Land and his desire that it be real. Troy takes on the role of Devil's advocate to argue that the Land is better than the "real" world from which they both come. Troy reminds Covenant that he is a leper in the "real" world and Troy, himself, is blind. In the Land their physical ailments are cured. Who wouldn't prefer the Land? Covenant even begins to doubt whether Hile Troy is real or was made up subconsciously by Covenant's own imagination as a sounding board for all his doubts, not just about the Land, but also about whether he should be doubting the Land's reality. That one must choose between the Land and the "real" world is another manifestation of either/or thinking. For Troy, who was blind and about to be burned to death, of course the Land is preferable. His purposes in the Land are so much more important than the hypothetical war games which constituted his work for the Defense Department. But Covenant can't yet accept the Land as real. He knows that there is no cure for leprosy, that blind people don't simply start seeing. He suspects that they are too willing to believe because it coincides with their deepest desires. Covenant's inability to believe despite what his senses tell him is reflexive of the twentieth century philosophy which questions the reality of anything that does not fit our objective scientific expectations.

At first Donaldson gives only Covenant's point of view in his interactions with Hile Troy in *The Illearth War*, but beginning in Part II The Waymark with Chapter Eleven, "War Council," Donaldson changes the point of view character to Troy — the narrator is always third person semi-omniscient, but at this point he reveals what is happening through Troy's perspective and reveals Troy's thoughts. For the first time in the 1st "Chronicles," Donaldson gives credence to the perception that these "Chronicles" might not be all Covenant's dream (unless, of course, Covenant is dreaming things from Troy's perspective, but this is unlikely since none of Covenant's cynicism is evident). And just as Covenant discovers new ways to perceive the world through his health sense — his ability to distinguish a flourishing tree from a dying one, his ability to sense murder — Troy's sight is an entirely new sense to him who has known the world only through sound and touch and resonances. The fact that sight is familiar to us and we take it for granted gives further support to the idea that there can be senses of which we are unaware (like the ability to tell if someone is good or ill), that are quite common in the Land. But unlike Covenant's capacity to sense pleasure and pain through his fingers and toes which threatens to take away his ability to be able to cope in his "real" world if he believes such changes, Troy's newly gained sight is a great blessing to him, yet it is only operable during the day or with sufficient firelight; at night he reverts to his previous blindness.

Donaldson uses Troy's inherent blindness symbolically to reflect his ignorance about the enemy he is fighting. Troy relies too greatly on his logical ability to gauge how quickly a manethrall can cover the distance between the plains of Ra and Revelstone to give warning that Foul's army is on the march. As a result he can be shocked and dismayed by his miscalculations and by the magnitude of Foul's army. He is, therefore, susceptible to despair, but his own confidence in his abilities makes him continue to plot and strategize and find alternatives, even desperate resolutions to the impossible tasks he has undertaken.

Troy represents another interpretation to the concept of the power of command, which is a main theme of *The Illearth War*. Elena misuses the 7th

Ward, the Power of Command, when she breaks the Law of Death to call forth dead Kevin to fight against Lord Foul, to do what he could not do in life. Troy uses his power to command in more productive ways. From Troy's perspective, Elena represents the Land itself and she encourages him to use his tactical skills in service to the Land. Her faith in him makes it possible for him to assume command of the Wayward. He uses his position to make decisions for others (even the Lords) without explaining his tactics to them, thus robbing them of choice in the decisions of the war. The Wayward follows Troy's orders and is thereby a no-more-effective tool than Troy's strategies permit. As Donaldson explains in the 2nd "Chronicles," to get beyond the limitations of the one making decisions, others must voluntarily make their own personal choices and thus not function as tools. Only those who are not just obeying Troy's orders but act on their own personal choices have the potential for greater success. Callindrill refuses Troy's commands and decides to remain alone in Doom's Retreat and use his Lord's power to bring the hills down on Raver Fleshharrower's army. Though directed by Troy to summons Caerroil Wildwood, Mhoram makes his own choice to sing the Forestal's personal song, which could have been a fatal decision for him, but in this way he surpasses Troy's ability and acts not as a tool but as an independent being.

For Donaldson Hile Troy represents our misplaced faith in the muscle solution to disputes. Elena recognizes that battles won't solve the Land's problems and thus chooses to follow Amok to find the 7th Ward instead of going with the army to fight against the Raver Fleshharrower. Elena voices the idea that wars do not solve world problems. Battle tactics or the muscle solution has been tried before, and it never ultimately works. It didn't work for Kevin. Elena wants to find another alternative to combat. The fact that Troy comes to the Land having worked for the Department of Defense in the United States is obviously a sarcastic comment on America's reliance on intelligence, troop power, overwhelming force, and superior state-of-the-art technologically precise and powerful weaponry, as well as the threat of nuclear devastation. In the Land Troy does not lead the larger army, but he tries to compensate with strategy and guile and by invoking the aid of the power of the forest. Donaldson, as a pacifist, wants to show that the potential solution of winning wars by being able to destroy more of the enemy is not a viable resolution at all. But to make other options more credible, he must first show that our instinctive response of combating power and force with our own power and force cannot ultimately succeed. Here Troy's inherent blindness becomes symbolic of man's inability to see how ineffectual power and strategies and wars truly are.

Hile Troy also is an either/or thinker. When he learns to doubt himself because he is finally told the truth that Atiaran had inadvertently summoned him when she tried to bring Covenant back to the Land, he begins to question whether he can win, and if not, whether his failure will be worse for the Land than if he had never taken on responsibility. He berates himself, believing that if he tries and loses, the Land will be worse off than if he had never tried because the Lords and all those in the Wayward will have put their faith in him rather than looking for some other, better hope. He will be the cause of their despair. Troy finally recognizes that Covenant's unwillingness to let the people of the Land believe he can/will solve their problems with Lord Foul is a better solution than making promises he, Troy, can't fulfill.

Donaldson has his little joke with Troy when he has Troy claim that after the war, he will take a vacation for a few years: "'I'm going to sit down in Andelain and not move a muscle until I get to see the Celebration of Spring.'"[5] Troy becomes apprentice to Caerroil Wildwood in Morinmoss and eventually Forestal of Andelain for several thousand years longer than he had planned for his "vacation" to last.

On the macrocosm level of interpretation, in our real world, Troy's name has resonances to one of the great battles of all time, the Greeks' siege of the fortified city of Troy in the days of classical heroes, about 1200 B.C., made renowned in the epics of Homer. But how should this symbolism lead us to a clearer interpretation of Donaldson's purpose? Hile Troy represents the futility of relying on armed combat. The Trojan War was costly for the Greeks and devastating for the Trojans who were not defeated by an overwhelming force because their strong walls protected them, but were destroyed by the tactic of Odysseus's trick of armed soldiers hiding in the belly of a hollow wooden horse, which the Trojans themselves brought within their city gates. Hile Troy also uses guile and a costly bargain with Caerroil Wildwood, the Forestal of Morinmoss, to save his army from destruction. But it is only the older power of the forest that can destroy Foul's army and defeat the Giant Raver Fleshharrower. The muscle solution, or the belief that wars can resolve conflict, fails in the Land as it does in our real world. Combat has never satisfactorily resolved the enmity between peoples or any two sides of a religious or political dispute. The result may be a winner and a loser but not peace nor acceptance of each other. Also, we cannot raise large enough or powerful enough armies to fight earthquakes, hurricanes, tornadoes, storms at sea; neither can we fight pollution, global warming, or erosion of our natural resources with any known weapons.

Troy's gift is his ability to predict what can happen given certain scenarios — Fleshharrower stops before Doriendor Corishev, does not surround the ancient city of the King and Queen of Berek's time. Troy makes the Raver act in anger by taunting him so that he first attacks using the power of the Illearth Stone, allowing the Lords' army more time to escape out the back of the city toward Garroting Deep. Fleshharrower uses the time to make a scepter to hold the Illearth Stone and thus concentrate his power. Fleshharrower attacks with a tornado-like (sirocco) force of nature, the Vortex of Trepidation, to create fear. Troy's leadership or command ability can be neutralized — he becomes paralyzed when the danger includes the bat/eagle-like birds of prey that fly within the Vortex of Trepidation or when the overwhelming number of the enemies in Foul's army is so vast that it defies his comprehension. Troy is also challenged by the Bloodguard's fidelity — he believes that it is an affront to his power of command. He needs sleep, and though he tries to match their devotion and prowess, he cannot. The Bloodguard's Vow was sealed by Earthpower, and Troy knows doubt.

And, therefore, Troy himself is susceptible to despair. He tries to commit suicide by throwing himself off Kevin's Watch, either instinctively or in reaction to his overwhelming despair at learning that the Giants are all dead, that the seer and oracle Mhoram dreamed of the Bloodguard fighting for the Despiser (even before learning that they have taken control of a piece of the Illearth Stone), that Quaan has not been able to slow down Foul's army enough and it will be arriving at Doom's Retreat within three days, and that his plan to ambush that army will inevitably fail because the Giant Raver leads a force much larger than Troy anticipated. Troy also tries to commit suicide in Doriendor Corishev by eluding his Bloodguard Ruel's watchfulness, then standing exposed to the sirocco in the open remains of a meeting hall. Each time he is prevented from self-destruction. Here he is contrasted with Covenant whose main motivation is to survive, go on, stubbornly resist.

Overall Troy is an old-fashioned hero; he continues to fight even after being blinded anew and having his sword taken from him. He is able to kill a man-like creature with Manethrall Rue's Ramen rope weapon. Troy also asks for Covenant's ring at the end of *The Illearth War* when the Lords can perceive that Elena is fighting dead Kevin by herself and Troy wants to aid her. When given the ring, Troy tries to utilize its power, but Caerroil Wildwood stops him and claims the cost of his aid in allowing the Lord's army to pass unharmed through Garroting Deep: Troy is turned into an old stump of a tree with new leaves sprouting from his upraised fist to begin the reforestation of Gallow's Howe. Then Troy becomes Caer-Caveral, an apprentice Forestal to Caerroil Wildwood. As the Forestal, Troy no longer needs sight: music is all the power he needs now.

At his death in *White Gold Wielder*, Hile Troy represents a different view of dying, neither suicide nor mercy killing, but rather self-sacrifice. Troy tells Sunder not to hesitate to strike at him; he is prepared and even eager for the release of death. Also, Troy knows that the motivation for Sunder will be his great love for Hollian, and such intents are positive. The last Forestal does not command Sunder but invites him to strike. Though Sunder strikes for personal reasons, based on his love for Hollian, Troy knows that only through the breaking of the Law of Life can Covenant accomplish his feat at the end of the tale. Troy's death is another example of the eye of the paradox. Troy's sacrifice did not create sorrow in the observers, but rather hope because so much good comes from it. When Sunder stabs him, Troy ends as the now-burning tree stump, into which he had been transformed by Caerroil Wildwood. The psychological baggage that the "real" world characters bring to the Land influences their actions in the Land, but their experiences in the Land also help them work through their problems in the "real" world and move toward more positive insights about themselves.

Within the Land itself, history reveals much of the character, the principles, the capacities and weaknesses of the inhabitants. Like Tolkien, Donaldson provides a rich back story and depth to his fantasy world. Also like Tolkien, this history implies a Golden World in the past when the Lords were more knowledgeable and more powerful, and yet also flawed by their own potential for despair. Unlike Tolkien, Donaldson provides the possibility of regaining the Golden World even after its loss or destruction, but in keeping with Donaldson's eye of the paradox solution, Linden accomplishes the healing of the Land through acceptance (not denial) of the Sunbane and, using the new Staff of Law, recreates the beauty of the Land.

The King and Queen of Berek's time lived in Doriendor Corishev until the Shadow wormed its way into the King's Council, making the King greedy for the power of life and death over others, and then the Queen was compelled to rebel against him. A civil war was fought between the King with those who feared to disobey him and the Queen with her Champions, the greatest of whom was Berek. The Queen's forces fought bravely, but the hosts of the King fought ferociously with a madness and a frenzy which pushed them to maim and desecrate their victims. As war becomes when it is desperately fought and rules of humanity are lost or forgotten, the viciousness and carnage caused despair in those who championed the Queen until one by one they fell. Berek alone was left to answer the King's challenge to single combat. Their battle was even until the King's ax chopped off Berek's hand. Then Berek fled. He ran to Mount Thunder where the Earth itself promised him aid if he would pledge to heal it. When the Fire Lions defeated the King and his army, Berek created the Staff of Law to help him fulfill his promise to heal the Earth. Thus was Earthpower first used. Berek established the first Council of Lords; the first Lords later became known as the Old Lords. For 2,000 years they used the Earthpower and the Staff to restore beauty to the Land.

Among the other important Lords of antiquity were Damelon Giant-friend, for whom the Giants built Revelstone; Loric Vilesilencer, whose epithet defines his importance; and Kevin, who later became known as Landwaster. Damelon was especially important to the Giants because he prophesied omens of optimism and promise that gave the Giants hope for a successful return to their Home. Later they realize the prediction referred only to the end of their exile. Loric rendered the viles impotent so that they must create not beget others to carry on their race. Though Kevin performed the Ritual of Desecration, the peoples of the Land have great sympathy and reverence for him because they recognize that the despair he experienced that led to his horrific act is like their own individual despair, just multiplied exponentially because of his greater power and responsibility.

At first Kevin was a magnanimous ruler who met the threat of an attack by the *Haruchai* with gifts rather than defense and inspired the Vow of service of the Bloodguard. He was extremely knowledgeable and insightful enough to realize that power was not the ultimate answer to Despite and foresighted enough to preserve his knowledge in sequential Wards so that if the wisdom of the Lords were to be lost, it could be recovered, but each Ward would have to be mastered before new, more powerful lore could be found and utilized. For example, the Lords have to know how to create, bend, and break a Word of Warning before they can recover the 2nd Ward that is protected by such a Word.

In spite of (or perhaps even because of) the vast amount of knowledge Kevin had concerning the uses of power, he was especially susceptible to despair. When he realized that none of his powers could rid the Land of Lord Foul, he succumbed to the temptation for desperate measures. He believed, falsely, that if he were willing to perform the Ritual of Desecration, though it would destroy the Land he loved, that Lord Foul would be destroyed as well. But he was not both seer and prophet as Berek had been. Tamarantha later explains that Kevin was seeking absolute answers and had lost the paradox of ambiguity. Kevin hid his seven Wards to help the survivors of the Desecration to rebuild the Land and sent the Bloodguard, the Ranyhyn, and the Giants away because he could imagine a time that the Land could recover from the Ritual of Desecration. But he predicted incorrectly that Foul would be destroyed. He was blinded by his own despair when he could not defeat Lord Foul with the might of his armies, and he could think of no other way to defeat Foul except total destruction. Therefore, Kevin challenged Foul to meet him in Kiril Threndor to perform the Ritual. Though Foul was diminished for thousands of years, he was not destroyed by the Ritual of Desecration, and Kevin himself perished.

Centuries after the Desecration the peoples of the Land migrated back to their original villages and began to build their society anew. It is paradoxical that the inhabitants of the Land revere Kevin despite his horrific act of destruction. Perhaps they admire his motive — to rid the Land of Despair/ Despite. Or perhaps they empathize with his ignorance and weakness, associate with his frustration and despair, and cannot imagine themselves being able to concoct any better plan. The story of his attempt and failure is one of the tales which unites the people of the Land and motivates them to attempt pure service.

The most significant result of the new Lords' reaction against Kevin's solution of Desecration is their adoption of the Oath of Peace. They vow never again to let their destructive emotions rule their decisions. The results of this oath (like the Bloodguard's Vow and Hile Troy's promise to pay Caerroil Wildwood's price himself) are both beneficial and detrimental to the Lords. By remembering the Oath of Peace, the Lords refrain from acting in anger or hatred even toward their enemies. But the stoicism required to uphold the Oath also limits their ability to unlock the secrets of even Kevin's 1st Ward. Kevin had learned his power without restricting himself from exerting any more power than was needed to subdue the enemy. He had even discovered the Power of Command which would take away the volition of anyone so commanded, though he had not used it.

By taking the Oath of Peace, the Lords limit their own choices and make themselves either/or rather than both/and characters. Either they abide by the Oath, or they are not worthy as Lords. Mhoram discovers the fallacy of this either/or thinking when he discovers the secret to the Ritual of Desecration and learns how to control the *krill*. At the same time he learns that he has not changed in his motivations or basic character though he has more power available to him when he is not limited by the Oath. Donaldson's view of vows, oaths, or pledges is negative. Promises may provide incentive for some characters, but they inevitably limit choice. And in the case of the Bloodguard, they absolve the *Haruchai* of the need for making personal decisions. Covenant may make pledges, but he does not hesitate to change his mind and make a new and different choice after he reevaluates his situation. Thus, he remains a both/and character. So overall, in Donaldson's view that the most important human trait is the necessity of freedom to choose, vows or oaths, rather than being a sign of honor, are a detriment, limiting the full potential and effectiveness of a character.

The main heroes of the Land existed in the Golden Age of the past, before the Ritual of Desecration, from the time when the Land was united under a King and Queen, through the time that Berek, the Lord Fatherer, taught the Lords to use Earthpower to its full potential, and to the time when Kevin was a wise ruler. After the Ritual, individual communities re-formed, but much lore has been lost. Whereas before the Desecration, it is suggested that every community knew both the *rhadhamaerl* and *lillianrill* lores, after the exile the separate communities passed down from generation to generation only that lore which best helped them control their immediate environment. Thus, the *rhadhamaerl* lore is remembered by those who lived in stone houses; the *lillianrill* lore is preserved by the tree-dwelling communities. Because each separate community is tightly knit, there isn't very much interaction between the two, now-separate cultures except in Revelstone. There the new Lords begin their long service to the Land when the Giants deliver Kevin's 1st Ward. And the limitations they place on themselves by taking the Oath of Peace hinder their comprehension of the old power.

The new Lords, therefore, are left with an overwhelming sense of inadequacy because their history tells them of the potential for more power and greater ability to control the Earthpower, but they are unable to harness these powers. Their sense of inferiority to the Old Lords supports the declining world theory, in which a Golden Age from the past can never be recaptured because of the weakness and inadequacies of the present inhabitants of the Land. Our own real world has succumbed to a similar depression as we acknowledge the overwhelming problems we face, our own culpability in helping to create these problems, and realize we also do not know how to recreate our world without the problems of pollution, global warming, nuclear weapons.

The inhabitants of the Land, like many peoples in our own world, create legends that might solve their problems and allow them to regain knowledge or an attitude they think is lost. Atiaran admits to Covenant that the people in the Land believe that their great hero Berek will return if he is needed, much as King Arthur and Jesus Christ have been predicted to return as well. The song Atiaran sings for Mithil Stonedown tells the whole tale of Berek's battle against the King and the Shadow, not only his revulsion and guilt when forced to recognize and accept the carnage of battle, but also his despair before his bargain with the Earthpower of the Fire Lions, and his renewed optimism when he pledges to use his new knowledge of Earthpower to heal the earth.

In essence Donaldson wants to lead the modern age through this progression. We have wallowed in the despair of recognizing the wasteland we have made of the world and our own heart of darkness, and more than ever we need the hope for the future that a return to an epic vision will give us. But before we can heal our problems of pollution, global warming, our own capacity for total destruction, we must believe that we can and thus find the power in our own world (as Berek harnessed Earthpower in the Land) to heal the hurts we ourselves have inflicted on our world.

Therefore, Covenant's resemblance to Berek is not fortuitous but an important part of Donaldson's design. Covenant's interactions with Lord Foul during the time periods of the 1st and 2nd "Chronicles" allow the societies of those time periods in the history of the Land to learn to overcome despair. The devastation of the Land in the 2nd "Chronicles" is much worse than in the 1st, making the Land seem more similar to our own real world, and yet still it can be healed without Desecration. Therefore, though Covenant is also associated with Kevin Landwaster through the ultimate power of the white gold wild magic of his ring, and though Covenant sometimes seems to embrace Kevin's destructive options, as when he claims as his purpose that he will completely demolish Foul's demesne (a destructive solution), Covenant opts in the end to embrace the paradox as Berek did and find a more successful solution than destruction/despair.

Along with the importance of the characters' individual past experiences, and the significance of historical figures and events to the character of the peoples of the Land, the "Chronicles" explore the larger philosophic concept of history as a playing out of some over-arching plan (in which perhaps a Creator can take a role to aid in fighting despair and rebuilding, re-growing, or rediscovering the beauty of the Land). The question, which the modern world sees as an either/or dialectic — either there is predestination or there is free will — to Donaldson is another example of the eye of the paradox. Of course, there is the power of choice, free will, as it is essential for the condition of being human. And yet in the Land, through the working out of prophesies or hindsight in the interpretation of omens, for societies the culmination of individuals' moral choices create the inevitability of their present condition, and only better choices by another group of dedicated individuals can reshape the future for a better world.

Donaldson acknowledges the possibility of predestination or an over-arching plan for the world as much as he mandates the necessity of choice or free will for individuals. Therefore, ambiguity exists about how much (if any) influence the Creator can exert over the Land, and the confluence of events surrounding Covenant's sojourns in the Land is both chance (fated, predestined) and the result of choice. At the Council of Lords, Lord Osondrea claims she believes Covenant's trek from Mithil Stonedown to Revelstone is part of a larger purpose because his trip is accomplished in a fortuitously short time. She believes that it must have been fated, though it was the choices of Atiaran and Foamfollower that actually achieve the task.

Thus fate and choice can be combined in the eye of the paradox. We do not have to find scapegoats on which to place blame for our current condition; we simply have to make better choices to clean up the pollution, reverse the effects of global warming, negate the ultimate destructive power of superweaponry; in other words, we must acknowledge, embrace, and fix the problems of our world, to recapture the epic vision which suggests that man does have control over his environment. If Covenant, an alienated, flawed, diseased, impotent man, can learn this lesson through his experiences in the Land, surely modern man can, too. Donaldson thereby emphasizes our ability to remember and learn from the past.

CHAPTER 4

They Could Not Go Home Again

Thomas Wolfe's *You Can't Go Home Again* (originally published in 1940) is about a writer not accepted by his own community because of the ideas he publishes. If is often said that prophets are not welcome in their own towns because they advocate change, which is scary to us, especially in our day when changes are more prolific and come more rapidly than we can adjust to them. New ideas provide new awareness, taking us from innocence to experience, and we believe that we cannot then recapture our innocence or re-experience our comfort zone. Donaldson disagrees that we cannot recapture innocence; after all, Foamfollower, who worried that he would become what he hates because of his frenzied blood-lust and desire to kill the Cavewights and ur-viles of Drool's army, becomes the savior that was prophesized to the *jheherrin*. The fate of the *jheherrin* and their ability to break Foul's curse and produce the *sur-jheherrin* gives proof to the redemption of Foamfollower, whose baptism of fire in Hotash Slay makes him the Pure One of the *jheherrin's* prophecy. In addition, Covenant fuses his venom and wild magic in the Banefire and eventually has the venom burned out of him by Foul himself who uses the wild magic to try to break the Arch of Time, but Covenant blocks the attempt. Linden tells Berenford at the end of the 2nd "Chronicles" that Covenant had achieved something that should have been impossible: "'He made himself innocent.'"[1] Donaldson gives the ironic man his heroic status as Covenant fights his most significant battle against Foul so far. The recognition that experience and innocence can co-exist and are not mutually exclusive is another form of the eye of the paradox. Covenant's experience of not fighting Foul at the climax of both "Chronicles" but laughing at despair and sacrificing himself to block Foul's abuse of power illustrate another aspect of opposition — that two opposites can negate each other when combined. The battles between the *skest* acid-creatures and the *sur-jheherrin* mud-beings and between Hamako, enhanced with the heat of the power of the Waynhim, and the Arghule ice-creature with a *croyel* also illustrate the juxtaposition of opposites negating each other. Power cannot be fought with greater power, but it can be absorbed by its opposite and rendered useless. Thus is peace achieved (at least temporarily).

Donaldson also asserts that involvement changes those who participate in the crises of their times. Most of the characters from the Land are faced with their own inadequacies, see into their own hearts of darkness, risk becoming what they most hate, and certainly grow in wisdom from their losses and the cost of their fidelity. Thus, the heroic fantasy beings that interact with Covenant and strive to take some responsibility for the demands of their world become more like modern man in their awareness. Often because of this change, they cannot or do not return to their own communities. However, Donaldson also says that the change is necessary for the Land's inhabitants to be effective, showing once again the eye-of-the-paradox view that a dual perspective is essential.

The peoples and beings of the Land can be interpreted in several useful ways. If the Land is a dream for Covenant, then they are a reflection of Covenant's inner struggles and needs. They are aspects of the multiplicity of Covenant's identity, each personified separately. They are psychological aspects of modern man which result in unresolved conflicts and must be faced and understood for Covenant to become a fully actualized human being. But if this is an alternate real world, then these groups, characters, and beings should be analyzed as separate cultures and individuals to explore how they function together as a society, why they might have developed differently, and what each group can tell us about the Land. I will focus more on the second analysis. They each interact with Covenant, and we can learn more about him from their interaction, but more important, they change because of their contact with him. As he is forced to look inside himself and acknowledge his own heart of darkness after the rape of Lena, the other characters all become less mythic and more modern characters from their experiences with Covenant as each in turn must also acknowledge his or her weaknesses and face some hard truths about him- or herself. As a result of their changed perspectives, the Land-born characters are able to accomplish feats that might have been impossible for them before their interaction with Covenant. In addition, in Covenant's interaction with them, he loses some of his ironic cynicism and becomes more effective as he allows himself to embrace more heroic traits.

As beings separate from Covenant's psyche, they also serve to illustrate for us different answers to the question "What is the nature of man?" Some of these other characters obviously are other men: the Lords, the *rhadhamaerl,* the *lillianrill,* the Ramen, the Bhrathair, even the *Haruchai,* though the Bloodguard's ability to defy sleep and death because of their Vow might argue against this characterization. Even among these groups, some are closer to the lives of animals than others, for example the Ramen; some are loners like the

Unfettered Ones; and others especially need community. And yet still other beings in the Land are clearly not human — the Giants, Ranyhyn, *Elohim*, Wraiths, Waynhim, *jheherrin, sur-jheherrin*. Of these, the Giants have the most to teach humans about joy and recovery, seeing the world in a new and productive way. All have characteristics for man to evaluate. Even the evil creatures, such as the cavewights and ur-viles, will aid in this self-awareness for us, but they will be discussed in a later chapter.

The three main peoples of the Land could be seen to represent animal (Ramen), vegetable (*lillianrill*), and mineral (*rhadhamaerl*). Was this intentional the same way the scarecrow (strawman), tin man, and cowardly lion so neatly companioned Dorothy in Oz? I doubt it. But Donaldson's focus on Earthpower, on the divinity of the natural world, makes it a possible interpretation. How is this reflective of our world? We are destroying our own beauty, our "scenery," as we blow up hills to make way for roads or pollute the earth with radioactive and other kinds of waste with no concern about how such wastes will make their way into drinking water or crops or simply make the land itself too toxic to inhabit. We are cutting down large, old trees and killing off (sometimes just for sport) whole species of animals. We are laying waste to our mineral, vegetable, and animal resources. And the power — in the case of the Land, the Earthpower — each of these peoples finds in nature is also reflexive of our electric power generated using damned up water, the energy of coal- or wood-burning or now gasoline-burning combustion, solar power and even atomic power; most of our modern power sources have their roots in the earth or nature. The difference between our world and the Land is that somehow, through better control of Earthpower and the Law controlled by the Staff of Law, the citizens of the Land can create heat or light without destroying the wood or stone that produces it.

Taken all together, the people of the Land show respect for the earth and its minerals and stone, the vegetation (especially trees), and animal life (especially horses). The reckless logging without reforestation that has depleted whole forests, the blowing up of mountains to make way for railroads, and the wanton slaughter of entire herds of animals such as the bison of the Old West should not have been possible had we *lillianrill-, rhadhamaerl-*, or Ramen-like peoples to look after our vegetable, mineral, and animal resources. These are the guilts we, as Americans, particularly face. In the whole world, our disregard of other living things has resulted in the total extinction of many species, and only our recent protection of some endangered species has stemmed and, in some cases, reversed the trend. Donaldson clearly wants us to see our interdependence on other beings as similar to our need to preserve better the resources of this world. The peoples of the Land function as models for us in respecting the earth. Elena greets the lake above Revelstone and recognizes the power this natural resource holds for the Land. Anyone who enters Andelain recognizes and is reinvigorated by its natural vibrancy and beauty. Though Donaldson does not personify natural power (as ancient cultures did through their pantheon of gods representing the Sea, the Sun, etc. or as Tolkien did trees in his Ents), he suggests that there is tremendous Earth-power available to the Forestal or Colossus or even any knowledgeable Lord who can call on it. We never know quite how Prothall with the help of Covenant's wild magic calls the Fire Lions, but the volcanic eruption does aid the Company in escaping from Drool Rockworm's trap in *Lord Foul's Bane.*

Certainly the 2nd "Chronicles" serves, as did many modern twentieth century novels, to illustrate the wasteland we can make of our world. Obviously, in fantasy such points are often made in the extreme, but do we truly believe ourselves incapable of the forced growing of plants, the artificial control of seasons, temperatures, rainfall, droughts, and periods of sunlight? And how do we know what effect this would have on that vegetation, or on us if we eat such force-grown vegetation? Though Sunder and Hollian accept the deterioration of the Land, and, in fact, do not seem to know the Land was ever different, and they can cope with the abnormalities the Sunbane inflicts on the natural cycles or seasons of growth, they eventually can also recognize the truer health of Andelain and want to restore such health to all the Land. Therefore, allegorically, the experiences in the Land can help encourage us to work toward restoring the natural beauty and health of our own world. Of course, in the 2nd "Chronicles," the harnessing of power requires the blood of forced human sacrifices, but even that could symbolically reflect the cost in lives we sometimes choose to pay for our natural resources (as our experiences in Iraq in protecting our oil interests taught us in the early twenty-first century).

Nevertheless, as with other aspects of Donaldson's Secondary World, the peoples are believable and realistic in and of themselves. I'll begin my discussion of the peoples of the Land with the various cultural groups: the *rhadhamaerl*, the *lillianrill*, the Ramen, and then discuss the Lords and the Bloodguard. All are of mankind, but each group inhabits a different geographic area and has developed skills to work with the materials at hand. Senior claims these "races" follow a typically American pattern, with agrarian settlements, tree cities, nomadic plains peoples, and even the mountain settlements of the *Haruchai*. He also states that unlike the more strict class distinction, for example those evident in Tolkien that reflect a more structured, hierarchical British society, the people of the Land form more of a melting pot and intermingle, especially in the Loresraat and in Revelstone. The Lords come mostly from the *rhadhamaerl* and *lillianrill* groups because the Ramen rarely leave the plains of Ra where the Ranyhyn roam and also because Lords' power is learned and called forth through their staffs much as the power of stone and wood are controlled by the gravelingas and hirebrands, and the Ramen use weapons but not Earthpower (other than the horse-healing Earthpower of the *amanibhavam* plant).

All the communities Covenant encounters have several characteristics in common: they are democratic, often with a Council of Elders or Heers for decision making; nevertheless, no politics, no conflict exists between opposing philosophies (and certainly none of the complexities of Frank Herbert's political intrigue in the *Dune* series). No differentiation exists according to wealth — in fact, there don't seem to be luxuries, though the Lords do house valuable art in trust for everyone in the Land (except, of course, in Brathairealm, which is set up as a dystopia society/political structure). Respect for learning/education/lore flourishes. Most groups are small in number, the exception being Revelstone, the home of the Lords. Many of these details about the people of the Land make more sense if the more valid interpretation of the "Chronicles" is that all Covenant's experiences in the Land are part of his dream, since obviously one individual does not disagree with himself about politics. Covenant comes from a small town near Haven Farm. And he is American.

Rhadhamaerl

The *rhadhamaerl* community is the first Covenant meets, and it turns out to be very significant. This community has much in common with Covenant's own town since some of the buildings in his home town are made of stone, whereas the *lillianrill* live in a large tree, the Ramen wander the plains, the Lords inhabit a fortified structure, and the *Haruchai* reside in mountain communities. If the Land is Covenant's dream, his rejection by his own community might foster a great need for acceptance by a unified community, and even for an important place within that community. So though his resemblance to Berek Halfhand frightens Covenant, the modern man, who is always aware of his leprosy and conflicted about how he feels about himself, he may unconsciously be searching for a way that he can act heroically, distance himself from his ironic view of himself. And since so much of his world is broken by his leprosy, it is easy to see why he dreams about health and the ability to mend the unfixable. Of course, his rational mind keeps arguing that such dreams can only lead to madness and death if he neglects the reality of his disease.

The *rhadhamaerl* work with stone. They are a strong people, usually shorter and stockier than others of the Land, with broad backs and powerful muscles to aid them in their work. Trell, the powerful gravelingas in Mithil Stonedown, is shorter than Covenant, and most others are shorter than he. They dress simply in earth-colored clothing, a short tunic with trousers, often with a pattern to identify their own family woven into the cloth at the shoulders of their clothing. Trell, Atiaran, and Lena (and eventually Elena) wear a white leaf pattern. Their homes are made of stone and are structured to form a circle, looking inward to the center of the village. That center becomes a large meeting place in which the entire community gathers to hear Atiaran sing the song of Berek Halfhand, in other words, to celebrate and reinforce their communal heritage and purpose. In times of battle, the gravelingas can fortify the stone to withstand the destructive power of monsters with stone suckers and in Revelstone even to withstand the power of the Illearth Stone wielded by the Giant Raver Satansfist.

Their names are simple, with family heritage being shown through connection in the female line. Elena's name contains reference to her mother Lena, as Atiaran was daughter to Tiaran. They use no last names but are identified by their important relationships: Atiaran is Trell-mate, and he is identified as Atiaran-mate. Another Stonedowner, Triock, one who woos Lena, is identified as the son of Thuler, but his name does not contain his father's name. He is also identified by his job; he is a Cattleherd.

The graveling pots of the *rhadhamaerl* provide heat and light for the community. Through the calling forth of the Earthpower, Trell makes the large container holding the graveling lightweight enough for him to carry, though it is filled with firestones. As Trell carries the large pot of graveling for the Gathering, Covenant asks Lena how Trell can manage such a heavy load, and she explains that his lore helps him to bear it when he has awakened the graveling. Anyone versed in the *rhadhamaerl* lore can call forth or extinguish the heat and light power of the stones, thus allowing "fire" to be carried safely on long journeys. Therefore, even Lena and Atiaran, who are not gravelingas themselves, can use the stones.

All in Trell's family (and presumably the others in the village as well as many Lords) can recognize hurtloam (a form of healing mud) and use it to heal wounds, even internal wounds that cause bruising but do not break the skin. Lena cures Covenant of the wounds he inflicted on himself during his long descent from Kevin's Watch, but the hurtloam also works on Covenant's leprosy, restoring his ability to feel through his fingers and toes. The pain he is surprised and almost pleased to feel from Triock's knife cut across his fingers is one of the first examples in Donaldson's work of Nietzsche's idea that we need the Dionysian frenzy and pain as much as the Apollonian control and reason. He lost such sensations when he contracted leprosy. Mhoram also heals Covenant's forehead with hurtloam during his second journey to the

Land. And Prothall uses it to release the spell placed on Llaura that had forbidden her to tell the Company of Drool's planned ambush, so it has power to cure or heal psychological hurts as well. Foamfollower thinks hurtloam might help Pietten, who seems abnormally attracted to blood as a small child, but chooses instead to use the last of his hurtloam to aid a dying Cavewight. It heals Hile Troy's burn wounds and gives him a Land sight to replace his previous blindness.

Through his craft, Trell is also able to mend the pot that Lena breaks when she is shocked at Covenant's news of the return of the Grey Slayer (Lord Foul). He has skill in his hands but also uses lore and a song or chant to rejoin the pieces of the pot. The pieces stick as he reassembles them; then finally he runs his fingers over the crack lines that were left until even those disappear, and the pot looks as good as new. By Tolkien's definitions of fantasy, the desire to explore time and space is illustrated through Trell's act, since our world believes that in the linear view of time, if something such as glass or pottery is broken, it cannot be mended not only to look unbroken, but also be whole as if never broken as Trell is able to wipe out even the lines which formed the original cracks. He can also foretell the weather through "reading" the stone. In the 2nd "Chronicles," Sunder and Hollian use his orcrest, her *lianar*, and Covenant's *krill* to read and even to change the Sunbane and bring on a sun of rain early, effectively speeding up time.

Through the art of *suru-pa-maerl* the Stonedownor people try to heal the wounds made to the earth by finding and melding together stones. This task is consistent with the purpose of all the peoples of the Land to honor the earth and try to remake its beauty, which was lost during the Ritual of Desecration. It illustrates a belief that creativity belongs to some Creator and as humans try to recreate the lost beauty, they are trying to see the original form, not create their own new forms. In addition, it supports the idea that the *rhadhamaerl* control/master and serve stone: they call forth the Earthpower of the stone, but they also use their skills to re-form the beauty of the stone (as the Ramen use their skills to heal injured or sick Ranyhyn). This control and service is a dialectical kind of interaction.

Near Trothgard after the Lords have recovered the 2nd Ward, many *rhadhamaerl* form the natural stones of the area into the Rock Gardens of the Maerl, a bruised and contorted but laughing face that can best be perceived from a high perspective. On closer examination the unevenness of the stones creates contortions and makes the face seem pocked or bruised. The eyes look wounded, and the path of the road gives the impression of a deep scar across the face. Notwithstanding its blemishes, the face exhibits a wide grin. The first impression of irrepressible love of life despite misfortunes makes most of the Company share a contagious joy at the sight. This alone is another example of the eye of the paradox, the inextinguishable joy in spite of the abuse that produced a scar and bruising. But Covenant's story of the woman he met in the leprosarium who smiled the same way, while juxtaposing the same oppositions, focuses more on the danger the woman put herself in by not adequately caring for her disease. The two perspectives of the same art work illustrate a more profound example of the eye of the paradox, which simultaneously presents us with conflicting emotional responses to integrate.

The attitude of the *rhadhamaerl* toward creating with stone supports the Declining World theory within the mythic world view of the inhabitants of the Land, and also supports that there was a Golden Age in the past and the purpose of those in the present is to recreate that age as closely as they can in an imperfect and broken world. This view of the inhabitants of the Land, not of Donaldson, indicates the limitation of the heroic world view alone. Knowledge is the key to rebuilding the world after the Ritual of Desecration. Apparently, before that act of Kevin's despair, most peoples of the Land were aware of all the major lore or forms of Earthpower, but when the *rhadhamaerl* were wandering the lands by themselves, they remembered, found useful, and passed down the *rhadhamaerl* lore, and thus it was preserved. Perhaps their environment, which does not contain many trees or other animals, determined their choice. This theory is also supported by the style of the tale Atiaran tells the Stonedown, which gives it a Biblical feel. She uses terms such as "'*It came to pass* that there was a great war'"[2] (emphasis mine) in telling the tale of a Lord's actions at least 3,000 years before her own time.

The result is a kind of specialization of skills within the Land, which symbolically leads to the animal/vegetable/mineral division discussed earlier. The *rhadhamaerl* focus their skills and interest on the minerals, the rocks and stones, of the Land. Though they don't "worship" stone the way the Ramen seem to reverence the Ranyhyn or the way Covenant asks if the Lords worship trees, they respect the earth. Though the Fire Lions or molten lava seems to be personified and might be associated with animal power in the Land, it is a part of the earth itself, neither its vegetation nor its inhabitants, and thus the calling of the Fire Lions is more closely connected with *rhadhamaerl* lore. As the stones themselves can be made hot, if that skill is exaggerated, the rocks could become molten lava moving downhill; the hotter the lava, the more quickly it could move and then it would resemble hungry lions charging down a mountain.

In the 1st "Chronicles," the Stonedownors are basically "home" in Mithil Stonedown; that is, they have returned to the area of the Land in which their ancestors probably lived before the Ritual of Desecration, but their home is not the same as it was during the idealized past of the Land. However, all the members of that community who eventually leave Mithil Stonedown — Trell,

Atiaran, Lena, Elena, and Triock — do not return. They all die based on decisions they make as part of their interaction with Covenant. In the 2nd "Chronicles," when Sunder leaves Mithil Stonedown, he must sneak away, and he cannot return or he would be sacrificed for his own village or to the Clave. Therefore, they are modern characters in the sense of not truly living in a utopian world, though it might seem to us who live in an ironic world (using Northrup Frye's definitions) that their strong sense of community makes them more ideal than we are. But they perceive the world as declining and their skills and connection to the earth as not as strong as they had been.

The *rhadhamaerl* people have formed a strong community. Though the *rhadhamaerl* have no formal religion, they participate in a kind of Deism that permeates the Land in their reverence for Earthpower. No mention of churches is made, but they still celebrate important passages or rituals such as marriage. Their customs involve the community. When a couple wishes to marry, as Lena explains to Covenant, they announce their intention to the village leaders. The council observes the couple's interactions over the next season to make sure that no hidden conflict exists and that the affection between the two is genuine. When it is time for the ceremony, it is very simple. The Elders call the entire Stonedown together and publicly ask the couple if they wish to be together and work together to improve the Land, and when they answer in the affirmative, they are united. Since the community is small, there are no last names, and the couple becomes known as the other's mate, as Atiaran is Trell-mate. There is no reference to the couple themselves receiving gifts from the community, but rather they are responsible to teach something new (a new game and/or dance and/or song) to the community at their wedding. When Trell and Atiaran marry, using a stone of *orcrest* which Trell found, and knowledge Atiaran learned in her studies at the Loresraat, they give an immeasurable gift to the community. She sings as he crumbles the stone in his hand, and when the dust hits the ground, lightning springs from the ground to the sky, thunder sounds, the blue sky is immediately covered by gray rain clouds, and rain falls. Thus is Mithil Stonedown's famine broken. Donaldson always emphasizes service. Other ritual gatherings occur in which their important history is recounted, sung by whoever is the most knowledgeable. Atiaran, having studied for a time at the Loresraat, sings the legend of Berek Halfhand. Those who listen sit or stand in a semi-circle and move forward to hug her in appreciation when she finishes.

The *rhadhamaerl's* sense of service refers to the Oath of Peace as well as to the Land itself. When Triock attacks Covenant for his rape of Lena, Atiaran commands Triock to remember the Oath and put the good of the Land itself and the importance of Covenant's message to the Lords above his own anger and desire for revenge (even if it is just). She also wounds the earth herself with her knife rather than harm Covenant when she leaves him in the care of Foamfollower. Later Trell is hard pressed to remember his Oath of Peace, and through his conflicting emotions, finds in his *rhadhamaerl* lore enough knowledge to begin a Ritual of Desecration within the Close of Revelstone.

The role of the gravelingas changes dramatically between the 1st and 2nd "Chronicles" since in order to wield power, Sunder, as the graveler, must cut himself and use his own blood to trigger the use of the Sunbane's power. Also, he is required to perform the human blood sacrifices for the village, even if it means he must kill his own wife and son or his mother. Not only does this archaic practice reflect the declining world view that important lore has been lost in the intervening years between the 1st and 2nd "Chronicles," but it also supports the Clave's use of blood and the sacrifice of the lives of the peoples of the Land to enhance its power. Philosophically, the Clave must use lies to convince people to support its political power. The newer view of a government all too willing to sacrifice its own people to maintain its tyrannical power has a frighteningly close resemblance to some modern countries, such as — to name only a few — Bosnia, the Sudan, and Iraq. Though Donaldson writes fantasy, his insights are often extremely relevant.

Individual *rhadhamaerl* people play important roles in the first two "Chronicles." They are important for their family relationships and their connection to Covenant and his responsibility to them for his treatment/rape of Lena as well as for their own knowledge and skills as Stonedownors. Violence against one family member also affects the others closely connected with that person emotionally. The same is true of other tragedies, like Covenant's leprosy and how it changed instantly not only his life, but also the lives of his wife and son, Joan and Roger. In the 1st "Chronicles," the Trell-Atiaran-Lena family group with Lena's daughter by Covenant, Elena, and Lena's suitor Triock, are all characters essential to the story.

Lena first finds and befriends Covenant on Kevin's Watch. She explains many aspects of the Land to Covenant, from aliantha or treasure-berries for food and sustenance to hurtloam, which on his first visit "cures" him of the symptoms of his leprosy, his inability to feel through his hands and feet, and of his impotence. She introduces him to her family and through them to the Stonedown. However, Lena is a much more important character psychologically for Covenant, for it is through his interaction with her that he must face his own heart of darkness. When the hurtloam has allowed Covenant to act on his physical/sexual desire for Lena (even leprosy did not rob him of the desire, just the performance) and he rapes her, he forever after must deal with his sense of guilt and shame. It really doesn't matter that he believes his experiences in the Land to be a dream, that as a leper he should be incapable of sexual intercourse and therefore can be surprised by his overwhelming desire and ability, that Lena herself seems to desire a relationship with Covenant (though not as violent nor as quick a sexual relationship), nor that afterwards Covenant feels remorse and tries to make amends to Lena through his bargain with the Ranyhyn that she loves. His guilt will inform all his other insights and choices. After the battle of Soaring Woodhelven, Covenant realizes that Lord Foul "raped" the Wraiths at the Celebration of Spring in exactly the same way he himself had raped Lena. Again, Donaldson is confusing the truth of whether Covenant's experiences in the Land are real or a dream. If his experiences are just his dream, his subconscious is reminding him to acknowledge his own faults, and this epiphany teaches Covenant about his integral relationship to Lord Foul. This acknowledgement and his guilt over the number of creatures of the Land he had personally killed at Soaring Woodhelven lead to Covenant's fast, his determination to do no more killing, his bargain with the Ranyhyn, and eventually result essentially in his own personal Oath of Peace. Covenant is profoundly affected by his sense of responsibility toward Lena.

As a modern novelist, Donaldson is simply acknowledging the awareness that no one in the modern world can escape: that we are all capable of evil, that we all have a heart of darkness that might surprise us at any time. Though his tale is set in a myth-like other world, coexistent with our own, but which has many attributes we recognize as more consistent with the medieval past of our world (horse travel, swords, and bows and arrows — and mystical power — rather than the guns and rockets of today), the psychological awareness of the novels is essentially modern. And through their interaction with Covenant, some of the peoples of the Land come to be aware of their own hearts of darkness, their susceptibility to becoming what they hate, their ability to destroy that which they most love. So even that which they most fear and least understand, the potential for ultimate self-destruction, the Ritual of Desecration, becomes possible first for Mhoram and then for Trell within the Land during the 1st "Chronicles." Thus, though the feel of Mithil Stonedown, of the Land, of the simple communities of people within the Land, remind us nostalgically of our now-more-idealized-because-presumed-simpler past, Donaldson does not let that be the only view we have of the Land; he forces us to incorporate modern awareness into the idealized view, creating another aspect of the eye of the paradox which is one of his purposes in writing the Covenant books.

Covenant's rape of Lena and its contrast to Foul's of the Land is the most important (though not the first) juxtaposition of a modern world view with an idealized view as presented in the Land. Donaldson wants us to accept and act on both world views — to reverence and be of service to the Land but without losing the epiphanies, the awarenesses (knowledge learned), the experiences we gain by living in the modern world. Because modern fantasy usually abandons the modern world and all its often-depressing self-knowledge to prefer a more idealized earlier time, as if we could recapture the earlier innocence despite having gone through the experiences of our times, Donaldson's "Chronicles" stand out as unique and more significant than most other fantasy novels being published at this time. He brings us face to face with the paradoxes and forces us to acknowledge and integrate the polarities together. Also, Covenant's actions have physical as well as psychological repercussions within the story. His rape of Lena is a horrific act, and yet without it, Elena would not be born.

Lena plays another role in the 1st "Chronicles" when she is an old woman and Covenant has returned for the third time to the Land and is traveling through the preternatural winter, finally to confront Lord Foul. Despite his constant doubt in the reality of the Land, his need to hang onto his own perception of what is true, he plays the role her madness calls for in the Land and lets her believe she is his "Queen," thus solidifying the connection between himself and Berek, which he had always tried to deny. The change in his interaction with Lena also signals his changing perception of the Land and his changing world view. As the perpetual winter of the Land in *The Power That Preserves* threatens to overwhelm the Land's earlier heroic world view with a more ironic one, Donaldson again forces the juxtaposition of the two views by making Covenant strive to act in a more heroic way, to use his power for the good of the Land.

Lena's mother is another important character. The Circle of Elders of Mithil Stonedown chooses Atiaran, Lena's mother, to guide Covenant to Revelstone so he can deliver his message to the Lords, thus initiating the first half of his first quest. She plans their route to include a stop at Soaring Woodhelven and a detour through Andelain to try to witness the Celebration of Spring. Both these incidents have a tremendous effect on Covenant, as do their experiences first at a Waymeet that is provisioned for travelers and later at another within which he finds a murdered Waynhim, which precipitates the abandonment of this service by the Waynhim. Since he has met the people of Soaring Woodhelven, their slaughter by Drool's army devastates him and contributes to his fury in killing. He realizes later that since Drool knew where to find the Company because he could sense the touch of Covenant's boots on the earth, boots not made in the Land, Covenant has perhaps helped Drool make the choice of where to attack. Therefore, his guilt is compounded by his knowledge as well as his sense of outrage at himself for killing so many Cavewights personally. The attack on the Celebration of Spring also creates an epiphany for Covenant, who realizes that Foul is doing to the Land exactly what he did to Lena, again adding to his sense of guilt. He already feels guilt over his rape of Lena and her unselfish protection of him to facilitate his quest, but the other incidents connected to Atiaran also exacerbate Covenant's sense of guilt.

Atiaran herself is plagued with self-doubt. She never finished her course of study at the Loresraat, and though she knows more of the old tales than others in her community and is revered there for her superior knowledge, her quest with Covenant seems to exceed her capacity. At first she just feels rushed, that they must arrive at Revelstone in time for the Lords to take the appropriate action to regain the Staff of Law. But after Triock tells her of Covenant's rape of Lena, she becomes conflicted in how she interacts with him. She forbids Triock to take vengeance by reminding him of his Oath of Peace. Yet when she turns Covenant over to Foamfollower, her anger and self-blame becomes evident. Covenant can see that she is upset and tries to encourage her, and she spits back at him vehemently that she should use her own knife to kill Covenant, not only for her own personal, family grievances, but also for the good of the Land. She knows that he, as the white gold bearer, can save or damn the Land, and she is convinced he is more likely to damn it. She blames Covenant for not being willing to use his wild magic power to save the Wraiths at the Celebration of Spring, not really accepting that he does not know how. At the same time she blames herself for desiring personal healing and taking the detour to see the Celebration of Spring. As a result of her unresolved conflict, she hurls her knife into the Earth so she will not be further tempted to forget her own Oath of Peace. While not a sacrilege, for a Stonedowner to wound the earth is unthinkable.

She is later referred to in the second book, *The Illearth War*, as the student who tries to summon Covenant the second time but ends up bringing Hile Troy to the Land instead and being burned from the conflagration which is about to consume him as Troy hangs from the window of his "real" world apartment to escape the fire that is destroying it. Her motives for the attempt remain mysterious. Is she acting to help resolve the needs of the Land or for her own personal vengeance? Later in the story it is revealed that she returned to the Loresraat to learn more but that she also had a hard time containing her anger at Covenant.

Trell, Lena's father, is a powerful *rhadhamaerl* gravelingas. His ability to bring the firestones to life and light and heat and then carry what should be an extremely heavy pot of graveling to the community services and his ability to mend the broken pot attest to his skill with stone. His power to destroy is equally great: in *The Illearth War* when Trell first confronts Covenant, without even being aware of what he is doing, Trell pushes his fingers into the stone floor of Revelstone, gouging out chunks of stone as if it were as soft as clay. When he realizes what he is doing, that he is harming what he loves most, he is horrified. Later, his own personal despair leads him to discover the secret of the Ritual of Desecration, but ironically, the object of his destruction is the stone of the Close. Again, he attacks that which he most loves and formerly worked all his life to preserve. Mhoram and Tohrm the Hearthrall almost are not equal to halting Trell's Ritual. From his despair Trell discovered how to augment his power but only for destruction. Trell, too, has been changed by his interaction with Covenant. He directs his anger outward at Covenant first when he meets him by chance at Revelstone. Then in *The Power That Preserves*, his anger is focused inward upon himself, is intensified by his guilt and despair, and results in his attempted Ritual of Desecration.

Triock is another stonedowner from Mithil Stonedown who plays an important part in the 1st "Chronicles." His love and devotion to Lena, whom he had wanted to marry, extends to Elena, the illegitimate child she bears as a result of Covenant's rape. Triock resents Covenant, for Lena continues to believe all her life that Covenant will come back and marry her, and, therefore, she will not marry Triock. Triock selflessly gives over his own desires and needs to serve Lena and Elena. He also is powerful and skillful, and with the *lomillialor* rod given to him by the foresighted Mhoram and the knowledge he learns of how to use it through study of *lillianrill* lore at the Loresraat, he and Foamfollower are able to recall Covenant to the Land (though Covenant also believes his own weak, close-to-death condition might have made it easier). Elena tells Covenant that Triock was truly her father as she grew up and that even though he harbored resentment himself, he raised her not to hate Covenant. He undertakes at Covenant's request/command a task he believes to be impossible, to find a way to communicate using the *lomillialor* rod with the Lords in Revelstone. He might have succeeded if *turiya* Herem Raver had not taken over his companion Yeurquin and eventually Triock himself, forcing him to trap and bring Covenant to the Colossus. Later he explains to Covenant how Elena is trying to destroy the Colossus. Yet in the end, when the Raver has left him and claimed the Ramen because it cannot approach too close to the Colossus, Triock tries to distract Elena and manages to get Covenant's white gold ring back for him, but dies as a result of his valor.

After his initial attack on Covenant, Triock tries desperately to remain a heroic character, to hide his resentments against Covenant from Lena and Elena. Triock understands better than Covenant that Foul cannot be fought with hate. He lies to Covenant about the fate of the Giants, then lectures him, "'We have sworn the Oath of Peace. Do not ask us to feed your hate.'"[3] He knows that no good for the Land can come from such emotions. He challenges Covenant to decide what he is fighting for, not just against. When Covenant's purpose against Foul appears to be based on his hatred, Triock refuses to join him in order to keep his Oath.

Of all the Stonedownors who aid Covenant on his various quests, Triock is the best example of one who is more effective when he has learned to combine the heroic and ironic qualities in himself. At the beginning of *Lord Foul's Bane*, Triock is still a pastoral heroic character. When he learns of Covenant's rape of Lena, he becomes a black-or-white, either-or person capable of murder. He goes from being a peaceful cattleherd in love with Lena to an angry, jealous, murderous, vengeful man intent on stalking and killing Covenant. Triock's loving care for Elena restores his goodness, and Mhoram's trust of Triock with the *lomillialor* rod encourages him to learn its uses. Later he surpasses his original skill and strength with Foamfollower's aid, to recall Covenant to the land. When he refuses to go with Covenant to confront Foul, he remains true to his Oath of Peace. But when the Raver possesses him, Triock fully experiences the eye of his paradox. Covenant sees without comprehension the dual awareness in Raver-possessed Triock, who acts as if he were two men struggling for dominance inside one body, one angry and the other afraid but defiant. Covenant almost cannot recognize him. Though Triock fights to fulfill his Oath of Peace, the Raver in him finds out his hatred, and Triock hears *turiya* Raver through his own voice cry out his great resentments against Covenant and against all the Unbeliever had cost the Stonedowner. Even when the Raver leaves Triock to control the Ramen, anger and anguish remain. But the cunning and the struggle are gone, leaving only self-condemnation at having to acknowledge the deep feelings he has tried to repress. His possession by Elena's power is not as complete as the Raver's was. Triock still fights Covenant and utters many hateful things, but within himself he is aware of the wrongness of his actions and tries to thwart her as well. Even as he watches her prepare to destroy the Colossus, the chief enemy of the Ravers, and can do nothing physical to stop her, still he tries to distract her by yelling at Covenant the truth about how Foul is controlling Elena. As he does so, he is also reminding her how much she is acting against her own will.

Triock's conflicts within himself—his need to acknowledge his own hatred for Covenant, his self-loathing for his own weakness, and his desire to uphold his Oath of Peace—finally unite when he finds the eye of his paradox and, at the fortuitous moment when Elena can perceive that the Lords are fighting back against *samadhi* Raver, Triock performs his most heroic act to regain the wild magic, white gold ring for Covenant. He becomes most effective at the height of his inner conflict, when his ironic and heroic sides collide and juxtapose. Thus, Donaldson is saying that not only can his characters never go home to their previous innocent existence after being exposed to the ironic world view of Covenant and their own awareness of individual culpabilities and negative emotions that cannot be controlled by Oaths or sheer will power, but Donaldson is also stating that the changed characters are truly more effective for good only when they have learned to juxtapose the oppositions of their personalities.

Therefore, new hope exists for our own modern world because our inevitable ironic world view, rather than being a detriment to our epic, heroic ambitions, is an essential component in our ability to be effective. Man is not a futile animal; he is capable of becoming an effective force by virtue of his guilt, his anger, his sinfulness, if and only if combined with his hope, his idealism, his desire for good.

Triock is the best example of the Stonedownors in the 1st "Chronicles" to illustrate this concept because Lena never has to face a heart of darkness in herself. Atiaran and Trell face self-doubt and despair but not combined with hope. Elena does not reach the apex of her character until after she has made her greatest error in using the Power of Command and thus destroying the Law of Death, but then she immediately dies and is later recalled to a life of servitude by Foul and forced to lead the fight to destroy that which she most loves. At the moment when she is relegated again to death, her true heroic side re-emerges, but she can no longer act.

Elena is the most important of the *rhadhamaerl* people who interacts with Covenant in the 1st "Chronicles." She is High Lord during Covenant's second visit to the Land and the beginning of the physical war against Foul. She is an enigma to Covenant for she is his daughter, but one whom he never sees as a child, never sees grow up, and meets when she is a forty-year-old woman. Also, she is attracted to Covenant and he to her, so there is a sexual tension between them. They can play as family members do when they dunk each other in Glimmermere, but she also offers herself to him sexually and tells him he cannot rape her since she is willing.

While the other Lords and Hile Troy's army are marching to face the Giant Raver *moksha* Jehannum Fleshharrower, Amok leads Elena and Covenant with two Bloodguard on a separate quest to find Kevin's 7th Ward. Because sound is necessary to propel a boat over Earthroot, Elena tells Covenant about her experience at the secret Ranyhyn rite in the mountains of the Southron Range to which Myrha, her Ranyhyn, took her as a child. The Ranyhyn at this ritual drink from the lake with its dark waters reflecting no sunlight and run around in a frenzy, scaring young Elena, until she realizes that they expect her to drink also. Then she understands that she is sharing in her generation's horserite to honor and tell the tale of *Kelenbhrabanal*, Father of Horses, who was killed by Lord Foul, whom they name Fangthane the Render, when he offered himself to Foul as a sacrifice to save the other Ranyhyn but was betrayed. The ritual involves celebrating their pride and experiencing their grief and rage, so obviously the Ranyhyn have understood the eye of the paradox to be able to combine these disparate emotions.

Throughout her life Elena refers to Lord Foul as Fangthane, showing her connection with the Ranyhyn.

Elena also is given another clear lesson of containing contradictory emotions. When she is called back from death to wield the Staff of Law to perpetuate Foul's unnatural winter and attempt to destroy the Colossus, which is the Ravers' biggest bane, she clearly acts as Foul commands, but Triock tells Covenant that she is still aware of who she was in life and abhors what she is being forced to do in death. As she is defeated and sent back to her death, her last words to Covenant come from the real Elena, "'Covenant ... Beloved! Strike a blow for me!'"[4]

Before Elena drinks the EarthBlood to gain the Power of Command, she reminds Covenant that Foul's greatest risk is their greatest opportunity. Juxtaposing these opposites makes perfect sense to us. Even comprehending that our own greatest risk might be our best opportunity as an example of finding the eye of the paradox does not confuse us; we need to learn to combine other oppositions like Unbelief and acceptance the same way. Then though she is warned by Amok of the limitations of the Power of Command, though she knows that Kevin himself never dared it, though Mhoram has warned her against hazarding peril she doesn't fully understand, though Covenant begs her to desist when he perceives an ill in her, and though Kevin calls her "Fool!" when she begins to give the Command, she still chooses to use the power of the 7th Ward without completely understanding it or its consequences. So she commands Kevin from the grave, breaking the Law of Death, and sends him to fight Lord Foul for her. But because Kevin has already been conquered by his own despair, it is easy for Foul to defeat him again and, using the Illearth Stone, send him back against Elena. This result illustrates Donaldson's view that knowledge must personally be learned to be useful. Kevin understood this and deliberately arranged the knowledge of his seven wards so that the Lords would have to learn the lore from the first to discover the second. But the unpredictable power of the white gold awakened the power of the *krill* and that action prompted Amok to appear. Since none of the Lords have completely understood even the 1st and 2nd Wards, and the next four Wards are still hidden, any use of the 7th Ward would be what Donaldson calls unearned knowledge and therefore dangerous.

Although Elena is an important character in the 1st "Chronicles," she is not idealized by Donaldson. Like Frodo in Tolkien's *The Lord of the Rings*, Elena faces her greatest test at the end of her quest, and she fails it, precipitating her own death. Thus she has no opportunity to learn from experiencing her own heart of darkness as Covenant has. Therefore, she is a character who cannot go home, and she doesn't have time in her life to embrace both her heroic and ironic perspectives to become truly effective. She is finally able to heal herself of her hatred toward Foul and laugh at despair but only with the help of Foamfollower and the other Lords. Their laughter is strained at first and still filled with anger, but soon the simple act of laughing becomes contagious and they find joy and emotional relief in their shared mirth. At this point they are effective in diminishing Foul. When she returns to her death, Elena is at peace and has become the High Lord of hope and promise that she was before she broke the Law of Death.

All these characters eventually leave their homes in Mithil Stonedown and are not able to return because each dies in the course of following his/her life's path. In the 2nd "Chronicles" there is less freedom to travel because of the danger of being sacrificed by another village or being taken to Revelstone to become another human sacrifice of the Clave. Nevertheless, both Sunder, the current graveler of Mithil Stonedown, and Hollian, the eh-Brand of Crystal Stonedown, leave their homes to follow Covenant. Hollian's power to foretell the future of the Sunbane is accomplished through her wooden *lianar*, so obviously in the intervening 3,500 years in the Land, there has been some crossover between the power of the *rhadhamaerl* and *lillianrill*. Now all power supposedly comes from the Sunbane, and stone and wood are only the conduits, so in the 2nd "Chronicles" the wood of a torch can no longer be preserved and crumbles into ash when the fire triggered by the blood is let go. Also, for this reason, Sunder can learn to use the *rukh* of one of the Clave's Riders to control the coursers. His success with the mastering of different conduits of the power of the Sunbane allows him, and eventually also Hollian, to learn to control the *krill* of Kevin as well (which is not tied to the Sunbane or its power source of blood).

Sunder and Hollian cannot go home and must eventually remain in Andelain because only there can they be together. Sunder brings the dead Hollian to Andelain, and she is brought back to life when the Forestal Caer-Caveral goads Sunder into killing him, breaking the Law of Life, allowing the dead to cross back into life without being summoned. Only the remaining Earthpower of Andelain can sustain her life, so they must make a new home and find a new purpose there.

One other *rhadhamaerl* character is important but whether he can or cannot go home to his original village isn't really relevant; gravelingas Tohrm is the *rhadhamaerl* Hearthrall during the time of the siege on Revelstone. He is significant because he is able to stop Trell's attack against the Close. He gains power and protection from Mhoram who accompanies him into the conflagration and even shares with him the secret knowledge about the Ritual of Desecration. Then, when Mhoram is ready to ride out against the Raver Satansfist, Tohrm is the only one who isn't exhausted or stressed. He has already faced his crisis as he fought Trell's Ritual of Desecration, and he won, so no challenge can ever be as great. This victory is very important because the Ritual of Desecration that Kevin performed in his despair appeared to be unstoppable, all-powerful, and completely devastating. Nothing better illustrates Donaldson's view that one must go through crises to become whole, or that our own most difficult challenges can also be our best opportunities if we face them with hope and courage.

Lillianrill

On their way to Revelstone, Covenant and Atiaran stay the night with a *lillianrill* community at Soaring Woodhelven. Like the Stonedowners, the Woodhelvennin have a close-knit community, democratic in nature, with Heers who are entrusted to make important decisions, and a hirebrand, Baradakas, who in his control over wood parallels Trell. The *lillianrill* are taller than the *rhadhamaerl*, slimmer, and fairer. Their form-fitting clothing, which matches the tree's colors, allows them to move easily about their tree home without worrying about its being snagged on stray branches. They all live in the same tree community, with their children playing by jumping easily from branch to branch.

Baradakas tests Covenant using his community's test of truth, by throwing a *lomillialor* rod to see if Covenant can catch and hold it. The test is based on the belief that the wood itself can reject one who is not good, at least if the power of the person being tested is not greater than the power of the wood itself. Covenant tries to catch it, but it slips through his half-hand. But then he picks it up with his left hand. In keeping with the proliferation of paradoxes and ambiguities that abound in the "Chronicles," it is not clear whether the wood tries to reject Covenant or not or if his power is greater than the test, for though he can hold onto the *lomillianlor* rod, it feels slippery. Therefore, Covenant himself is not sure if he passed the test. As usual Covenant turns his self-doubt into anger when he challenges Baradakas to repeat his claim that the wood rejects him. Later as the hirebrand is not needed for the council meeting, some insight directs him to offer Covenant a staff that he had made for himself. This action supports a belief in an over-arching universe, in which some events can be foreordained or predestined, or perhaps in Covenant's unconscious mind, he wants a talisman of power to counterbalance his helplessness. Covenant later uses this staff and the wild magic at the Celebration of Spring and when he kills to avenge the destruction of Soaring Woodhelven.

Llaura and Pietten are the only two survivors of the attack on Soaring Woodhelven, and somehow both have been corrupted. Llaura, who was one of the Heers who greeted Atiaran and Covenant as they passed through, is aware of what was done and tries to escape to avoid springing the trap on the Company. But Pietten, who is only a small child, is unaware of his fault. The pattern is the same as for most evil in Donaldson's work, for they both are used to destroy that which they most love. Her community is burned, but Llaura reveres the Lords and does not want to cause harm to them or to cause their quest to fail and knows a trap has been set for them. Llaura is given the knowledge of the danger and also is made unable to tell the Lords. When they find her, Foul is assured that the trap will be sprung because the Lords will delay their departure in order to help Llaura to communicate with them. Thus she is frustrated and depressed because she blames herself for the predicament she puts the Lords in, though, of course, Lord Foul is actually to blame.

Pietten is afflicted in a similar way. He is fascinated by the Ranyhyn and comes to serve them as a member of the Ramen, yet his actions lead to the decimation of the herd as well. He doesn't even understand that his intention to drive the Ranyhyn from the Central Plains to safety is merely a product of his own madness. Again, his actions help bring about the exact outcome he wants to prevent.

Birinair is the *lillianrill* hirebrand for Revelstone during the quest for the Staff of Law. He stands guard before the burned tree and uses it to provide light for the Company as they fight the attackers at Soaring Wood-helven. He also leads the company into the catacombs of Mt. Thunder because his power is less perceptible than the Lord's power Prothall would have used to light their way. He is as knowledgeable as the High Lord about the maps of the catacombs of Drool's domain. Because of this awareness, when he recognizes something and excitedly rushes off down a side passage, he is caught and dies in the Word of Warning left by Kevin to guard the 2nd Ward. Prothall's sense of responsibility and guilt is increased because he believes that Birinair died due to his position in the front, leading the company.

Rillinlure, a healing wood dust used by the *lillianrill*, is like hurtloam and can be mixed in food to provide renewed strength and endurance. Mhoram mixes both into the food of the Waymark after their forced march toward Garroting Deep and again at Revelstone during the siege. Any unusual healing ability contributes to the disease/health dialectic of the books. The special Gildenlode keels and rudders the Giants will need for their ships to return Home are fashioned by the *lillianrill*. After the slaughter at *Coercri*, the *lillianrill* reshape the Gildenlode wood into *lor-liarill* arrows that automatically burst into flame when they hit a target for the Waymark's use against Satansfist's catapults. The importance of Earthpower is constantly emphasized.

Ramen

The Ramen are a nomadic community that follow and serve the Ranyhyn. They have shelters but are more often found roaming the plains. They do not ride themselves. They do use the fragrant but poisonous-to-humans *amanibhavam* grass to help heal the Ranyhyn's wounds or sicknesses. In their fighting groups consisting of one Manethrall and four Cords (later the ratio is more like eight or ten Cords to one Manethrall), they protect the horses from wandering *kresh* (wolf-like beasts). Though they can use spears (at least Pietten does), they rely mostly on stealth, their ability to blend into the landscape and disguise their presence, and quick movements with the rope cords which they wear either around their waists or in their hair. Even a Cord can kill one of the fierce *kresh* by concealing herself in the tall grass until the wolf-like beast is almost past her. Then standing quickly and readying her rope, she loops the rope around the beast's neck, and planting her feet squarely on the ground, allows the beast's own momentum to be the force that breaks its neck. Even if the *kresh* is large and powerful enough to pull her from her feet, she is smart enough to hold fast to the rope and agile enough to spring to her feet again, ready to apply additional pressure with the rope if necessary to strangle the beast. In fighting ability they almost rival the *Haruchai*; though they do use simple weapons, it is their personal skill in close fighting that makes them successful.

Lithe agrees to accompany the Company on the quest for the Staff of Law into Mt. Thunder because the Ramen have an instinct for direction and know how to find sun and fresh air. When she is torn between what seems like the most logical way to get out of the catacombs and what her instinct is telling her, Mhoram encourages her to trust her instinct, learned though many seasons of running in the open to serve the Ranyhyn, rather than logic. And she is successful. The path she chooses leads them out of the catacombs.

Again supporting the theme of paradox that underlies the entire "Chronicles," one Ramen woman has two names. In *Lord Foul's Bane*, she is the young child Winhome Gay, who has not yet attained her cording. She tries to serve the fasting Covenant some food and acts insolently toward him, showing her spirit. Then in *The Illearth War*, she is the messenger who volunteers to take news to Revelstone that Foul's army is on the march, but at that time she calls herself Rue. She gives her rope cord to Hile Troy, as he marches off to war and shortly thereafter dies.

The Ramen's creative form of art is *anundivian yajna*, though even at the time of the 1st "Chronicles," it is a dying art. It consists of the ability to meld and reshape bone into a sculpture. Elena learns this skill from her interaction with the Ranyhyn in her childhood; from the bones of Myrha, the

Ranyhyn that had chosen her and that sacrificed itself to save Covenant's mustang from the landslide, Elena creates a marrowmeld sculpture of the head of Covenant. When he mistakes the artwork for the head of Bannor, the parallel between the Bloodguard and the Unbeliever is strengthened. He reads the face as gaunt and purposeful, yet enigmatic. The sternness and unyielding quality of its expression makes him think of the Bloodguard. Again on the level of interpretation of the "Chronicles" as the external playing out of Covenant's internal selves, his uncompromising harshness with himself which makes him so like the strict *Haruchai* is captured by the marrowmeld.

Elena's bone sculpture has a much more far-reaching impact on Mhoram. Bannor explains, in uncharacteristic detail, the story of Covenant's misinterpretation of Elena's art, and as Mhoram understands the connection between the absolute judgments made by both Covenant and Bannor, the High Lord loses his power as a seer. But his resultant intuitive insight is far more important and dangerous, so much so that he feels that he has to keep it secret from the other Lords. Through the juxtaposition of the Bloodguard and the Unbeliever, Mhoram has also discovered the great paradox that can lead to the Ritual of Desecration. He fears to tell anyone else of his new awareness of the greatest of destructive powers, and so for his silence he feels guilty.

Obviously the Ranyhyn and the Ramen's love and caring for the magnificent horses is a reflection of Covenant's wife Joan's ability to "break" horses for a living, or rather her seduction of them into compliance. Covenant's fear of horses and unwillingness to ride a Ranyhyn comes from his "real" world fear also. This association supports the idea that the Land is a dream-like creation of Covenant's mind based on his past experiences in his "real" world.

The Ranyhyn, though not human, are the closest to epic, heroic beings in the "Chronicles," and thus deserve some analysis at this point. The great horses are varied in size and coloring, but all have a white star marking their foreheads. They have more stamina and seem to exhibit more wisdom and yet share none of the guilt or despair of the humans of the Land. Though they do not speak with voices, they have the ability to choose to whom to offer service and they comprehend speech and communicate with each other and with Elena. Without speaking to her, they indicate, at the horserite they share with her, that they want her also to drink from the tarn and share their frenzy and celebration. The drink endows Elena with the knowledge of why she and the Ranyhyn have gathered: to celebrate and mourn *Kelenbhrabanal*, Father of Horses and Stallion to the Herd, who attempted to sacrifice himself for his herd but was betrayed by Fangthane, their name for Lord Foul. When the leaderless herd was attacked again by the *kresh*, the Ranyhyn fled the plains of Ra and were not able to return until the Ramen volunteered to care for them. One hundred of them offer themselves to Covenant during the quest for the Staff of Law and understand his conditions for refusing them: they are to visit Lena once a year and be available to come if he calls. Pietten seems to be able to read their emotions, their fear of Covenant, though he is just a child.

The Ranyhyn illustrate Tolkien's purpose for fantasy to explore the depths of time and space in their ability to anticipate the need of the Lord or Bloodguard they have chosen to serve and to traverse whatever distance is necessary to arrive shortly after the call is whistled. They must leave the plains of Ra long before the call is made in order physically to cover the distance to their Lord or Bloodguard. And since they arrive immediately after the whistle, they must know, perhaps even before the Lord is aware, of the need. After Mhoram swims in Glimmermere and redresses himself, he comes to an important decision. He would have to take on the heroic action of challenging *samadhi* Satansfist himself to affect the battle and provide hope for the other Lords and defenders of Revelstone. Covenant can't help. As High Lord, it is his responsibility. But he cannot do it alone, so he calls on the strongest, most faithful, greatest power he knows for aid, his Ranyhyn Drinny, not knowing if his whistle will be answered by the great horse. After all, Satansfist's army stands between the Plains of Ra and Revelstone and the preternatural winter is deadly. After he whistles, Mhoram waits as if he knows Drinny will arrive, trying to be worthy of the effort he knows the horse will make to get there. Then finally he sees a blur of brown coming towards him. To answer his call Drinny would have had to leave weeks earlier, travel from the plains to the mountains to make his way around the great army encamped in his way. Obviously the journey has been difficult, the cold, the lack of food, the strenuousness of the path. But when Mhoram sits atop him, he becomes the High Lord who can do the impossible if only to match the epic accomplishment of the Ranyhyn. Drinny is immortalized along with Mhoram in the sculpture "Lord Mhoram's Victory."

Lords

The Lords' power can include the lore of the *rhadhamaerl* or *lillianrill* skills since, obviously, the lords might come from those cultures, and much of the Lords' power is used to try to heal the Land of the blights brought on by the Ritual of Desecration. But the power they try to master through study in the Loresraat of Kevin's Lore from the 1st Ward, and eventually, after the quest for the Staff of Law from the 2nd Ward also, includes the power to defend the Land from Lord Foul and his armies and to fight against physical attacks on the peoples of the Land using military power. This power inevitably involves the destruction of "evil" creatures such as Cavewights, ur-viles, griffins, *kresh*, or child-giants who have been possessed by Ravers. For a conscientious objector such as Donaldson, dealing with the necessity of war for some causes, in some circumstances, and choreographing how such battles should be undertaken within his Secondary World was undoubtedly an ethical dilemma. But since his purpose is to show the limitations of the muscle solution, he has to have his characters try it. This paradox is exemplified in the contrasting values of Kevin's Wards and the Oath of Peace that all the peoples of the Land swore to uphold after the Ritual of Desecration. The crux of the problem comes from the emotional involvement that usually accompanies wars. The Oath of Peace advocates control of emotions, restraint of anger and hatred. Its Code reads:

> Do not hurt where holding is enough;
> do not wound where hurting is enough;
> do not maim where wounding is enough;
> and kill not where maiming is enough;
> the greatest warrior is he who does not need to kill.[5]

The dispassion needed to uphold such an Oath would be best exemplified by the Bloodguard, yet they, ironically, have taken no such oath, and in doing their job of protecting the Lords, they do not hesitate to kill rather than simply capture or main. Other inhabitants of the Land have a harder time maintaining their devotion to peace. Both Triock and Atiaran wound the earth with their knives rather than hurt Covenant, against whom they are rightly angry. Trell gouges out fingerholds in the rock of Revelstone to keep from further attacking Covenant. Trell eventually best understands the paradox when he discovers the secret to the Ritual of Desecration, and Mhoram, too, finally understands that the reason the lords have not been more successful in comprehending Kevin's Wards is precisely because of their Oath of Peace. The ability of the lords to be successful in war, to use what weapons and power are available to them to fight the enemy is antithetical to the restraint of withholding power or deciding exactly how much power is necessary to subdue without killing an opponent bent on killing and destroying them. Here is another manifestation of the eye of the paradox for Donaldson.

Power can corrupt is still a truism, but more than that, Donaldson is telling us that power can be uncontrollable. In some ways, we cannot know enough about power or its aftermath to use it conscientiously. This attitude is particularly appropriate for the modern era, which has seen a proliferation of atomic, biological, and chemical weapons for which we have no idea what consequences we would face after their use. Covenant wields the ultimate power in the white gold ring, the wild magic that destroys peace, but he cannot call up the power consciously nor control what he does with this power. When he does inadvertently use it, usually in anger, and kills cavewights at the battle of Soaring Woodhelven, he immediately regrets his own destructive power and feels guilty about killing even enemies. Then in the 2nd "Chronicles" when he has decided that he wants to use the white gold wild magic to aid the Land, he is hampered by the unpredictable nature of the venom within him, which enhances the power of the while gold so that he cannot control it. While both Tolkien and Donaldson would quail at a simplistic allegorical connection between the power of the rings in their Secondary Worlds and atomic power, nevertheless a case can be made for such a comparison, if only to prove the point that such power in the hands of an enemy would be devastating and could destroy our entire world, and in Donaldson's case, also to show that we do not know enough about nuclear power or lasers or any other form of power that could be both helpful or potentially destructive to be sure it would be used only constructively. Without knowledge of all possible potential uses of the power and complete control so that it is used only for good, the best approach to power is restraint or refusal to attempt to use it until one can have full knowledge of its consequences. This attitude is taken by Covenant (though for additional reasons based on his unbelief) in the 1st "Chronicles" and might have served Elena better than her desire for and mistaken confidence in her own ability to control power, even the Power of Command.

Nevertheless, the Lords feel a need to learn how to use whatever power is available to them. The Lords have chosen their way of life, or have felt called to the service of the land. They possess no special magic in themselves but acquire knowledge through the study of Kevin's lore at the Loresraat at Trothgard, which allows them to call upon power or magic within the land itself, Earthpower. The exception to this rule is Mhoram's abilities as seer and oracle. The most consistent distinguishing trait among the Lords is a sense of inadequacy to their chosen tasks. None has mastered all the Lore that was once known and contained in Kevin's Seven Wards which were left behind after the Ritual of Desecration and of which only the first two (and later temporarily the 7th) have been recovered.

Despite their inadequacies, the Lords represent our best intentions, our most pure service, in the layer of interpretation of the story in which Covenant dreams the Land and they represent parts of his inner character. And since Donaldson always forces his reader to acknowledge more than one possible layer of interpretation of the characters, it is also valuable to evaluate them on face value, as they appear to be and are made to act within the story itself. In this way, the Lords do not function symbolically as a group but have individual personalities.

Prothall is High Lord during the quest for the Staff of Law; he is old at the time Lord Foul's message is delivered to the lords by Covenant, and he feels inadequate for the task, but there is no one else to take the responsibility. His guilt is heightened when he lets Birinair lead in his place in the catacombs of Mount Thunder, and Birinair dies. One of Prothall's most important characteristics is his understanding of the psychology of those around him. He knows when to confront Foamfollower and shock him with his question, "'Do you rave?'"⁶ to bring him back to himself away from the bloodthirstiness and anger Foamfollower feels toward the servants of the enemy and his desire to kill them all, which could lead led him to become what he hates. Also, Prothall trusts his own instincts in leading the Company on a longer journey in order to go by way of the plains of Ra and allow Mhoram to be offered to the Ranyhyn. He allows Covenant to be offered as well, but the bargain Covenant makes with the Ranyhyn — that he wouldn't choose any of them — is even more important for the successful completion of the quest because it means that the great horses are there to bring the Company to safety away from the Fire Lions and Drool's army at the end of the quest.

Elena is High Lord at the beginning of Foul's attack, and her role was discussed earlier. Mhoram is the most important Lord of the 1st "Chronicles," for he is present throughout and High Lord in *The Power That Preserves*. During the first quest, he loses both his parents in Drool's attack on the Company at Soaring Woodhelven, and his song expresses another of the dialectics we need to learn to join: "Hold peace and grief/and be still."⁶ Obviously peace and grief are antithetical, but he needs both. Later, he knows to trust Manethrall Lithe in the catacombs of Mount Thunder to find the way out for the Company.

In his role as seer and oracle, he knows that the Lords need to send an embassy to the Giants because something is wrong. During the battle against Raver *moksha* Jehannum Fleshharrower, Mhoram accompanies Hile Troy to Kevin's Watch so that Troy can understand the strategy that will be needed to defeat the Raver. Mhoram uses the *lomillialor* to communicate with the marching army and later is foresighted enough to know that he will not need the communication rod any more and gives it to Triock. But his most important task is his most dangerous one: Troy requires that Mhoram call Caerroil Wildwood to bargain with the Forestal of Garroting Deep for the safety of the Lords' army in exchange for the Raver Fleshharrower and his army. When Mhoram's initial attempts are unsuccessful, he resorts to singing the Forestal's own song, an effort dangerous and possibly fatal if the Forestal takes offense. However, the desperation of the situation convinces him that only this attempt is perilous enough to work. Again, the extremity of the peril is balanced with the hope and need for success.

During the time period of Covenant's third visit, High Lord Mhoram, at ninety years of age, becomes one of the Land's greatest heroes. Before Covenant's second visit, in the labyrinth of Kurash Qwellinir, Mhoram had met and come into contact with *samadhi* Raver who becomes Satansfist and who was intimidated by what he learned of Mhoram. But more important, by the time of the siege on Revelstone, Mhoram has learned the secret to the Ritual of Desecration. When Bannor explains the story of the bone sculpture that Elena made of Covenant and Covenant's mistaken identification of the subject of the sculpture as Bannor, Mhoram intuitively understands the connection between the White Gold Wielder and the Bloodguard: both require absolute answers, either the Vow or abandonment of service to the Lords, either the Land is real or it is a dream. This either/or thinking illustrates the limitation of the Bloodguard and also Covenant's inability to understand the eye of his paradox at this time and accept both views as true. Mhoram's realization has other consequences. He recognizes the double-edged nature of power — that the same power is apt for good or evil. He learns the secret of the Ritual of Desecration from Elena's marrowmelt bust of Covenant, and the epiphany fills him with fear and hope. The juxtaposition of these opposites is another representation of the eye of the paradox. As a consequence of his new knowledge, Mhoram loses his ability to foresee the future in dreams. But he learns to harness the same power that causes Desecration and to use it for good against the Raver; thus, as a High Lord he is more effective than he was because of his knowledge of evil.

Mhoram himself tries to call Covenant back to the Land when the Raver Satansfist has destroyed Revelwood. But Covenant has just come upon the young girl threatened by the timber rattler in the woods near Haven Farm and refuses the summons. Mhoram tells him of the Land's great need but eventually reverses the invocation, releasing the compulsion he is using to bring Covenant to the Land. He recognizes that Covenant's motivation to stay in his "real" world, to save the life of the young girl, is an honorable desire. He is still afraid that without Covenant's help, the Lords may fail, but as was articulated by Lena's poem "Something there is in Beauty," should the Land be destroyed, its beauty cannot die as long as it remains in Covenant's memory. Mhoram takes comfort in the fact that Covenant will always remember the unspoiled Land, and this belief supports the "immortality through art" theme of much of Western literature; the "Chronicles" themselves have given us a picture of the Land that will not be lost as long as the books are still published or remembered by readers. This awareness on Mhoram's part of the need for voluntary participation and free-will choice is developed more fully by Covenant when he explains the necessity of freedom to Linden in the 2nd "Chronicles" and is one of Donaldson's essential themes. Also, Mhoram eventually realizes that by keeping the key to the Ritual of Desecration secret from the other lords and even from Trell, he is not allowing them the free will to reject the power or to find another way to combat the despair that could lead to Desecration. The Wasteland isn't the only possibility, even in our modern world.

Mhoram's interaction with Trell is significant for the story. Mhoram knows that Trell is in pain, but decides not to mistrust him nor to have him watched. Trell somehow intuits that Mhoram has knowledge of some secret power and at the same time is suspicious that Mhoram might be willing to hand over Revelstone to the Raver intact. Though we never have Trell's point of view, by some logical or intuitive process, he learns the secret of the Ritual of Desecration and begins it within the stone hall of the Close. It takes the *rhadhamaerl* lore of Tohrm, the secret knowledge that Mhoram shares with him, and the protection of two other Lords for the Hearthrall to counter Trell's power and stop the Ritual. Mhoram later feels guilty for not trusting Trell enough to share his secret knowledge of power when Trell asked him since then Trell might have found the courage to resist the despair or temptation of that power. Mhoram then corrects his mistake and shares his dangerous knowledge with the other Lords.

Mhoram's great heroism is a result of the desperation of the siege and his belief that there is no other hope of help to be expected from Covenant when the gem of the *krill* first loses its light, then turns the color green of the Illearth Stone. At first, his reaction appears to be depression and giving up; he leaves Revelstone and goes to Glimmermere, where Earthpower is still viable. He dips himself in the lake, and the cold brings back his desire to live. When he emerges, he has decided what he has to do, so he calls his Ranyhyn, and amazingly Drinny has anticipated the call and found a way around the Raver's army to answer him. Mhoram is willing to sacrifice himself for the Land and to use dangerous power if necessary to save the Land because as High Lord, he lives for service. Because of his new knowledge and power, he is able to pull the *krill* from the table into which Covenant thrust it, in an obvious parallel to King Arthur's claiming of Excalibur. Although he is no longer a seer and oracle, he knows what must be done, and asks the others to accomplish almost impossible tasks first. By doing so, Mhoram feels that if he fails, the others can still continue the fight without him, for they will have confidence in their own abilities. They will have faced crises, as Torhm has, and prevailed. Then he rides out alone against the Raver because his personality will not allow any other choice. He cannot give up and is willing to attempt any challenge, even face his own knowledge of the ultimate destructive power and yet refrain from using it. Having found the eye of his paradox, he rides out against Satansfist. When his staff is shattered as he strikes the Raver across the forehead, and it looks as if the Raver is about to kill him, the unnatural winter wind stops, and Mhoram feels the presence of Covenant in the *krill* and rises to kill Satansfist. Mhoram becomes known as one of the great heroes of the Land. Later, the Clave chooses to name the equivalent of a High Lord, its puppet leader, the na-Mhoram, to use Mhoram's reputation of service and self-sacrifice for the Land to disguise its real intent in the 2nd "Chronicles." However, none of the na-Mhorams of the Clave, once he has been taken over by the Raver, is a true Lord.

The *Haruchai* / Bloodguard

The *Haruchai* are reminiscent of the Fremen Fedaykin in Frank Herbert's *Dune* series. Men grow self-reliant and strong from an uncompromising environment. Herbert discusses how the Fremen are raised much as the Padishah Emperor's fighting force, the Saudaukar, are trained, through exposure to the harshest physical conditions. The Saudaukar are the fanatical soldiers who are trained on a ferocious prison planet that kills about half of all who are sent there but turn the rest into a military force in which each Saudaukar is the match for any ten ordinary (but also well-trained) fighters. They do not shrink from violence, and thus terror weakens their opponents' resolve as well. The Fremen Fedaykin differ from the Saudaukar only in that they are also fighting for religious beliefs in their *jihad* against the Emperor. The *Haruchai* differ in that they are more like martial arts masters who use the force necessary to defend the Lords but do not revel in inflicting pain, torture, or death. In prowess they would be a match to Herbert's forces; in philosophy they, unlike the Lords, are not limited by the Oath of Peace, but they do not relish killing.

The *Haruchai* people, who flourish in the mountains of the Land, are a combative culture that uses physical combat to test skill and determine leadership, so theirs is not a democratic society. Covenant's first impression of the Bloodguard focuses on their solid impassivity. Their inexpressive mien and alertness convey their prowess and skill. In appearance they resemble Stonedownors. In short tunics, with bare legs and feet, they appear instantly ready to perform their chosen purpose: to protect the Lords. They originally came down from the mountains to make war on the Lords but were greeted with such largess by Lord Kevin that the only way to repay this generosity was through their Vow of service. Five hundred *Haruchai* swore to serve the Lords and thus become the Bloodguard. Their Vow, however, since it was recognized by Earthpower when it was made, allows them to defy sleep and natural death. Their expressions give no hint of the age of the Bloodguard as if time cannot affect them.

They are also a people who are self-reliant to the point of disavowing weapons of any kind. As a part of Covenant's inner psyche, the *Haruchai* represent his most fiercely independent but also his judgmental side. Covenant wants his lawyer Megan to fight against those who pay his bills for him, depriving him of any reason to go to town among them and thus cutting him off from all society. Covenant himself breaks the taboos of separateness enforced on lepers when he enters the tent of the gospel preacher Dr. B. Sam Johnson or the nightclub The Door. In our real world, Donaldson himself is a martial artist and undoubtedly prefers the philosophy of using skill solely in self-defense to the portrayal of violence so common today in our mass media as a solution for any kind of problem. And Donaldson is always more creative in his solutions.

The Bloodguard maintain their Vow through the first half of the 1st "Chronicles." However, the Vow is another example of either/or fallacious thinking, and Covenant recognizes it as unnatural and somehow wrong from the very beginning; for the Bloodguard there is either pure, unquestioning service through their Vow or Corruption, which to them signifies weakness and thus unworthiness. Corruption is also the name they give to Lord Foul. Though Covenant berates Bannor, the Bloodguard assigned to serve him as Ur-Lord, and constantly questions his total devotion, the absoluteness of the Bloodguard's belief in their Vow is similar to Covenant's total insistence that the Land is a dream and that only his "real" world can truly exist. Therefore, both are alike in their extreme views. Covenant eventually finds his eye of the paradox and learns to embrace both beliefs. When the Bloodguard realize that they can be corrupted by Lord Foul through the Illearth Stone fragment they took from the Raver Kinslaughterer, and Bannor, Terrel, and Runnik are forced to kill Korik, Sill, and Doar, whose right hands have been maimed to resemble Covenant's, the remaining Bloodguard give up their Vow and, all except Bannor and a few others, return to their mountain homes. For them, the truth is either the Vow or Corruption.

Though the *Haruchai* seem impassive, Donaldson tells us that the extremity of the passions they keep concealed casts a shadow on their stoicism. The 2nd "Chronicles" gives us a better understanding of the people themselves, without the Earthpower of the Vow that allowed them to eschew sleep and natural death. This was their eye of the paradox: when they promise service, they hold themselves to rigid standards. All their feelings are extreme — their love for their home and mates, their pride of their own prowess, their sense of loss for what they have given up to maintain their promises. They judge all others by the purity of their devotion to their chosen duties but judge themselves most harshly of all. This fanaticism best illustrates their either/or world view. Donaldson states that some weaknesses, culpabilities are necessary for real, effective people. Those who require extremes of themselves are quicker to give up at the first real challenge to their understanding of themselves (like the Giants at *Coercri*) and are thus more susceptible to Despair and destruction.

There are too many named *Haruchai* to give a detailed analysis of the role of each on the various quests, so I will mention only a few. Bannor is assigned to protect Covenant on the quest for the Staff of Law. He was one of the original *Haruchai* to take the Vow and had served the Lords for 2,000 years, long after his wife had died. With the other Bloodguard he obeyed when Kevin sent them away before the Ritual of Desecration. Therefore, he and First Mark Morin know and could be demanded to give the name of the 7th Ward to Amok, thus allowing Elena to use the Power of Command. Since Elena's use of the Power of Command leads to her own death and the Bloodguard cannot save her, inevitably this act enhances Bannor's sense of culpability.

Elena must see the similarity between Covenant and Bannor (at least subconsciously if characters in Covenant's dream can have subconsciousnesses) because the *anundivian yajna* sculpture she creates resembles both men. Donaldson is constantly pointing up the similarity between the two. So psychologically, Bannor may be one of the most important aspects of Covenant's personality that he must understand through his dream. Our first impression of Bannor and the other Bloodguard is that they are epic or at least romantic characters; by Frye's definition, they have control over natural death itself, an ability to communicate mentally together, and an almost supernatural control over their environment and others through their superior fighting skill. The purity of their service and their self-sacrifice to the Lords for the benefit of the Land might make them seem ideal characters. However, they do not really make choices, which to Donaldson is essential. They made one choice when they swore the Vow, but now all their reactions are like instincts. They follow the Lords; the Lords make all the important decisions, and the Bloodguard merely use their superior abilities and devotion to protect the Lords. Conversely, Donaldson clearly sets up the imperfect, doubting, alternately super-powerful and helpless Covenant as more ideal because he can embrace the both/and of the world's polarities; he can find the eye of the paradox where they are united.

After Bannor and the other Bloodguard abandon the Vow, Bannor comes closer to what Donaldson would call an effective person. His fighting abilities remain the same, though he seems older, so effectiveness is not entirely or even primarily connected to prowess, but he makes choices for himself. He joins the Ramen to serve the Ranyhyn until he meets up with Covenant and Foamfollower. After Covenant defeats dead Elena, Bannor chooses to return to help the Ramen lead the Ranyhyn into safety in the mountains, then to deliver the ends of the Staff of Law to Revelstone before returning to his mountain home. His most important decision is his choice no longer actively to fight Lord Foul, Corruption. Foamfollower explains to Covenant how difficult this decision is for Bannor because he must renounce vengeance, retribution for the violation of his thousands of years of service to the Lords. Foamfollower acknowledges how sweet revenge can be, yet Bannor walks away from that possibility. Like Triock, Bannor instinctively knows Covenant cannot fight Lord Foul with force or anger or hatred and therefore will not need Bannor's superior fighting strength and might come to rely on it rather than finding a better solution.

In the 2nd "Chronicles," the dead Bannor begs Covenant to "'redeem my people. Their plight is an abomination. And they will serve you well.'"[7] They are a strong people but susceptible to being ensnared by the Clave if they come too close to Revelstone, which they do to find out what has happened, first five alone and then in larger and larger groups. The Clave likes to sacrifice *Haruchai* to the Sunbane because the mountain people are so potent. Covenant frees Brinn and many others when he storms through Revelstone after freeing himself from the Soothtell. Six *Haruchai* agree to accompany Covenant, Linden, Sunder, Hollian, and Memla toward *Coercri*, where they meet the Giants of the Search. Two return with Sunder and Hollian to try to rally the peoples of the Land. Brinn, Cail, Ceer, and Hergrom sail with the Search for the One Tree. During this quest all the *Haruchai* are lost one way or the other: Hergrom and Ceer die; Brinn challenges the *ak-Haru Kenaustin Ardenol*, the Guardian of the One Tree, who is also in *Haruchai* legend the ultimate antagonist by which *Haruchai* can measure their worth, and because he wins, he stays behind to become the new *ak-Haru*; and Cail eventually returns to the *merewives*, but not until he has fulfilled Bannor's promise. So like modern man they, too, cannot return home. Both Brinn and Cail become more effective as *Haruchai* once they have acknowledged their weaknesses: both are susceptible to the *merewives* and are almost lost. Then Brinn wins his battle by falling first. Cail can resist the compulsion of the Clave because he no longer believes himself invulnerable. Their acknowledgement of their weaknesses makes them more effective.

Giants

Giants in Covenant's mind could be the result of his noticing the huge statues of heads which adorn the courthouse during his walk into town. As such, they would be connected to justice/judgment, and paradoxically, since his divorce was granted at the courthouse, also with injustice. As representatives of aspects of Covenant's personality, they could be closest to his role as writer for they love long tales and get the same kind of deep, enduring joy out of telling and hearing great tales as Covenant did out of writing before he was afflicted with leprosy. So they are closest to the naïve and idealistic Covenant and farthest from our ironic world view that comes to dominate Covenant's mind because of his leprosy. Of all the Land's inhabitants, the Giants are the quickest to laugh. They were perhaps created as large figures because they are closest to the mythic stature Donaldson wants to recreate for our world. Like the Bloodguard, the Giants don't seem to need weapons though they can wield swords for even greater power. The Giants do need sleep and cannot defy death, though they are longer lived than others in the Land. They are also proof against even the extremes of cold and heat. They can endure the *caamora* of putting their hands into fire without physically burning their flesh, but they still suffer pain from that act and, thus, use it as a way to remind themselves of what is truly important. The pain and purity of the *caamora* is an excellent example of Nietzsche's Apollonian vs. Dionysian dialectic, in which pain is a part of the Dionysian frenzy, desirable because it lets us know that we are alive.

The Giants have already understood the eye of the paradox. The song that identifies them includes dialectics they have already conjoined:

> Stone and Sea are deep in life,
> Two unalterable symbols of the world:
> permanence at rest, and permanence in motion;
> participants in the Power that remains.[8]

Stone is solid; the sea is liquid. One remains where it is unless some force makes it move; the other is constantly being pushed and pulled by the tides of the world. Yet for the Giants, both together provide their means of transportation: their ships are made of stone and they sail over the sea, so both are necessary to their livelihood and adventure. Both have power and yet the power in stone must be called forth by someone knowledgeable in that lore, and the power of the sea can be corrupted by the Illearth Stone into a tsunami to destroy *Coercri* by Kinslaughterer. The Sea also contains powers, like the Nicor that may be called or the Soulbiter that comes uncalled for. The poem could suggest that the two opposing powers are separate and both are respected by the Giants, but the fact that they unite these two forces in their defining song suggests their understanding that these elements need to be juxtaposed.

Diamondraught is a potent healing liquor, which the Giants brew, and which functions like the *rhadhamaerl*'s healing mud hurtloam and the *lillianrill*'s wood dust *rillinlure*. All provide solace, strength, and the will to persevere, often ironically by providing first a deep sleep.

Saltheart Foamfollower is one aspect of his personality that makes

Covenant a loveable character. If the Land is Covenant's dream, then his friend Foamfollower must represent part of his own personality, the part that willingly shoulders burdens and joins the quest, that is appalled at his own desire to kill and knows it turns him into what he hates, but also that takes on the extreme pain of Hotash Slay voluntarily and by that ultimate *caamora* regains his innocence enough to be able to lead the dead Lords in laughter against Lord Foul. If all these traits are within Covenant, then all his protestations and bargains and unwillingness are rationalizations or excuses, and we should know that his character will force him to act when the need arises.

Foamfollower can be interpreted as an independent being also, and as such he has much to teach Covenant. His most important lesson is to appreciate all the senses and move away from our narrow reliance on sight and touch. The Giants focus their perception of Truth on hearing: "'Joy is in the ears that hear, not in the mouth that speaks!'"[9] This saying emphasizes the importance of story telling, essential to a writer. But it also reinforces the idea that it is not the circumstances of our lives that matter, but how we react to them. Whatever we are told, if we can find joy in that tale, we can be happy, but it is our responsibility for hearing the joy, not the responsibility of the teller to speak of joy.

If even Foamfollower, a larger than life, almost epic-like hero, can experience his own heart of darkness, it reinforces the absolute truth of that epiphany for us and suggests that no world view, even an epic one, can now exist without taking our dark knowledge into consideration. We cannot have our own former innocence but must find a way to incorporate all our truths, even the ugly ones, into the eye of our paradox.

Foamfollower cannot go home in several ways. Like all the Giants, he has lost the knowledge of how to sail to the Home of his Giant ancestors. The Giants, like the *Haruchai*, had made an extravagant vow: to explore the entire earth. They do learn the folly of their vow but too late; at that point they have lost the knowledge of how to get Home. But also Foamfollower leaves *Coercri* when he sees how the other Giants are in despair because *turiya* Herem Raver has been able to control one of the three child-Giant triplets. Therefore, Foamfollower cannot dissuade and will not share the fate of the other Giants when they are attacked by Kinslaughterer. He is not tempted by the ultimate Despair maybe because he has already undergone the crisis of his life when he acknowledged that he was becoming what he hated and yet passed beyond that awareness. Perhaps the other Giants' inexperience in recognizing that they could have weaknesses and culpabilities added to their despair and decision simply to accept the fate Lord Foul sent to them. In some ways, they were either/or characters also; since they believed themselves strong and incorruptible, when the triplets succumbed to the Ravers, their belief in their ability to resist evil is shattered, so they simply give up and await their own end in death. Though Foamfollower, who has already gone through his own particular crisis, does not feel he can stay in *Coercri*, he also does not physically fight the child-Giant Raver, so he carries guilt with him over the annihilation of his people. His own personal soul-searching when he is afraid he is becoming what he hates and his embracing of his own guilt through the *caamora* saves him from the fate of the other Giants. To the *jheherrin* he identifies himself as the last of the Seareach Giants. Since Giants use the *caamora* to feel and expiate the pain of guilt, Foamfollower is prepared to stand and perhaps even to welcome the extreme pain and cleansing of the volcanic Hotash Slay. In this way Donaldson shows that some culpability, some guilt may be necessary, and we need to confront some evil within ourselves and still accept ourselves to avoid the either/or of judgmental responses during times of crisis.

Though Foamfollower plays no role in *The Illearth War*, he reappears in *The Power That Preserves* as one of Covenant's summoners and his companion for most of his trek towards Ridjeck Thome and Foul's Creche. Without him Covenant's quest fails, for though Covenant can use the might of the wild magic to destroy the Illearth Stone, by some intuition he knows that laughter is needed to diminish Foul, and he cannot yet defeat Foul himself. He has finally recognized the futility of using force against the Enemy. Force can defeat an evil being, but the very act of using force — robbing the Enemy of the freedom of choice — keeps that evil in the world. What he needs to do is to diminish Lord Foul's ability to cause despair, to turn the focus of the Lords away from Foul to themselves. The best antidote is joy. He asks Foamfollower to laugh, to take joy in the knowledge that Foul has been defeated and laugh away his own fear of despair. Foamfollower laughs, sarcastically at first, but finally he hears the joy in the tale of the defeat of Foul's power and heals himself and laughs with joy. The infectious quality of his laughter guides the dead Lords past their rage, and their laughter heals them as well, further diminishing Foul. This release is exactly the way to defeat Despair. Lord Foul cannot fight against pure joy. In fact, the more joy that they express, the less power Foul has, so he begins to fade. It is as if he is being unmade as he grows younger and less solid. As a youngster, barely existent, he has lost his essence and power. Then Foamfollower does not regret even his impending death because he has "'beheld a marvelous story'"[10] and found joy and purpose in the tale.

For the 2nd "Chronicles" and the voyage with the Giants on Starfare's Gem, the earlier reference to Covenant's creativity in writing his novel is relevant. He likens the process of his writing to sailing across treacherous seas. Donaldson is using the ocean as a metaphor for modern life (the temptation of sirens, the unpredictability of tempests, the danger of Nicor). Covenant sees his own life like a sea voyage in which his leprosy is a storm he did not anticipate, which knocked him completely off course. So he feels a great connection with the Giants. The Sea is a home away from Home for the Giants of the Search who have journeyed to the Land because of Seadreamer's Earth-Sight which convinces them that some great wrong needs to be redressed in the Land. Seadreamer has beheld a vision of the Sunbane.

Four particular Giants play an especially significant role in the 2nd "Chronicles": Grimmand Honninscrave, the Master of Starfare's Gem; his brother Cable Seadreamer, the mute Giant whose vision sends the Search on their original quest to the Land; the First, Gossamer Glowlimn, the Sword-main and Leader of the Search; and Pitchwife, her husband, a deformed Giant of great joy, whose job it is to wive or mend the stone of the *dromond* should any damage be inflicted upon it on their voyage. Also important to the plot are Mistweave, the Giant Linden heals and who takes over the *Haruchai* Cail's place as Linden's protector, and Galewrath who calls and lassos the Nicor to move the *dromond* and also aids the First to rescue Brinn and Cail from the *merewives*.

Hollinscrave's most important relationship is with his brother, Sea-dreamer. Hollinscrave lives with guilt because his own carelessness caused the blow that bereft his brother of speech. The Search undertakes its quest to see what is wrong in the Land because of Seadreamer's EarthSight. But Hollinscrave can see how much such visions hurt. So he asks the *Elohim* for the gift of his brother's voice, thinking that if Seadreamer could just articulate the visions his EarthSight is giving him, his suffering might be eased. But Seadreamer can have only one or the other. Donaldson reiterates that knowledge comes with a cost. After Seadreamer's self-sacrifice at the One Tree, Hollinscrave begs Covenant to provide a *caamora* for Seadreamer as he had for the Giants at *Coercri*. But because Covenant's power is growing so strong that he cannot control it, he has to deny Hollinscrave. Therefore, Seadreamer is one of the visions the crew and passengers of Starfare's Gem see when they stray into Soulbiter.

Hollinscrave is most important to Covenant's story because he is able to kill Gibbon, the na-Mhoram. Hollinscrave kills Gibbon's mortal body and the Raver must flee. When *samadhi* Raver tries to take over Hollinscrave's body, the Giant is able to maintain control, trapping the Raver in his body. Perhaps *samadhi* Sheol thought that since he had been able to possess a child Giant once, he could take over Hollinscrave. The internal battle between the Raver and the Giant is presented through Covenant's point of view. At first Covenant thinks Hollinscrave has killed the Raver, but he soon realizes his mistake when he perceives the internal battle being waged between the Master and the Raver. When the Raver attempts to take possession of the Giant, Hollinscrave does not lose himself or cower in fear but struggles to maintain control over his own identity and at the same time retain the Raver's essence within him, so that *samadhi* cannot flee or possibly possess someone else. But the strain is excruciating, and Covenant cannot tell how it will be resolved as the Master's face fluctuates between the grim purpose of the Giant and the insanity and desperation of the Raver. Finally Grimmand Honninscrave gains control of himself and begs Thomas Covenant to end his life and thus slay the Raver. Yet even knowing that Honninscrave would consider this to be a worthy death and wanting to kill the Raver, Covenant cannot strike against his friend. While the Master strives mightily to contain the Raver, his appeal goes unanswered. When no one in the Company can move, the Sandgorgon Nom reverently grants his wish and "rends" the Raver, taking on cognitive awareness and the ability for mind speech that the *Haruchai* can understand. In this way Hollinscrave resolves his great grief over the loss of his brother and chooses the purpose of his life by the way he decides to end it. Hollincrave's ability to master the Raver is a good model for Linden, also, when *moksha* tries to possess her. Donaldson leaves ambiguous whether the Raver is actually destroyed, but *samadhi* plays no further role in the tale.

Seadreamer saves Covenant from eels after the *Elohim* silence him and saves him again at the One Tree, this time from Covenant's own ignorant folly, because his EarthSight has told him what will happen if Covenant cuts a limb from the One Tree. He sacrifices himself, having pre-knowledge of his fate. Before Covenant can approach the One Tree, Seadreamer jumps over the rocks and scrambles up the roots sticking out above ground. He is near the branch which Covenant has picked out, but he does not immediately reach out to grasp it. His EarthSight allows him to know that the repercussions of his act will be fatal for him, so he pauses for a last beseeching look at the Search before he breaks off the branch. The earth reacts creating a cacophony of outrage, the blindness of a myriad of tiny suns screaming their denial and calling forth the wild magic. Seadreamer dies, but when Covenant releases the power of the white gold wild magic, the venom in him makes it too powerful, and Linden must pull him back from destroying the whole earth or awakening the Worm of the World's End. Therefore, he cannot dare to use his power to provide the *caamora* of solace for Seadreamer that Honninscrave requests; thus Seadreamer becomes one of the *dromond's* dead, like Hergrom and Ceer, visible as they pass through Soulbiter.

The role of the First runs counter to our sexist stereotypes about women warriors; she is the Swordmain and leader of the Search. The only decisions she leaves to Hollinscrave are those that involve his role as captain of the *dromond*. In this way Covenant helps to break down stereotypes still sometimes evident in the modern age. Gossamer Glowlimn is daughter to Brow Gnarlfist, the Master of Wavedancer, and sails with him often when she is a child. Thus, she sees firsthand the terrible sacrifice her father makes to save his ship when it has been crippled by the Teeth. Since Pitchwife is also instrumental in the affair, he tells the tale. When Soulbiter tears a breach in the hull of Gnarlfist's *dromond*, Wavedancer, Pitchwife immediately heads below to try to mend the hole. But with the water pouring in, he cannot even approach the breach. Then amazingly the water no longer flows in, and Pitchwife realizes that Gnarlfist is using his own chest to block the hole and allow for the repairs. Knowing the Master would have limited air, Pitchwife hurries to prepare his pitch and setrock to mend the wound. Though hastily he seals the breach, he does not understand that in so doing he is sealing Gnarlfist's doom. The same pitch that so readily bonds stone to the *dromond* also seals Gnarlfist's chest to the hull. Pitchwife both blames himself for foolishing overlooking the consequences of his actions, but also acknowledges that he is fulfilling his own purpose and Gnarlfist's by saving his companions aboard Wavedancer at the same time.

This incident, like so many others, contains the dialectical emotions of unbearable loss and joyful success. Pitchwife feels responsible for Gnarlfist's death. Yet, the First gets him to see the opposite view. Because of his role in her father's self-sacrifice, the First notices Pitchwife anew. She does not see him as a failure but as the person who gives meaning to her father's death. Her love for him comes from their shared experience and the shared emotions of both sorrow and joy. After this incident, the First learns the skills of the sword and becomes the leader of the Search. Her personality mostly matches the powerful, objective, decisive role she has taken on, but every now and then, her feminine side breaks through, for example, when she asks Linden to tell her that Pitchwife is all right when they are all in the dungeon of the Sandhold. Linden's health sense allows her to perceive the others and their states of health, even in the dark. She can tell the First that Pitchwife is merely unconscious but will be all right. She can even perceive that Pitchwife, though hit hard, has no broken bones. The First thanks her, but Linden can also feel her silent tears of relief.

Though Giants can fight and be deadly with just their fists, the First relies on her sword and feels less effective when she drops it into the sea during the crisis with the Raver-eels. The Kasreyn uses the opportunity of the capture of the members of the Search to reprimand Rant Absolain subtly for his gift of a sword to her by hanging it in her sheath but too far away for her shackled hands to grasp. Most of the time, however, she represents the strength of the group, taking on overwhelming odds or impossible tasks like threatening the mound of the Cavewights so that Covenant can leave to confront Lord

Foul. She represents trust and faithfulness even when Covenant tells her that she should embrace doubt as well.

The Giant who is perhaps most important to Covenant's overall quest is the one who can find joy when others have forgotten how. Pitchwife has been deformed, bent over, with problems in breathing because of his lungs, all his life. Yet he embraces the Giants' mantra, "'Joy is in the ears that hear, not in the mouth that speaks.'"[11] And because of who he is, he has learned to see beneath the surface to the real character underneath. When he and the First are tested by the *Elohim*, both are offered a sight of Pitchwife without his deformity, but both can also reject that view because it is Pitchwife's personality that makes him lovable, not his outward appearance. The First can tell that the *Elohim* who impersonates her husband, though resembling Pitchwife outwardly in all ways, cannot present the essence of Pitchwife. He is a physically perfect Pitchwife, no longer crippled but able to stand proud and tall, as Pitchwife might have grown to be. And her initial response is to cry for what Pitchwife could and should have been. But immediately she checks herself and laughs because clearly the *Elohim* could not mimic the joy which is the basis of Pitchwife's personality. Pitchwife himself laughs at his wife's report.

Pitchwife knows when to liven the mood with a song or a tale, picking up everyone else's spirits. He can sense the moods of Covenant and Linden and sometimes knows exactly what to say to help them past a personal crisis. And yet, at the end, when Covenant has lectured the First that she needs doubt as well as faith, Pitchwife admits that he does doubt. Yet he stays by her side and will not let her order him away to safety, even in the face of immanent death. After Linden has healed the Land of the Sunbane, her spirit returns to Kiril Threndor, and she perceives Pitchwife and the First. They are exhausted. Using her power Linden gives them the best gift she can think of: a sense of victory and hope. Then she does more, for when Pitchwife stoops to pick up the body of Covenant, he can stand up tall. Not only is his spine straightened, but his internal organs are healed as well. He can breathe freely for the first time. With their hearts high, they bear Covenant's body and the Staff of Law from Kiril Threndor, the First purposeful and confident, but Pitchwife mischievous as always with a spring in his steps, as if he can hardly contain his joy.

The *Elohim*

The *Elohim* are a most unusual group in the "Chronicles." They do have a community, for which Infelice is the leader or spokesperson, and they seem to make decisions democratically, yet they are most independent beings. Their purpose is to study their "würd" (or "word" or "wyrd") separately to discover truths about the world. They are called the heart of the Earth. They are independent, self-contained, and secretive, and they feel no compulsion to explain their motives or their actions to Linden or the others of the Search. Maybe the eye of the paradox for the *Elohim* includes all potential interpretations, including destiny or doom. But they rarely decide to do anything about the truths they discover, unless the potential danger is particularly dire, and then they choose one of their members to bear the cost for the whole community as the Appointed. Like the stars in their creation story, the *Elohim* act as they do because it is their nature to do so, and most of the time they stay out of the affairs of other peoples or the Land. Infelice tells Linden that she is mistaken in her understanding of and desire for power. Rather, they want her to comprehend also, as part of the eye of the paradox, the helplessness of power. Because they are a different kind of being from Lord Foul, though they are Earthpower incarnate, his actions don't affect them, nor can they change or defeat him. They do not see Earthpower making them "powerful" beings. So, though they seem very wise in their self-reflection, and Linden perceives them as Earthpower personified, they are also cold and self-centered. The *Elohim* at the *clachan* seem to be carefree and vital beings, yet Linden perceives conflict and even their abhorrence/threat toward the Search.

They seem all-knowing and can perceive several possible outcomes for the quest for the One Tree. In this way they represent the concept of predestination, though they also allow for free will since they recognize that there can be several possible outcomes based on choice. However, they do not allow the freedom of choice to others, and they make one choice when they close Covenant's mind, which they claim means they share the responsibility because they are providing the Appointed Findail for the quest, but they do not discuss this choice or their decision-making process with Covenant or the other members of the Search who are affected by that choice. In addition, this decision is not unanimous; Linden can interpret the bell-sounds, which seem to be the *Elohim's* private speech, to indicate that a debate is still ongoing about whether their purposes are good or they wish evil on the Search. Certainly the members of the Search do not understand the silence that is imposed on Covenant. It might have made them interesting to the Kasreyn so that he could be induced to provide supplies and materials to mend the *dromond* in order to have access to Covenant, and it might also have protected Covenant from the compulsion of the Kasreyn's *geas*, but it causes Linden to learn to possess Covenant with her health sense in order to free him of his stupor, an act which appalls her as the ultimate evil.

Chant and Daphin represent opposing viewpoints among the *Elohim*. Chant's testing of Covenant mostly involves his trying to talk Covenant into giving up his ring; Daphin is gentler with Linden. Chant wants to imprison Vain but is not able to do so because Linden understands the nature of the Demondimspawn well enough to know that if they leave, Vain's programming will compel him to follow. The events of the *clachan* and the *elohim-fest* and the audience with Infelice at which the Giants and Linden ask their boons illustrate another view of time since they seem to take up considerable time, yet when the Search is transported back from *elemnesdene* to the *maidan*, the Bloodguard, who were sent out much earlier, believe that no time has passed.

Findail is the Appointed who travels with the Search but rarely helps them. However, his knowledge of the *croyel* that Kasreyn calls his son and his willingness to kill it to keep Covenant from letting his white gold wild magic free not only save the company in Bhrathairealm but also teach them about *croyels* so they can recognize the one of the Arghuleh. Findail is an enigma in many ways. Of all the *Elohim*, only he has a sour expression. He seems indifferent to the fate of Covenant and Linden, yet he does not leave. He isn't affected by weather and doesn't even get wet in the rain, nor does he need shelter on Starfare's Gem. He fights against Vain and tries to kill him, but cannot escape even though he has shown that he can just evaporate into thin air. He fights to the end against Vain's purpose but allows himself as the Appointed to be used to create the new Staff of Law.

The Bhrathair

Bhrathairealm is a desert community, but the lavish accoutrements of the Chatelaine and their ruler, the *gaddhi*, seems to deny the harshness of the desert in their backyard. They are an extremely hierarchical group with a ruler, Rant Absolain, who is really just a figurehead for his Kemper; Kasreyn wields the true power. Those of the court try to curry favor using their beauty and flirtatious mannerisms, but all are afraid because their positions and their very lives could be forfeit on a whim. As representations of possible political structures, that of the Bhrathair is probably the worst (except, of course, the deliberate evil of the Clave). It is certainly a visibly armed community with the *Hustin*, vicious mindless servants, constantly in evidence. The *Hustin* are another way to evaluate what it means to be human as they are machine-like fighters which all look alike and receive their orders via a wavelength too low for the human ear to hear, but they can bleed if hurt and can die. They make no decisions for themselves. Perhaps Donaldson, the conscientious objector, is depicting soldiers as mindless automatons or these particular creatures as a mixture of man and machine, like man without his own will. They are appropriate servants for the Kasreyn who uses psychological compulsion to get his way.

Rant Absolain is a weak ruler, playing at having power. His response to his awareness of how he is manipulated by the Kasreyn is to manipulate others, get his petty revenges, and get drunk. One of his favorites, the Lady Alif, is the most interesting of the court, the only one who seems to have a mind of her own. She tries to save Covenant from the Kasreyn by bringing Rant Absolain to Kemper's Pitch; unfortunately that plan backfires because one of the *Hustin* that Rant Absolain believes are loyal to him has just been killed by Hergrom. His retribution leads to Hergrom's death and the Company's awareness of the Sandgorgon Dom. Later Lady Alif and Caitiffin Rire Grist change their allegiance to help the Search escape and probably affect a coup in Bhrathairealm after the death of the Kasreyn.

The Kasreyn represents another example of either/or thinking. He desires immortality and bargains with the *croyel* for the ability to come back to life if killed and thus live forever. He is a mage whose magic centers on circles and gyres. He captured the Sandgorgons in Kasreyn's Gyre and can use circles of magic to make the members of the Search unconscious. On the other hand, he also admits that everything he does must have some kind of flaw in it, like the ability of a Sandgorgon to escape its prison if its name is called, at least until it has killed the one who called it. He is covetous of Covenant's white gold ring because, since it is an alloy, it is imperfect, and with that power, Kasreyn could create perfect spells. But because his mind has been blanked out by the *Elohim*, Covenant is not susceptible to the compulsion of Kasreyn's golden ocular *geas*. Linden succumbs, but the *Haruchai* Brinn does not. The fact that the *Haruchai* can be immune to some compulsions and that Honninscrave can contain *samadhi* Sheol Raver teaches Linden that she can exercise choice, even when *moksha* Jehannum Raver possesses her.

Other Important Inhabitants of the Land

There are many other important beings in the Land: Vain, *jheherrin, sur-jheherrin,* Waynhim, Wraiths, Unfettered Ones, and Forestals. They represent the variety of Donaldson's imagination. All are new to fantasy literature. Each in his own way helps Donaldson explore the question "what does it mean to be human?" by providing a contrast. Some are made, not born, creatures. Vain is perhaps closest to a computer; he has been programmed by the ur-viles who created him, but he is also an enigma because neither Covenant nor anyone else in the Company (besides Findail who won't tell) knows what purpose he is to serve. The *jheherrin* are cast off failures of Lord Foul's breeding program, so they are made, but when they are freed, they are then able to reproduce, and their offspring become the *sur-jheherrin*. The Waynhim are like the ur-viles, but obviously they have the power to make their own choices.

The Wraiths are totally unlike humans, in that they are beings of light and melody. And the Unfettered Ones, though human, have separated themselves voluntarily to work in solitude. The Forestals live powerful, immortal lives until they choose to set aside their task of protecting the forests of the Land. All play important roles in the "Chronicles."

Vain

Vain's self-absorption and complete disregard for the others of the Search unless Linden is in danger suggest he is appropriately named. Saltheart Foam-follower gives Vain to Covenant, so everyone accepts him more because of Covenant's love and respect for Foamfollower than for any affection or concern for Vain himself. The Waynhim of Hamako's *rhysh* tell Covenant that Vain personifies the purpose or weird of the ur-viles and are surprised to find no ill in Vain. He does not make friends: he doesn't talk to anyone; he stands motionless by himself most of the time; he seems completely self-sufficient in that he rarely needs to be rescued. Only once, after the *Elohim* have imprisoned him and he escapes, do the *Haruchai* have to rescue him from the Callowwail River that is trying to melt him down, yet he is fully restored as soon as the sun hits his body. Once he shows Covenant where Linden is being held in Revelstone so that she can be rescued, and he takes the initiative to carry Linden to safety across the graveling-like firestones. Most of the time, however, he remains unmoving and unresponsive. Because wherever he stands, he seems to become part of the *dromond* or floor, when the ship tips dangerously to one side, the *Haruchai* can brace themselves by holding onto Vain's legs to rescue Linden.

It is clear that the *Elohim* fear or hate his purpose and that the two beings together — Vain and Findail — represent complete opposites. When Linden obeys Vain and embraces the two of them together so that she can make a new Staff of Law, their completely dialectical characteristics are evident. Findail is the incarnation of Earthpower, but he is also self-absorbed and amoral. Also, he resents being forced into his role as the Appointed by the *Elohim*. Vain, created by the lore and theurgy of the ur-viles, is completely unconcerned for any other purpose but his own and rock solid in his programmed purpose. Linden must combine the fluidity and ethereal quality of Findail with the black obsidian purpose of Vain. Together they form the new Staff of Law, but the juxtaposition of their oppositions is not enough. Vain represents impersonal Law but not the motivation for applying that Law; Findail provides the ability to apply the Law but cannot determine its purpose — he is too self-centered. The white gold wild magic provides the power to unite these two disparate opposites, but Linden, the Sun–Sage, is also needed. Intuitively, she understands that only a human being can supply the purpose. She infuses her health sense and passion for healing, her awareness of the Land's perfect potential, her great love of Andelain, Ranyhyn, Giants, and beauty. The purpose of her being is intricately woven into the Staff of Law.

Jheherrin *and* Sur-jeherrin

The *jheherrin* and *sur-jheherrin* are connected and provide an important clue in the question of "what does it mean to be human?" The *jheherrin* are mud-creatures, who call themselves soft ones, the un–Maker-made, all deformed in some way, representing creatures Foul made himself and then discarded as imperfect, and they have become sterile and timid in their powerlessness. They divide themselves by their shape into different *Befylam*. The *aussat Befylam* are the flawed creatures who rescue Covenant and Foamfollower; the *fael Befylam* are the crawlers; the *roge Befylam* are the Cavewight-like creatures; there are others that resemble beasts — wolves and horses. The legend of the Pure One given to the *jheherrin* as their only hope for salvation supports the concept of predestination, that there is an overarching plan which guides the fate of the world. Yet the free will of the Pure One is also needed. Because Covenant has learned that it is wrong to hide the truth even if it costs him the aid of the *jheherrin*, he confesses to them that he is not pure. He knows how deeply he is disappointing them and does not want them to give in to despair because their great hope is dashed by his imperfections. So he reminds them that he has nothing to do with their prophecy. The fact that he is not the Pure One does not negate their intrinsic worth. Another Pure One may yet come. And, in fact, when Foamfollower submits to the pain of the baptizing *caamora* of Hotash Slay to convey Covenant across the lava flow so that he can continue on to find Foul, the cleansing power of the fire and pain purify Foamfollower of his bloodlust, his anger, his guilt, and he is able to laugh at despair, at Foul, in the end. Therefore, the *jheherrin* understand that it is Foamfollower who fulfills their legend, and from this redemption they are able to leave Foul's demesne and begin to reproduce themselves. This tale they pass on to their offspring and descendents, the *sur-jheherrin*.

The *sur-jheherrin* play one important role in rescuing the Company from the *skest* or green acid creatures of Sarangrave Flat. They make themselves known when they have heard Foamfollower's name spoken by Covenant as he tells of meeting his old friend in Andelain. They volunteer to use their mud forms to absorb the acid of the *skest* in grateful repayment for their liberation so that the Company may escape.

Waynhim

The Waynhim play a surprisingly important role in the first two "Chronicles." In appearance they resemble ur-viles except they have grey skin rather than black and are slightly smaller than ur-viles, but they fight in a wedge like the ur-viles. Like the ur-viles they have short limbs and can travel upright or on all four limbs. Their eyeless faces include pointed ears and thin mouths. They rely on smell instead of sight as their primary sense. Their wide nostrils help them smell their world. Like the Giants, the Waynhim teach us to use other senses besides sight and hearing and touch to understand the world around us.

Covenant's first experience with them is through the Waymeet which they were supplying for travelers in the Land until Jehannum Raver murdered a Waynhim. At this point Covenant doesn't actually meet any Waynhim, for they withdraw their aid to the Land and are not mentioned again until the Lords try to heal *dukkha*, *dharmakshetra* Waynhim, who has been deformed by Lord Foul with the Illearth Stone. The Lords fail. Nevertheless, later a company of Waynhim chooses to become involved in the fate of the Land again when Raver Satansfist is attacking Revelstone. Mhoram has been waiting for a sign that his ride out against the Raver was the right thing to do, and he interprets the attack by the Waynhim as that sign.

In the 2nd "Chronicles" they play an even greater role. Because Covenant rescues *dhraga*, the Waynhim used as bait by the Sunbane-warped creatures of During Stonedown, the Waynhim's community or *rhysh*, including Hamako, takes him in, restores him with the aliantha-like *vitrim* and shows him how they are preserving some vegetation and animals from the Sunbane. And finally with their own blood, eight members of the Waynhim give Covenant preternatural power and ability to run for a day or two across the Center Plains without stopping so that he can try to catch up with Linden and the Stonedownors who have been captured by a Rider of the Clave. While Covenant is with Hamako's *rhysh*, Hamako explains that the Waynhim's purpose is their weird. Like the *Elohim's* concept of their purpose, their wyrd or word, for the Waynhim weird can mean both destiny and choice. They embrace the contradiction. Though fate may decree one's time of death, only that being can choose the way he accepts his fate, in cowardice or bravery.

Covenant again meets Hamako and what is left of all the *rhysh* in the Land, when he and the members of the Search are fleeing from the Arghuleh, the ice creatures of the North. The Waynhim are preparing to sacrifice themselves to fight against the Arghuleh. When Linden recognizes that one Arghule looks like a double creature, she realizes that the Arghule has a *croyel* on its back that has allowed the Arghuleh to change their nature and fight as a united group. Hamako accepts the ritual blood-giving of twenty Waynhim and uses that fire to confront and melt the Arghule with the *croyel*. This is another example of the need to juxtapose and unite oppositions; here it is fire and ice that are conjoined, and the result is the destruction of both Hamako and the *croyel*. It also breaks the threat of the Arghuleh and allows Covenant and his party to continue toward Revelstone.

Wraiths

The Wraiths represent the epitome of beauty in the Land. They are creatures of pure light and song, dancing flames that celebrate the coming of spring to Andelain. An Unfettered One studies them and with some small animals of the forest comes to release the Wraiths from their ceremonial dance when their Celebration is attacked by an ur-vile wedge; he sacrifices himself to free the Wraiths and allow Atiaran and Covenant to escape. The Wraiths are later protected by another Unfettered One until Triock brings the *lormilliar* rod to ask the Unfettered One to try to use it to contact Revelstone with a message, but *turiya* Herem Raver within the body of Yeurquin kills and eats the Unfettered One before his message can be delivered. Although the light of the trees in Morinmoss leads Covenant deep into the forest toward the Unfettered One who can heal him, Wraiths probably protect him from her knife. Though Covenant is unconscious, the narrator reports that after the healer heals Covenant's physical broken ankle, when she tries to heal the madness brought on by his eating of the *amanibhavam* flower, she sees deep into his soul and determines to kill him. But several gleaming lights flutter around her, confusing and distracting her, so that she cannot strike at Covenant. When she dies, with notes of music, the dancing lights retreat back into the forest. These may not be Wraiths, but they look and act and sing like Wraiths. And the power of the Forestals protects them. Therefore, they are still protected in Andelain by Caer-Caveral during the time of the 2nd "Chronicles" and lead Covenant to his meeting with his dead friends, at which time their gifts can be given to him.

Interestingly, Donaldson also provides reference to something which seems to have a purpose opposite of the Wraiths'. Wraiths are contrasted to the dancing flames Covenant sees when the Sunbane-warped creatures of During Stonedown have captured him and tied him to the stake and the man with the spider has triggered another venom relapse. He perceives some kind of dancing flame gyrating around the bowl in which he is bound. These flames do not sing but rather shriek as they bound about. Here, obviously, the dancing flames/figures are evil rather than pure, with destruction not celebration in mind. They may be creatures of flame or Covenant's perception of the Sunbane-warped viewed through the flames of the fire. Donaldson has provided no eye of the paradox here, no way to unite both views of the dancing, vocalizing flames; they remain the either/or of pure good and evil, but they do suggest that everything has a dialectical opposite.

Unfettered Ones

Unfettered Ones are people of the Land who have studied at the Lores-raat but feel called to perform solitary service to the Land through some sort of specialization. They take the Rites of Unfettering:

> Free
> Unfettered
> Shriven
> Free —
> Dream that what is dreamed will be.[13]

Then they perform their own chosen work like hermits, eschewing community and gaining a longer life of service. One such Unfettered was studying the Wraiths in Andelain and sacrificed himself to save them and facilitate Covenant and Atiaran's escape from the ur-viles. Later, in *The Power That Preserves*, the forest of Morinmoss brings the healer, another Unfettered One, to Covenant to heal his broken ankle and the madness brought on when he ate the *amanibhavam*, healing flowers for the Ranyhyn but poisonous to humans. She introduces an important theme of healing by taking on the hurts of the wounded herself, which later Linden will also do to heal the Sunbane. In addition, the Healer follows the pattern Donaldson has set up for most of his characters; the challenges of their lives seem to surpass them. She knows what she needs to do to heal Covenant but feels she hasn't the courage or strength to suffer his pain to free him from it. By breaking her own ankle to mimic Covenant's wound, she heals them both of the physically crippling break. When she tries to heal his madness, on the other hand, she sees his disease and tries to kill him, but is prevented by the Wraiths of the forest.

A third Unfettered One resides on the upper end of Glimmermere. Elena takes Covenant to meet him, and the Unfettered One tells Covenant that his dreams are true, perhaps helping him eventually find the ability to unite his Unbelief with his desire to believe the Land is real and resolve the most important paradox of the 1st "Chronicles." Later, Lord Loerya takes her children to this Unfettered One to try to keep them safe and also to free herself to concentrate on the fighting she must do during the siege of Revelstone. Glimmermere, like Andelain, is one of the last places to resist the Sunbane during the 2nd "Chronicles." Caer-Caveral, Andelain's Forestal, helps to protect the Land's perfect beauty despite the Sunbane. The Earthpower of Glimmermere, and possibly the power of the Unfettered One, protect the lake.

Forestals

Two Forestals play essential roles in the "Chronicles." The first, Caer-roil Wildwood, accepts the bargain of Mhoram and Hile Troy to allow the

Lords' army to pass unharmed through Garroting Deep in order to exact revenge on Foul's creatures and especially the Giant Raver Fleshharrower. But the price for the agreement is steep: Hile Troy agrees to pay any price before he even knows what will be asked and has, thus, volunteered to become Caerroil Wildwood's apprentice and eventually take over as a Forestal. By the time of the 2nd "Chronicles," he is the only Forestal left and has left Morinmoss to protect Andelain from the Sunbane. Hile Troy was present when Covenant told the Lords that Elena used the Power of Command and broken the Law of Death, allowing those who are dead to be summoned back to life. Troy, as Caer-Caveral, the Forestal, knows that he must encourage Sunder to kill him in order to break the Law of Life and allow the dead voluntarily to cross back into life. Sunder does this so that Hollian can remain with him, but the greater significance of this act is that Covenant is able to come back after Foul has killed him to place himself between Foul and the Arch of Time and absorb the wild magic, not allowing Foul to break the Arch of Time. That Caer-Caveral anticipated this need reinforces the concept of predestination or an over-arching universe, yet Covenant must still come to the realization that his own sacrifice is the choice he should make at the end.

None of these other inhabitants of the Land can ever return to what had been their homes, their former lives, with the possible exception of the Wraiths, though they no longer observe their Celebration of Spring ritual. Donaldson, similar to Robert Frost in his poem "The Road Not Taken," is saying that "knowing how way leads on to way, I doubted I should ever come back."[13] Or as Tolkien says in the "Road Song" from *The Lord of the Rings*, a person's fate must be pursued "with eager [or weary] feet until it joins some larger way, and whither then, I cannot say."[14] This belief supports the concept of an overarching plan or predestination but also the impossibility of humans to know the outcomes of their choices ahead of time. Donaldson also firmly establishes that free will is essential, thus joining these two disparate opposites in the eye of the paradox.

The other inhabitants also help Donaldson explore what it means to be human by comparing us to the made perfection of Vain, the ethereal existence of the *Elohim*, the beauty and frailty of the Wraiths, the helplessness and almost formlessness of the *jheherrin* and *sur-jheherrin*, the self-less purpose and devotion of the Unfettered Ones, the unity of the Waynhim's communal *rhysh* and their devotion to their understanding of truth, their Weird (like the *Elohim's* Würd, Wyrd, or Word). As representatives of Covenant himself, created by him as part of his dream to heal the psychological afflictions of his life, all the others he encounters can be parts of his own personality: his trusting, story-loving, Giant-like joy; his implacable judgment like that of the Bloodguard; his weakness and fearfulness like the cowering *jheherrin*;

his willingness to face and take on his responsibilities like the Lords and Unfettered Ones, all those who serve the Land. Thus, Donaldson is also supporting the modern view of the multiplicity of identity, the view that all of us contain many sides to our personalities, some of which are contradictory, yet we manage to embrace them all. And the unity of purpose possible for the different "races" in the Land also reinforces our interdependence with others and even with the earth itself, and is yet another way for Donaldson to reinforce the necessity of embracing difference, even contradictions, in the eye of the paradox.

New Characters from the "Last Chronicles"

Since the "Last Chronicles" is unfinished at this time, it is yet unclear if any of the new characters will be able to return to their homes. But already some have faced weakness or darkness in themselves and become more effective by finding the eyes of their own paradoxes. Donaldson is reiterating his view that to be a complete being, one must understand and accept both the strengths and weaknesses within him/herself, must take responsibility for decisions and actions, and must make choices based on a purpose larger than self-interest.

Anele, son of Sunder and Hollian, was brought back to life when Sunder killed Caer-Caveral with the *krill* to break the Law of Life and resurrect Hollian with the child she was carrying. He is the best hope for the Land and seems to be a being of great Earthpower. Others, including Lord Foul and Kastenessen, whose presence in Anele seems to burn Linden, as well as Covenant and Hollian, can take possession of Anele and use his voice. He claims that stone speaks to him and can become sane if holding *orcrest*, though it is a torment to him. The surface on which he stands — grass, dirt, or rock — affects his degree of sanity. He is plagued by guilt over losing the Staff of Law. His state of mind does not allow him to become effective in the defense of the Land, but his memory of where he left the Staff of Law enables Linden to go back in time to reclaim it.

Liand, a Stonedowner, helps Linden and Anele escape from Mithil Stonedown. He doesn't know his birthright of health sense because the *Haruchai* as the Masters of the Land have forbidden the use or knowledge or teaching of Earthpower and because Kevin's Dirt masks/inhibits the innate health sense that people of the Land had known. The fact that he is a *rhadhamaerl* allows him to learn the use of the *orcrest* that he finds in the Aumbrie at Revelstone. Later he uses his *orcrest* to open the eyes of the people from a *lillianrill* village to their health sense. When he travels through the *caesure* from Anele's past to the present before the gates of Revelstone, he is drawn into

Linden's mind and sees there her capacity for evil. Nevertheless, he is fiercely loyal. Certainly he is becoming more and more effective. Like Linden, he wants to heal others — Anele and even Longwrath. Like Sunder before him, he uses his innate *rhadhamaerl* abilities to find new uses for his *orcrest*, eventually even creating a storm to fight the *skurj*. Unlike the Masters, he wishes to absorb as many stories of the Land as he can and regain the wonder that Kevin's Dirt hides from him.

The *Haruchai* Stave brings Linden and Anele to Mithil Stonedown and imprisons them. He seeks them out in the hills above the South Plains when they escape and then chooses to accompany Linden. He suffers much humiliation from his service to Linden, rejection by the other Masters (in a ritual in which he must successively fight each of the three Humbled), a terrible beating from Esmer, and also bloody hands and feet from his almost ineffective battle with the Harrow. However, the Ranyhyn Hynyn offers to bear him and includes him in the horserite to which Hyn takes Linden. He learns how to close his mind to the other *Haruchai*. Even with only one eye and with doubt in his heart, Stave is as effective as a fighter and more effective as a friend to Linden. The Humbled — Galt, Clyme, and Branl —fight all the challengers for the privilege of being maimed to resemble the half-hand of Covenant and Korik, Sill, and Doar, who succumbed to despair when they gained part of the Illearth Stone from the Giant Raver Kinslaughterer at the Grieve and challenged Lord Foul. The Humbled participate in Linden's quest to Andelain more to prevent her from using Earthpower than to protect her. Of the other Masters only Handir, the leader in Revelstone, has been introduced, and he is not developed much yet. But already the *Haruchai* have learned that they are not invincible through their awareness of their ancestors' experiences with the Vizard, that they are not incorruptible through the breaking of the Vow by Korik, Sill, and Doar. The Masters have, at least, begun to doubt their chosen purpose, and to wonder if their goal of preserving the Land from any use/abuse of Earthpower is ill-advised.

The Ramen no longer inhabit the Land (nor do the Ranyhyn) though they return once approximately every ten years. Esmer calls them to the Verge of Wandering ahead of their scheduled visit to meet Linden. Manethrall Hami is the leader of the Ramen who help rescue Linden and her friends from the *kresh*, and then tests Linden and Stave. Mahrtiir, the Manethrall who accompanies Linden, longs for a more significant life. He is blinded by a spear in the horrific battle by the *lillianrill* village of many opposing forces: Roger and his Demondim, the Raver-maddened *kresh*, Esmer, the Harrow, Linden and her friends and the dispossessed *lillainrill* people. Nevertheless, after being blinded and despite his handicap, he is still effective and actually takes a more active leadership role, so one could argue that he becomes more effective. He directs the Cords to find a rocky area within Salva Gildenbourne on which the group can face the *skurj*, a strategy which turns out to be a brilliant military decision, as even the Cords can use the rocks to distract the *skurj* so that the Giants can attack them. Pahni and Bhapa, the young cords, volunteer to help Linden in appreciation for her medical skill in saving their cousin/half-sister Sahah from almost certain death in the battle against the *kresh*. Covenant's voice, through Anele, warns the Ramen of the consequences of their given allegiance but urges them to preserve themselves as they will be needed.

Esmer is the epitome of an unresolved eye of the paradox. He is the union of Kastenessen's power given to his abandoned human lover who used the anger and Earthpower to create the *merewives* and the *Haruchai* Cail who had succumbed to the *merewives'* song and returned to them when the Search had accomplished its goals. Thus, he embodies the anger of Kastenessen and Cail's unresolved sense of failure. He attempts to aid Linden, but apparently his conflicted, schizophrenic personality forces him to thwart her just as much. He embodies warring opposites but has not yet learned to embrace both, to find the eye of his paradox. Since it is difficult to ascertain what his real purposes are, it is equally hard to tell if he is being effective. He hasn't changed or grown so far.

Caerroil Wildwood challenges Linden to find the answer to his most pressing query, how the forests will survive when all the Forestals have died off. He protects Garrotting Deep with the power of his music. In the 1st "Chronicles" he is summoned by Mhoram who dares to sing part of the Forestal's own song. Caerroil Wildwood makes a bargain with Hile Troy to allow the Lords' army to pass through the forest unscathed in exchange for the opportunity to kill Foul's army and the Giant-Raver that leads it. Of course, the Raver doesn't actually die, but the Giant child does. The Forestal also demands a great sacrifice from Hile Troy whom he turns into Caer-Caveral, an apprentice and eventually the only Forestal left by the last book of the 2nd "Chronicles." In the "Last Chronicles" Wildwood begins his great war against the Viles due to Covenant's and Jeremiah's machinations when they and Linden have traveled to the Land's past. Later he grants Linden a boon she didn't ask for and adds powerful runes to her battle-blackened Staff of Law.

The Insequent are a powerful society who value knowledge and, like the *Elohim*, search for their knowledge and mastery alone, much as the Unfettered do. They have great enmity for the *Elohim*, considering them haughty and self-absorbed, though humility is not always one of their virtues either. The Mahdoubt values gratitude and honors friendship, sacrificing her sanity to protect Linden from the Harrow. She has studied time and can rescue Linden from the Land's past. Each of the swatches on her colorful, varied gown probably represents the gratitude of someone whom she has helped. Linden adds to her gown, sewing on the patch torn from her own shirt while the Mahdoubt is transporting them forward through time. She grants Linden the ultimate gift, the knowledge of her true name *Querl Estrel* by which she can be summoned.

The Theomach defeated the *Elohim* guardian and took his place on the Island of the One Tree until Brinn defeated him. Eventually, after he interferes with Covenant and Jeremiah's plans and redirects them to an earlier time and a greater distance from *Melenkurion* Skyweir, he accompanies them to Berek's camp and remains behind to undertake the tutelage of Berek, as the first High Lord strives to master the Earthpower to which he has pledged himself. He takes care that Linden will not change the past by her rather miraculous treatment of Berek's wounded men by calling her the first of the Unfettered Ones. The Theomach tells Linden that she knows his secret name, which she eventually realizes is *Kenaustin Ardenol*.

The Harrow has studied the made creatures of the Land and is able to unmake the Demondim that are threatening Revelstone. He covets Linden's forms of power, the wild magic of Covenant's white gold ring and her Staff of Law. His power appears to come from the accoutrements of his leather outfit and his knowledge. His eyes also have the same kind of power to compel Linden as Kasreyn's *geas* did. Both Esmer and Roger attempt to kill him in the plains near the *lillianrill* village, and Linden is forced to aid the Harrow and destroy the *caesure* that threatens him because he claims to be able to lead her to her son.

The Vizard single-handedly defeated five hundred *Haruchai* because of his ability to slip between moments and speed up his own time to pound the *Haruchai* senseless during the duration of three heartbeats. However, he considers himself less powerful than the Theomach, who had defeated the guardian of the One Tree. He also asks Jeremiah to make one of his structures to imprison the *Elohim*. When he tries to interfere with the Harrow's purpose, he also, like the Mahdoubt, loses his mind and his life.

Few new Giants have been defined by their personalities so far. The first Giant to appear in *Fatal Revenant* is Longwrath, the grandson of the First and Pitchwife, the third son of their third son, named Exalt Widenedworld, but renamed Lostson Longwrath after he was injured in a bout of practice with Rime Coldspray. At first the Giants think he might have been blessed/cursed by EarthSight as was Seadreamer. Longwrath can speak, though he iterates only his desire to kill some mysterious "her" and his criticism of other Giants who try to stop him as "fools." He easily escapes from all fetters and even stone shackles. When he kills his mother Sablehair Foamheart (Filigree) and beats his father Soar Gladbirth to unconsciousness, Rime Coldspray, who feels responsible for Longwrath's injury, with a small group of Giants, takes him as they sail aboard Dire's Vessel to *Bhrathairealm* to obtain iron shackles. However, Longwrath is able to slip from even his iron shackles, steal a sword from the armory of the Braithair, and board Dire's Vessel, clearly indicating his desire to leave. To try to understand his obsession, the Giants determine to allow his desired course to direct them. Once they arrive in the Land, Longwrath keeps shedding his shackles and running ahead of the other Giants. Thus he is unrestrained when he first attacks Linden. The other Giants recapture him and keep him apart from Linden as much as possible. Once Linden and her friends achieve Andelain, the Wraiths repel Longwrath with their music.

Rime Coldspray is the Ironhand of the Swordmainnir, the all-women group of Giants who try to restrain and understand Longwrath. She is strong but earned her position as leader by her cunning. When it becomes clear that Longwrath is directing Dire's Vessel toward the Land, she fears that her small group of Giant warriors may be too few to provide the needed assistance. When she joins forces with Linden and hears Linden's story, she still does not understand why Linden wants the added power that Lorik's *krill* will give her. She wants to know what Linden will use all her power to accomplish. As Covenant had told the First, Linden also tells Coldspray that doubt must be an element in whatever decision the Giant makes to aid Linden. Linden needs the freedom to make her own choices without interference from others, but she also wants the Giants to choose to aid her for their own reasons, not for hers. Though many characters want to control the future by limiting Linden's choices, Coldspray accepts the ambiguity, embracing the eye of the paradox. She claims that what Giants love about the great tales is the potential for failure and the uncertainty of the outcome. Foamfollower had said at the end of the 1st "Chronicles" that his life and death had meaning because he had been part of Covenant's first great tale in the Land. Rime Coldspray is willing to participate in Linden's quest for the same possibility, to be part of a marvelous tale.

Nine other Giants are named and instrumental in the fights against the *skurj* and the trek across Salva Gildenbourne. Two do not survive to reach Andelain — Scend Wavegift, killed by Longwrath, and Moire Squareset, killed by the *skurj*. Once the rest are all safe in Andelain, the Giants hold a *caamora* to celebrate the lives of the friends they lost, to accuse themselves for any faults that contributed to those deaths, but also to feel the pain and the sorrow of their loss, and to forgive themselves. They, therefore, can understand the eye of the paradox. Before participating in the *caamora*, each Giant tells tales of her relationship with the two dead Giants, with humor and respect. Then as she thrusts her hands into the flames, the pain helps her purge her grief. When it is over, Linden can perceive their change of mood. "They had assuaged their bereavement with fire."[15] Longwrath, of course, cannot participate in the healing *caamora*, not only because the Wraiths refuse him entrance to Andelain, but also because his single-minded obsession to kill Linden allows him no form of healing, not fire nor the Earthpower of Liand's *orcrest*.

Since Donaldson just introduced Giants into the "Last Chronicles" in the last one hundred pages of *Fatal Revenant*, perhaps we will learn more about Frostheart Grueburn, Stormpast Galesend, Onyx Stonemage, Cirrus Kindwind, Cabledarm, Latebirth, and Halewhole Bluntfist.

Clearly, from the new characters Donaldson has introduced in the "Last Chronicles," certain themes are evident. Ten are afflicted by some sort of madness: Joan, Jeremiah, Roger, Anele, Kastenessen, Esmer, the Mahdoubt, the Vizard, the Theomach (according to Roger), and Longwrath. Together with the characters from the earlier "Chronicles" who are also mad — Kevin, Lena as an older woman, Pietten, Foamfollower in his bloodlust period, the Bloodguard who believe they can challenge Lord Foul with their fragment of the Illearth Stone, Marid, the Sunbane-warped of During Stonedown, and even Covenant himself as he is fasting and riding through Morinmoss or after eating the poisonous *amanibhavam* plant, or existing in his *Elohim*-imposed catatonic state of blackness — this is a disproportionately large number of characters with questionable sanity. Although clearly capable of making decisions, Lord Foul himself and Kasreyn of the Gyre should probably be included in the group as well. Possession continues to be an evil with *moksha* Jehannum in control of Joan, the *croyel* affixed to Jeremiah's back, Kastenessen's hand replacing one of Roger's, *turiya* Raver able to possess a pack of *kresh*, and Foul and others able to take over Anele's mind and voice occasionally. Since several of these characters are both possessed and insane, the connection between insanity and possession is evident.

Longwrath's obsessive actions against Linden because of her potential danger to the Land appear clearly insane, but Infelice and the Harrow also fear what they perceive to be the inevitable repercussions of Linden's choices. Thus, the important lesson that Linden learns at the end of the 2nd "Chronicles" — not only to allow Covenant to make his own choices but to trust that his personality will allow him to make only good decisions — has yet to be learned by the *Elohim* or the Insequent, who still believe they know what is best for the Land and, of course, for themselves. Indeed, one of the central questions of the overall "Chronicles" continues to be how the Land can be real and be Covenant's dream if he is sane.

Several other characters are blind or have lost an eye: Anele, Mahrtiir, Stave. Hile Troy is blind before he gains his Land-born sight, and then he loses his ability to see as the Forestal. The eyeless ur-viles and Wayhnim aren't bothered by their lack of sight. Seadreamer was mute; Longwrath can speak but says only two things. The number of half-handed people is growing: first, there is Berek, then Covenant. The 1st "Chronicles" also add Korik, Sill, and Doar. The "Last Chronicles" provide Jeremiah, the three Humbled, and Roger once he exchanges one of his hands for one of Kastenessen's in the Land. More characters are losing one or more of their senses, much as Covenant lost his sense of touch to leprosy. Leprosy can also cause blindness though Covenant has not suffered that loss yet. However, despite these handicaps, the characters can still be effective.

At this point Donaldson may be the only one who knows how the "Last Chronicles" will end. However, it is interesting how many of the characters are beginning to resemble each other and Covenant physically. This similarity reinforces the argument that the story can still be interpreted as the external working out of Covenant's internal psychological conflicts. The more the characters look alike and resemble him, the harder it is for Covenant to see them as different from himself. Indeed, one of the central questions of the overall "Chronicles" continues to be how the Land can be real and be Covenant's dream if he is sane. And if, as Donaldson has stated, the "Last Chronicles" will show that Covenant and Lord Foul are one and the same, Donaldson will, by necessity, be showing us how to combine our sane and insane selves. Donaldson thus maintains the possibility that the "Chronicles" are part of Covenant's dream.

On the other hand, with eventually ten books in the series and so many well-developed, distinctive characters that readers have come to know, believe in, and love (and sometimes hate), the argument that the Land is real and its people individual and separate from Covenant is also powerful. In fact, since Covenant resolved the belief- and disbelief-in-the-Land dialectic in the 1st "Chronicles," the potential that the Land was merely Covenant's dream lost its power, especially as the point of view veered away from Covenant's character, first to Hile Troy and then to Linden. This ambiguity is especially true in the "Last Chronicles" in which Covenant's point of view has not yet been given.

Therefore, it has become more difficult for Donaldson to maintain both possible interpretations as equally likely. However, this dialectic and its both/and solution was the original illustration for the eye of the paradox, and undoubtedly remains central to Donaldson's overall purpose. Therefore, Donaldson may be using the growing similarity of his characters in the "Last Chronicles" to keep strong the possibility that all Covenant's adventures in the Land could still be part of his dream. If the two sides of the dialectic between the Land-as-real and the Land-as-a-dream remain equally weighted, Donaldson can maintain the need for the both/and resolution of the eye of the paradox.

CHAPTER 5

Something Evil This Way Comes

In Ray Bradbury's *Something Wicked This Way Comes* (published in 1962), he shows just how attractive evil can be. He also supports one of Donaldson's main themes: knowledge unearned can be dangerous. Bradbury took his title from Shakespeare's *Macbeth* in which one of the witches says, "By the pricking of my thumbs, something wicked this way comes" (4.1.43). For Macbeth the prediction by the witches that he would be King, though he doesn't know how this forecast will be accomplished, is a serious enough temptation for him to devise a means to fulfill the prophesy: the murder of Duncan. This little knowledge proves disastrous to both Macbeth and Lady Macbeth. Obtaining what one most wants without effort can be a mighty lure and obviously some are willing to compromise themselves for such an advantage, but it would not be a true benefit. In the Land, Kevin's Wards are prepared for the new Lords in sequence, so that they must master the knowledge in the first one before they have access to the second. When Elena goes after the 7th Ward because Covenant had brought the *krill* to life but without having found or learned any of the lessons in the four Wards that precede it, she is undertaking a very dangerous and eventually fatal mission. Sometimes, though, it is difficult to judge the difference between what is ill-advised and what is truly wicked.

The battle between good and evil is a central staple of fantasy novels, and possibly accounts in part for the popularity of the genre since readers receive vicarious pleasure out of what Tolkien calls the consolation of good triumphing over evil. Modern novels, on the other hand, have consistently questioned whether "winning" is even possible for flawed creatures and have pointed out that the means used to defeat evil may be just as evil. In other words, we may be capable of the same kind of horror we abhor. For Donaldson to find the eye of the paradox in this particular dialectic, the good/evil dichotomy, is especially difficult as most of us have strong either/or beliefs about good and evil, and it is easier for us to see evil as an external opponent, the "Other." Yet Donaldson's goal is to juxtapose these opposites even as he conjoins the epic vision of fantasy with the modern ironic world view. Through his eye-of-the-paradox solution, he can break the cycle of determinism, futility, and impotence in modern literature and open up for us the next stage of evaluating our world and ourselves with hope for a successful solution to our problems, no matter how flawed we are or how overwhelming and impossible our challenges seem to us now.

Most readers believe that it is easy to recognize what is good. We assume that virtue will be exhibited by characters of pure intention using only moral means. Fantasy and science fiction literature is full of superheroes: Luke Skywalker from *Star Wars* who learns to control "the Force" or Paul Atreides from *Dune* who has mastered the weirding way. Donaldson develops Mhoram and other Lords in this mold, at least before their interaction with Covenant. On the other hand, modern literature, when it acknowledges heroism at all, usually provides an anti-hero, a person reluctant to take on the role of hero because he is aware that it will be costly, probably even claim his life. Donaldson's hero Thomas Covenant is a reluctant hero with the potential for super powers who chooses to sacrifice himself rather than use his power to affect solutions in the Land. Thus, Donaldson is reversing our view of good as well as our concept of solving problems to move us away from two assumptions that have held us paralyzed in the twentieth century: that only purely good people can hope to defeat evil, and that the way to defeat evil is to produce a bigger, smarter bomb or discover a more potent power. Donaldson's entire "Chronicles" (so far) dispel both these myths. Yet there still is a conflict between good and evil that must be resolved, one that is more an inward than an outward battle, and Donaldson wants to provide new, unique, creative, and effective solutions for us.

Natural phenomena such as hurricanes or floods are not considered evil even though they can wreck much havoc. No malicious intent produces the capricious forces of nature. Evil is motivated by envy, hatred, pride, lust for power, or despair and consciously contrives wicked deeds to make others miserable, too. Donaldson focuses on despair and hatred by making his ultimate villain Lord Foul the Despiser. For Donaldson, the ultimate evil character is not one who deforms or enslaves or kills, though Lord Foul does all these, but Foul's greatest evil is that he attacks a person's character, takes away hope, causes despair, forces an individual to face his worst inadequacies and guilts and then feel paralyzed even to try to act.

Evil can be defined many different ways: as the absence of good; as something or someone who actively tries to corrupt good; as an atrocity of some sort, such as murder, betrayal, or possession; as deliberately initiating violence against others. The world has pictured an ultimately evil character many ways: as a tyrant bent on dominating the world; as one who tempts individuals to forsake the Creator; as the ultimate jailer and punisher, sometimes with the same punishment for all — fire and brimstone and the contiguous agony of burning and being unable to breathe well — or sometimes with a punishment based on the seriousness of the person's crimes, such as are found in Dante's nine circles of Hell.

Good and evil have been diluted today. As we have turned away from universal acceptance of an involved deity carefully watching what we do, we have accepted a God-the-clockmaker belief that the Creator merely created the world and then left us to our own devices. The creation myths of the Land all differ in some ways but all agree on the fact that something — perhaps the Arch of Time, perhaps the fact that the Rainbow connecting the worlds was torn from the sky above the Land — some obstacle causes a separation between the Creator and the Land, and He cannot get personally involved. We've seen an uninvolved deity in other fantasies as well: Savoy of Ursula LeGuin's "Earthsea" trilogy speaks the First Word of creation and then allows the rest of history to work itself out. Tolkien, an ardent Catholic, writes in his creation myth, the "Ainulindalës" from *The Silmarillion*, that Eru provides knowledge to each of the Ainur for their part in the song, but they sing the creation of Middle-earth using their own individual input and creativity, including Melkor's contributions which disrupt the harmony of the rest. While they are still singing and composing the creation song, Eru introduces two new themes to use the disharmony of Melkor to create an even greater, if sadder, song. Then once the third theme is sung, Eru shows the Ainur a vision of the history of the creation of the world that they have just sung, and each individual Ainur recognizes his own contributions to the result. After that Eru sends the imperishable flame to create the world but delegates the responsibility to the self-chosen Ainur who become Valar by taking on human form and working with the raw materials under their power to control and shape the earth according to the vision they have seen. Eru himself does not interfere in the affairs of Middle-earth, though he is nowhere prohibited from doing so. Manwe, as the most important Valar, makes the significant decisions that affect Middle-earth. Though LeGuin, Tolkien, and Donaldson do not include an involved deity to protect man, an intimate evil is allowed to exert power: the Shadow or Aspen in "Earthsea"; Melkor and then Sauron in Middle-earth; and Lord Foul, the Despiser, in the Land.

Donaldson complicates the ambiguity of whether a deity can/will intervene to provide justice or help by separating his Creator from the Land yet suggesting that he can test and make choices about who from the "real" world can be transported to the Land. From the few words they exchange, the beggar learns of Covenant's stubborn will to live and his generosity and empathy. He also tests Linden's dedication to healing, despite the nausea and helplessness he makes her feel. The beggar (the Creator) can even influence Covenant's thinking by focusing his attention on the question of ethics, although once Covenant is in the Land, he must have the freedom of choice. A further ambiguity is developed because though the Creator cannot reach through the Arch of Time to help the peoples of the Land, within his creation is Earthpower that can be called up by knowledgeable Lords. This contradiction both supports and denies the Renaissance Christian Humanist belief that because there is a deity looking out for our good, we can count on divine help in a time of crisis.

Donaldson thus raises a major dialectic that man has often tried to resolve through his religious beliefs: does fate or predestination control the outcome of historical events or does free will exist and is choice truly independently made by individuals? If everything is predestined, then God or Eru or the Creator has no need to interfere in the affairs of man because everyone's actions have already been decided. If free will is operant, then the Creator is limited in how He can intervene, limited even in whether He can help. Boethius in his *Consolation of Philosophy* logically illustrates how both predestination and free will can co-exist, and Donaldson agrees. In modern fantasy literature one good explanation of how to juxtapose these two seemingly contradictory views was proposed by Frank Herbert in his *Dune* series. When Paul Atreides has come into his power as the Kwisatz Haderach, he can perceive the threads of future events, or the different paths that the future can take; unfortunately, he cannot tell which decision of his will produce which future. The *Elohim* present a similar view of potential futures based on different choices. The many different possible outcomes are predicated on the choices made by the people involved. However, the *Elohim* choose to make a decision entirely by themselves, which limits the choices of others, without discussing Linden's or Covenant's roles with them or how Findail's sacrifice might be necessary because of the choice they make. They do say that they are sharing the burden of the potential future, rather than making a choice in which they would be spared from naming an Appointed. However, clearly Donaldson believes that it is unwise to be able to predict the future; the necessity of choice must come without fore-knowledge of the consequences and with only past behavior, the current situation, and one's own moral principles as guides. Obviously, those choices will significantly determine the future. Here the eye-of-the-paradox way that predestination and free will can be combined involves an understanding of the characters themselves, their world views, their previous experiences, their inadequacies and capabilities, yet for the choice to be completely free, it must be based only on what they know at that minute and what they desire for the future, not on any knowledge that if they make a certain choice, a particular future is assured.

In today's real world, society has watered down the concepts of saintly behavior and deliberate evil to distinctions we call good and bad. We seem to mean that each person is either trying to be a good person and mostly makes moral choices or that person makes bad choices or has developed a cynical world view due to upbringing, poverty conditions, or bad influences. We even explain away some of the atrocities committed by criminals by rationalizing that they learned their violent behavior from physical, sexual, or mental abuse as children from one or more parent or guardian or through the influence of the cavalier attitude toward violence in films, television shows, video games, and/or popular songs, or we name their evil deeds as temporary insanity. We accept crimes of convenience or passion as unpremeditated and believe they justify a lesser sentence than deliberately chosen, planned crimes.

Both Tolkien and Donaldson want us to acknowledge the more extreme forms of pure good and pure evil but for different reasons. For Tolkien our most important purpose is to fight constantly against evil, striving to resist the evil in ourselves and to defeat physically that evil directed against us or against others. Covenant believes this kind of battle is his task against Lord Foul as long as he perceives Foul to be an entity external to himself, that is, as his external antagonist. However, Donaldson has already raised questions about whether Foul is part of Covenant if the Land is Covenant's dream. Donaldson believes Tolkien was headed in the same direction with the character of Frodo as Donaldson himself is headed with Covenant. In referencing *The Lord of the Rings*, Donaldson says that he believes Frodo is becoming like Sauron because Frodo claims the Ring at the end of his quest as if he personally were going to challenge the Dark Lord with Sauron's own power. But Frodo is rescued from this ultimate confrontation by Gollum, who steals the ring and then either fortuitously or through the self-fulfilling prophesy of either Frodo or the Ring itself, is "'cast [himself] into the Fire of Doom.'"[1] Donaldson has not yet come to the part in his story in which Covenant becomes Lord Foul, but this eventual unity is his stated purpose for the "Last Chronicles." Covenant has already acknowledged the connection at the end of *White Gold Wielder*: he comments on the similarity between Lord Foul's appearance and his own. He has already admitted that his own evil rape of Lena was like Foul's destruction of the Wraiths. Also, he knows that there is a side of his psyche that hates lepers and therefore hates himself just as Foul does. Donaldson will not allow Covenant the luxury of renouncing Foul as the evil "other." While Tolkien sees good and evil as separate opponents, as does Frank Herbert, Donaldson and LeGuin represent both good and evil as coexisting within everyone, and our greatest task is to recognize and embrace this truth and yet still act with integrity to accomplish good for society as a whole.

In another way Donaldson's view of evil is slightly different from Tolkien's and that of most organized religions. In many creation stories the personification of evil is created very early whether it is Satan (Christianity), Melkor (Tolkien's Middle-earth), Loki (Norse), Set (Egyptian), Coyote (Native American), or Tezcatlipoca (Aztec). In the "Chronicles," however, Lord Foul comes later, and the three tree- and soil-hating Ravers are born earlier. The Ravers' hatred is innate and destructive. Lord Foul comes with man. In terms of the definition of evil, then, Foul is not instinctive, animalistic viciousness, though he certainly uses creatures like the *kresh* for their innate power and violence. Nor is he pure natural power such as a tornado or tsunami (or the Sunbane or the na-Mhoram's Grim) which devastates enormous areas and kills many but is not targeted on any particular person. The Vortex of Trepidation is like a hurricane (with an ability to create emotional fear) and Raver *turiya* Kinslaughterer uses his portion of the Illearth Stone to raise a tsunami to engulf *Coercri,* so evil can use or corrupt natural power. However, Lord Foul's evil is deliberate and focused not only on an individual but targeted specifically on the weaknesses, guilts, and vulnerabilities of his victims. His goal is not the death of his enemies but continued psychological torture by robbing them of volition, their own essential power and identity and hope.

Like Bradbury, Donaldson first depicts evil as beautiful. Therefore, Lord Foul is not recognized as evil at first (much as Satan and Melkor are both considered the most beautiful, powerful, and intelligent of their Creator's first creations). But over time the human weakness of pride, the desire to make choices not only for others but also to have followers who worship him as well as call him Lord, the resentment against any who thwart his will, and his pleasure in enacting revenge and punishment on his enemies corrupt Foul until he becomes the personification of evil in the Land. Thus for Donaldson, evil is desire for power over others, psychological viciousness, and ultimate selfishness, though ironically it also encompasses self-loathing. During the time of the King and Queen, Foul gained his title of Lord by being part of the King's Council. Only the Queen sees beneath his outward appearance and perceives him merely as a shadow, something that upsets the harmony and joy of the Land's version of the idealized Camelot. But not until 1,000 years later does Kevin recognize Lord Foul's true nature and expel him from the Lords' Council.

Within the Land, Lord Foul is accepted as a real and powerful force for evil. He has many names to the people of the Land: he is called Lord Foul, the Despiser, by the Lords; the *rhadhamaerl* and *lillianrill* name him the Gray Slayer; the Ramen use the name assigned to him by *Kelenbhrabanal,* Father of Horses — Fangthane the Renderer; the Giants call him Satansheart and Soulcrusher; to the Bloodguard he is Corruption; the *jheherrin* call him the

Maker because he created them and other beings like the ur-viles. In the 2nd "Chronicles" the na-Mhorams of the Clave, who have been possessed by the Raver *samadhi*, manipulate the beliefs of the inhabitants of the Land and call Lord Foul a-Jeroth. They suggest by their version of the creation story that the suffering of the inhabitants under the Sunbane is justified retribution because too often the peoples of the Land conspired with Foul/a-Jeroth in the past. But no matter the name given him, all agree that his most potent weapons are physically, his manufactured armies, and psychologically, the despair he can create in the hearts of the people, in spite of and sometimes because of their best intentions which are hampered by their culpabilities and inadequacies. Through other powers, such as the Staff of Law and the Illearth Stone and later the Sunbane, he can control the weather, creating a preternatural winter or manipulating the growth and decay cycles of plant life.

The peoples of the Land fear and abhor Lord Foul mostly for his physical violence, destructive propensity and ability, and betrayal. Those who study stone- or wood-lore perceive that Foul has no love for the power in the earth that they want to protect and nurture. The reference to Foul as the Gray Slayer by the *rhadhamaerl* and *lillianrill* probably refers back to his association with the Shadow that fell on the King's Council and the despair of the Queen's Champions as a result of the viciousness and carnage of the civil war. Thus, both these groups of beings identify Foul with his actions of betrayal and slaughter. The Ramen associate Foul with the *kresh* whose fangs can rend unprotected Ranyhyn. But the great horses themselves see him as a betrayer because, as communicated to Elena in the horserite she attended, when *Kelenbhrabanal*, Father of Horses, went to sacrifice himself to Lord Foul on the condition that the rest of his herd be allowed to live in peace, Foul betrayed him, killed him, and yet still sent the *kresh* to attack the Ranyhyn. To combat the Lords and the peoples of the Land, Lord Foul manufactures and breeds large armies of ur-viles, cavewights, *kresh*, and griffins. To accomplish his goal, first he corrupts the viles then forces them to create perfect fighters for him in the Demondim and the ur-viles. Foul does not personally fight but sends his minions, led sometimes by a Giant Raver with a portion of the Illearth Stone, to enhance his physically destructive forces.

The Giants and the *Haruchai* hate and fear Foul not as much for his physical ability to kill them, but for the psychological change that could take place within them through contact with him. In this belief both groups fear their own weaknesses more than Foul's strength. The Giants name him Soulcrusher, and when the Ravers are able to control the child-triplet Giants and one as Kinslaughterer attacks his own people, the Giants despair and lose their desire for resistance and simply wait passively for their own physical deaths. Foamfollower's greatest fear is that his encounter with Foul through

Drool's armies of cavewights and ur-viles will make him become that which he hates, will force him to use his own hatred, bloodlust, and power to fight against the sheer power and numbers of the opposing army, and thus forget who he is as a Giant, not just a fighter. The *Haruchai*, in naming the ultimate evil as Corruption, admit the possibility of the failure of their Vow, through their own doubt. The Bloodguard name Foul with the abstraction Corruption not because he has corrupted any of them or even that they think he could, but that they fear he might be able to and in their either/or judgmental world view, forsaking their Vow is the worst evil they can imagine. The Giants and *Haruchai* see Foul probably closer to the way Donaldson wants us to interpret him. Destruction and killing are evil, but in the hierarchy of evil deeds, far more serious is making someone become what he hates (the battle bloodlust of Foamfollower, the corruption of the three Bloodguard Korik, Sill, and Doar, the temptations of Kevin and Covenant and even Trell to destroy that which is beautiful out of desperation). Since the peoples of the Land can be easily possessed by the Ravers but the *Haruchai* and the Giants (except the young triplets) cannot, perhaps this contrast explains Donaldson's distinction between the differing perceptions of evil for the *rhadhamaerl, lillianrill,* Ramen, and Lords, who see evil as an exterior force and are not trained to combat it within themselves, and that of Covenant, the Giants, and the *Haruchai,* who recognize the battle taking place within themselves, between their own good and evil sides. In this distinction the people of the Land are more like older, pre-twentieth century heroes. When Trell makes the discovery of the secret to the Ritual of Desecration, like Kevin before him, he has not been tested with self-doubt and therefore is not prepared enough to resist the influence of Foul from within. Both the Giants, in their contests against the unforgiving elements, and the *Haruchai,* from their political structure of determining leaders by combat, have faced outward, physical defeats and risen to fight again, so their fear is not of the fight itself but of the inward loss of the will to fight or of forgetting their reason to fight or of not living up to their own standards of behavior. Covenant, having faced his heart of darkness early in the story and having moved forward from there, also recognizes that the inner battle to be and do good is perhaps our greatest challenge. We are our own most powerful antagonists.

But Lord Foul reaches yet another level of disgrace because his evil involves the psychological torture of his victims — making them feel impotent, completely inadequate for the task at hand and, therefore, to blame for their own weaknesses and lack of effectiveness, devoid of hope for personal or societal peace. Foul's primary attack on Covenant, and possibly the reason he chooses Covenant to bring to the Land, is to exacerbate Covenant's feelings of impotence, ignorance, and desire for lack of responsibility or even for death. Both times when Foul has a hand in the summoning of Covenant, he taunts Covenant, calling him Groveler and threatening to destroy completely even the possibility of hope. Foul never reveals his strategy but claims to have foolproof plans not for the death of many inhabitants of the Land because that would end their suffering but for prolonged torment and despair. How neatly this belief parallels the refrain from the leprosarium in Covenant's "real" world: "You cannot hope for a cure."[2] Foul's purpose is worse than merely enslaving or even torturing victims; even slaves can be free in their own minds. Foul wants to manipulate Covenant's feelings and perceptions to the point that he completely despairs and has no hope for the future. If Lord Foul can torture Covenant so much that Covenant continues the self-blame, self-loathing, and despair against himself, Foul has won.

Lord Foul can manipulate not only Covenant's feelings but also his perceptions. At the end of *The Power That Preserves*, Foul exacerbates Covenant's vertigo by making him think that he is falling. Then he presents false images to Covenant of his own leprosy growing and of Joan and Roger being afflicted by rapidly spreading cases of Hansen's disease, then Mhoram, Lena, Atiaran, and others from the Land. Since one of Covenant's main tasks in the 1st "Chronicles" is to determine what is truth based on what he perceives and what he knows in his mind to be true, this particular manipulation of Foul's backfires because it helps Covenant unite his knowledge that the Land can't be real and must be a dream with his strong perception that his experiences in the Land are real and thus find the eye of the paradox necessary to accept both.

Lord Foul is definitely an either/or character. He does not believe that Covenant can resolve the disparities between his Unbelief and his desire for the Land to be more than just his dream. Foul also believes that through his plans and machinations, he can reduce the number of choices that the Lords or Covenant has to one that will fulfill his own will. But like Tolkien's Sauron, Donaldson's Foul cannot perceive all possible choices: Sauron is blind to the plan of the leaders of the West to destroy the Ring, the talisman of ultimate power; Foul believes that anger and a deep desire for revenge will force Covenant to engage in a physical contest against Foul which cannot be won. Actually, his inability to acknowledge the eye of the paradox defeats Foul.

Lord Foul, as can the other characters, can be seen as a representative of part of Covenant's personality, the part that hates himself, that believes he deserves the leprosy with which he has been afflicted, that despairs of ever being able to appreciate beauty or life again, and that feels suicidal. The level of interpretation of the "Chronicles" as Covenant's dream sets up gratuitously hurting others as bad, not living up to one's own moral convictions or commandments like "Thou shalt not kill" or forgetting Atiaran's admonition to

Triock "'You swore the Oath of Peace'"[3] as worse, but worst of all is succumbing to depression, giving up, and accepting death or ultimate destruction as the only possible solutions to seemingly insurmountable problems. Since part of the eye of the paradox for Donaldson is the question of whether the Land is real or Covenant's experiences there merely represent his dream, if the fantasy part of the story is Covenant psychologically working out his inner demons, then Lord Foul, the Despiser, the personification of Despair, is simply one aspect of Covenant's personality, the one which is causing him the most conflict and the one over which he most needs to gain control.

On the macrocosm level, Lord Foul can also represent the twentieth century view that our world is changing so fast, deteriorating so completely, being abused and used up and exploited to such an extreme, and we are so helpless to stop the devastating changes, that little hope remains for a wholesome life for ourselves or our descendants. On the level of the "Chronicles" representing an intellectual debate of modern man's interaction with his environment, evil is our intolerance and persecution of difference (of race, religion, nationality, sexual preference), our neglect and, worse, our destruction of our natural resources, our reliance on the muscle solution and thus our stockpiling of weapons of mass destruction rather than relying on diplomacy or other creative solutions to solve world problems. Donaldson has not claimed to be an avowed Christian (one whose purpose is to re-establish faith in God as a determining factor in our decision-making) as Tolkien was a practicing Catholic; nevertheless, the loss of faith in a caring and involved God today as well as our contradictory belief that "evil" as it was understood in the Bible doesn't really exist any more, only wickedness and the insanity which corrupts serial rapists or murderers, leads Covenant to another dialectic that he must resolve by finding the eye of the paradox. He must recognize his heart of darkness but not let it paralyze him from trying to act morally. However, first Donaldson must convince us that the two polarities of good and evil exist, not just wicked actions, but conscious, deliberate, determined evil. On that level, Lord Foul must be evaluated as a separate character, an independent force outside of Covenant's dream, a real character of the Land.

To Donaldson Lord Foul takes on another meaning in the macrocosm of Covenant's and Donaldson's real world. He is a representative of the proponents of limiting the modern American novel to realism, abandoning even the possibility for epic vision, and of all the modern critics of fantasy writers or of other mainstream writers who embrace the imagination. Donaldson claims, "Clearly, proponents of the modern American novel would argue that seduction by epic vision can only lead to stupid destruction. That, of course, is precisely the attitude Lord Foul takes toward Thomas Covenant."[4] However, in Donaldson's "Chronicles" exactly the opposite happens: the epic character

Kevin Landwaster invokes the Ritual of Desecration when he has lost his epic vision; in other words, without an epic vision, we limit our choices to ultimate destruction. By limiting our literature to realism and thus restricting the possible world views of modern man, we may be condemning ourselves to giving up on solving the problems that we face because they seem so overwhelming — huge problems like toxic waste, terrorism, nuclear disasters. We need an epic vision, a belief that we can find a way to control our environment before we are even willing to tackle the tasks set for our generation. Thus, the solution for the inhabitants of the modern world and for modern literature is the same: embrace the eye of the paradox that includes an epic vision.

So far in the first two "Chronicles," Donaldson has not explained the change in the appearance of Lord Foul. Tolkien claims that Sauron loses his physical form when Isildur cuts the One Ring from his finger, and he also suggests that the nine kings who accept the nine rings for mortal men and thus become the nine Ringwraiths, lose their form when they become immortal and inhabit the un–Dead world and, therefore, need to wear black clothing to be visible to ordinary inhabitants of Middle-earth. Even Frodo will fade, claims Gandalf, if he often wears and uses the Ring until he becomes like a clear glass filled with light. Thus, power does not need the body but can function with just the mind — or the Eye of Sauron or the disembodied voice of Lord Foul. From the beginning of the "Chronicles," Lord Foul does not have definitive form. Covenant is transfixed by his "gleaming green penumbra,"[5] his penetrating eyes, and his satirical, belittling voice. Yet he did have substance and even beauty during Berek's time and through Kevin's early years as High Lord. Foul was diminished by the Ritual of Desecration and obviously either lost or is able to conceal his form during most of the time of the 1st "Chronicles." Then at the end, when Covenant turns the wild magic on Lord Foul, the Despiser is forced to become substantial; he can no longer hide his form in invisibility. Once he has been revealed by Covenant's power, he loses some of his power to intimidate, so the Giants and dead Lords are released from their overwhelming fear of the Despiser. Foul as the personification of Despair can also be forced to diminish, grow younger, and eventually disappear by the pure joy and laughter of the Giant Foamfollower and the Lords who no longer fear despair and can heal themselves by recognizing that "'Joy is in the ears that hear, not in the mouth that speaks.'"[6] Foul can also be frustrated by having his use of the wild magic power blocked and absorbed by Covenant. So evil is not undefeatable.

And Lord Foul is limited in his use of power. He acknowledges the necessity of freedom. He knows that he cannot simply take Covenant's white gold ring, though he commands Elena to gain possession of it to enhance her power against the Colossus. But for Foul to be able to wield the potency of the wild magic himself, he must convince Covenant to hand the ring to him voluntarily. The necessity for the freedom of choice, so central to Donaldson's view of power, is more fully developed in Chapter 6.

The Ravers, however, are under no restriction to respect the free will of their victims and will invade and take possession of anybody they can. Until the birth of the Giant triplets, no Raver dared to try to take over any *Haruchai* or Giant. Linden later discovers from her intimate contact with *moksha* Herem that Giants and *Haruchai* are free of compulsion because they have always believed in the potency and power of their own choices. So the more a character accepts the necessity of freedom or the importance of personal choice, the less susceptible that person is to outside coercion.

The Ravers resemble the nine Ringwraiths of Tolkien's *The Lord of the Rings*, in that they are undying, have no physical form but must take on the appearance of substance — clothing to appear like men in the case of the Ringwraiths or bodies that the Ravers can control (or a swarm of bees, or a congery of eels) — and these evil servants take relish in inflicting pain and fighting for their Lord. In their immortality they are a way to explore the concept of time and to reevaluate the idea of death. Tolkien calls death a gift to man, and Donaldson implies that eternal life without choice is a special kind of Hell. But Donaldson's Ravers are more evil than Tolkien's Nazgul. Free will is essential to the question of "what does it mean to be human?" but a Raver strips his victims of free will and uses their bodies to attack and/or betray their former friends. In their disguises, the Ravers can appear to be that which they are not; for years, the na-Mhoram is not recognized as evil by other inhabitants of the Land who wish to serve the Land, but as their highest good, one representing Mhoram, their greatest High Lord hero. Yet Donaldson keeps the potential for the unity of the dialectic alive by allowing these victims of the Ravers the choice of resisting and being tormented or retreating into their inner, secure-though-catatonic beings, even while they are appalled by what the Raver is making their mouths say or their bodies do.

We learn most about Ravers though Linden's point of view when she recounts her inner fight with the Raver *moksha* Herem, who takes over her body in *White Gold Wielder*, in Foul's demesne of Kiril Threndor. By then she has learned that some beings are able to resist the Raver within. Hollinscrave remained himself, in control of his speech and choices, while trapping the Raver *samadhi* until the Sandgorgon Nom could "rend" the Raver as he killed the Giant. And Linden herself is touched by *samadhi* Gibbon Raver once in Revelstone, when her instinctive reaction is to retreat into herself, yet she hates that weakness, that paralysis, in herself. So when *moksha* Raver possesses her, she does not flee; she accepts the memories, the feelings of nausea, the accusations coming from the Raver and remembers her own pureness of motive, her own purpose of healing, as she fights back and eventually drives the Raver out of her body. Only those who know that they have free will and can make choices that matter for good reasons may hope to resist evil, such as the sin of possession.

Donaldson's Ravers are older than Lord Foul, though it is easy for him to enslave them because of their extreme hatred of all things growing (especially trees). They are the original evil, which arose from the Lower Land to threaten the trees of the One Forest before man reduced and separated the forests by cutting down so many trees. *Moksha* and *turiya* "taught the despising of the trees to the once-friendly Demondim."[7] *Samadhi* tries to aid the King in his conquest of the One Forest. The *Elohim* decided in their wisdom to try to contain the Ravers by choosing an Appointed to unite the purpose of the trees; that Appointed is then caught by the Forestal within the stone of the Colossus of the Fall above the cliff of Landsdrop to help the Forest to forbid the Ravers from attaining the Upper Land. But all this happens before Lord Foul comes. Mhoram tells Covenant that while the Ravers are great tree-haters, Lord Foul is the enemy of man. The idea of despair is connected to men's emotions, not some specific place of origin, so Mhoram claims that men brought it with them as they migrated in from the north or south of the Land. Before men populated the Land, its life consisted mostly of huge forests of trees, and the greatest evil was the hatred of growing things, represented by the Ravers, born as triplets from the same forgotten mother. Their enmity is for life and growth, while Lord Foul attacks the inner emotions and essence of men. But Foul is the one who teaches them to take pleasure in the suffering of their victims when he makes them his greatest servants.

The Ravers are indistinguishable from one another; they have no redeeming qualities and represent the ultimate evil of not only possessing someone else, robbing him of free will, but also of taking pleasure in the fears and anguish of their victims. Though they are interchangeable, nevertheless separate Ravers take on differing personalities depending on which body each inhabits and controls. For example, *turiya* uses Triock's resentment of Covenant to make the Raver-possessed Triock especially vicious towards Covenant.

The three brothers are *moksha* Jehannum, *turiya* Herem, and *samadhi* Sheol. Jehannum is the first Raver referenced in the "Chronicles"; he kills a Waynhim within a Waymeet and then travels to Soaring Woodhelven, where his odd behavior causes the Woodhelvennin to become suspicious of other unknown travelers in the Land. Later he controls one of the three Giant triplets as Fleshharrower and leads Lord Foul's army against Hile Troy and the Lords in *The Illearth War*. As Fleshharrower he taunts the Lords, especially

Verement who faces Foul's army alone to maintain the Word of Warning barrier to Doom's Retreat. Then the Giant-Raver's glee at having trapped the Lords' army against the forest at Garroting Deep turns to dismay when he foolishly sends his army and follows it himself into the Deep, only to be caught and hanged by the Forestal Caerroil Wildwood at Gallows Howe. Near the end of the 1st "Chronicles," Jehannum takes over one of the Ramen who is then killed by the Colossus when Elena loses control of Covenant's ring.

During the 2nd "Chronicles" *moksha* Jehannum kills Nassic, Sunder's father, leaving a hot knife behind in his back, and he later reveals himself to Linden's health sense and perception when he has taken over Marid to affect Marid's punishment of being abandoned to the sun's first light without protective stone so that he becomes one of the Sunbane-warped and can inflict Covenant with venom. The Raver *moksha* Jehannum again triggers a venom relapse for Covenant as the bees which attack when he and his friends are traveling on the Mithil River and later as the man with a spider after Covenant has freed *dhraga* from the trap of the Sunbane-warped people of During Stonedown, which had been destroyed by the na-Mhoram's Grim.

Finally, *moksha* possesses Linden at Kiril Threndor. He can torture her with her own memories of the deaths of her father and mother and all the other times she is paralyzed and does not/cannot aid Covenant. And to further appall her, he uses his own memories of the atrocities he has committed by inhabiting other bodies. He creates feelings of nausea or pain and uses psychological persuasion by speaking within Linden's mind to convince her to retreat into herself in fear and revulsion, which would make *moksha's* control over her stronger and easier. However, Linden does not flee into herself but accepts the disgust and pain *moksha* makes her feel. Eventually, therefore, she is able to expel him.

The second brother *turiya* Herem names himself Kinslaughterer when he possesses one of the Giant triplets and at *Coercri* forces the child Giant to kill all the other Giants, even his own mother and father. His task is facilitated by the despair the Giants feel over their own perceived weakness that would allow a Raver to control one of these proud people. Since they have never had to confront and overcome their own weakness, when their big test comes, they simply give up and wait passively and hopelessly in their homes for Kinslaughterer to use his portion of the Illearth Stone to tear out each Giant's brain in turn. But when Kinslaughterer tries to raise a tsunami from the ocean to engulf *Coercri*, Lord Hyrim and three Bloodguard are able to stop him, though this action proves disastrous as Hyrim dies and the Bloodguard believe they can bear the fragment of the Illearth Stone against Foul himself, thus corrupting their Vow.

Later *turiya* Herem takes over Yeurquin to kill and devour the Unfettered One trying to communicate with the Lords using the *lomilliar* rod brought by Triock. And even though Triock flees this scene, he too becomes victim to *turiya* and is forced to set a trap for Covenant and take him to the recalled dead Elena, Foul's servant now, at the Colossus of the Fall. He eventually leaves Triock to inhabit one of the Ramen farther away from the Colossus. This Raver doesn't have as big a role to play in the 2nd "Chronicles"; he controls the eels and eventually both Cavewights when *moksha* possesses Linden.

The third Raver, *samadhi* Sheol, controls an ur-vile loremaster and first fights against Mhoram in the Shattered Hills. Through his touch, Mhoram learns that *samadhi* had conquered Berek's liege, the King, and slaughtered many of the ancient Champions of the Land. In the days of the Old Lords, *turiya* and *moksha* brought the Demondim to Foul for the creation of the ur-viles. As the Giant Raver Satansfist, *samadhi* Sheol leads Lord Foul's army in the siege against Revelstone in *The Power That Preserves*. Because by this time the Law of Death has been broken by Elena, he can call forth the old dead to fight at Revelwood and again against the gates of Revelstone. He, too, fights using the physical power of Cavewights and ur-vile forces, griffins, *kresh*, and other evil creatures, but also he uses psychological fear to try to break the will of the Lords and the other inhabitants of Revelstone. The power of the Raver is enhanced by the portion of the Illearth Stone he carries. When Mhoram rides out against *samadhi* Raver, at first the Giant Satansfist seems to run away, to retreat from battling the Lord in single combat. But, eventually, Mhoram catches him and deals him a fierce blow on his forehead, shattering the Staff of Law in the process. The Raver then feels his victory is inevitable and relentlessly bears down on Mhoram with the power of the Illearth Stone fragment, until suddenly the cold wind stops because Elena loses control over Foul's preternatural winter when Covenant regains his ring. At that moment Mhoram feels Covenant's life in the Land through the *krill* and rises to kill the Giant Raver.

Because *samadhi* Raver's worst defeat is at the hands of Lord Mhoram, it is rather ironic that this Raver is chosen (whether by fate, by Foul, or just by Donaldson) to lead the Clave by taking over each new na-Mhoram in turn down to Gibbon. Therefore, though he could not conquer Revelstone from without and is weakened in power as are his brothers when Lord Foul is minimized by the laughter of the Giant Foamfollower and the dead Lords, when Foul comes back to power, *samadhi* is able to take over Revelstone from within. This takeover cannot be accomplished until the people of the Land have had their health sense so eroded that they are no longer able to perceive a Raver. Therefore, there are always well-intentioned, devoted people of the

Land who voluntarily serve the na-Mhoram (taken over by *samadhi* Raver), believing they are thereby serving the Land. These innocent people, like Memla, believe that they are fighting against the Sunbane when actually all they accomplish supports and strengthens the devastation.

When Covenant and the remaining members of the Search reenter Revelstone and Covenant fuses his venom and wild magic in the Banefire, Gibbon Raver flees to the Hall of Gifts, perhaps to cause Covenant to risk destroying what he loves in order to fight with the Raver. Then Honninscrave thwarts *samadhi's* plan by killing the mortal Gibbon and later, when *samadhi* tries to possess the Giant, containing the Raver long enough for the Sandgorgon Nom to "rend" the Raver as Nom kills the Giant. In keeping with other ambiguities in Donaldson's work, it is not clear whether the immortal Raver has been destroyed, but *samadhi* plays no further role in the 2nd "Chronicles."

A further ambiguity surrounding the Ravers concerns their names. Donaldson admits that he doesn't have Tolkien's facility with invented languages but also claims that names and other foreign sounding words were deliberately chosen for their particular sounds. However, moksha, turiya, and samadhi are actual words which refer to Buddhist states of enlightenment. Samadhi, for example, refers to a trancelike concentration. Since the purpose of meditation in Buddhism is to avoid or suppress emotion, it is ironic that Donaldson chose these names for his Ravers, who cause the most violently abhorrent emotions in their victims.

The other wicked creatures in the "Chronicles" are not individually differentiated, except the Cavewight Drool, and basically act as tools for Lord Foul or one of his Ravers. The viles have been enslaved by Foul and corrupted. They make the Demondim. After generations of experimental creation, the ur-viles, the fighting force produced by the Demondim, seem devoid of redeeming qualities. The evil of the ur-viles and the other creatures is innate or inbred and closer to the destructiveness of natural powers such as hurricanes than the personal vindictiveness of Foul. Their unity as a fighting force gives them an enhanced ferocity.

The ur-viles are Donaldson's most imaginative addition to the lexicon of evil creatures in science fiction/fantasy literature. They are eyeless, ebony beings that combine their power and strength to become more formidable by fighting as a unit, a dark wedge with a powerful ur-vile loremaster at the apex to concentrate their power and menace. Ur-viles have short limbs that allow them to stand upright in the wedge or run on four limbs. Eyeless faces perceive the world through smell, through their large noses. Their small mouths can, nevertheless, snatch a wraith out of the air and devour it. If they have a language, it sounds to Covenant like the natural sounds of stones rubbing against each other in a deep rumble or a chant snarled in unison. Neither the Viles nor the Cavewights are evil at the beginning. Viles first create the Demondim to reflect their own mighty and proud race. Cavewights delved for and worked with metals to make beautiful things that they could trade with the Land's other peoples. Their association with Lord Foul corrupts them, and thus other races or peoples of the Land are taught to fear how Foul could make them into what they hate.

Covenant's first encounter with an ur-vile wedge comes at the Celebration of Spring when he, Atiaran, and the Wraiths are surprised by the ur-vile force, and the Wraiths, helpless to interrupt their ritual, dance straight into the wedge to be devoured until the Unfettered One comes to release them with words of power. Covenant, though powerful enough to stop the desecration because of his wild magic white gold ring, is ignorant of how to trigger or use his power. Therefore, he lives with the double guilt of failing to rescue the Wraiths as Atiaran clearly thinks he should, thus forcing the self-sacrifice of the Unfettered One and the small animals, and making the intuitive leap in logic that Foul is symbolically raping the Wraiths, the Land, exactly as Covenant literally raped Lena, thus exponentially increasing his own sense of guilt. To Donaldson both incidents are extremely important. Covenant must acknowledge his own heart of darkness and the magnitude of the destruction it can cause early so that he can and will find options other than physical combat later when face-to-face with Foul.

Donaldson's juxtaposition of opposites is not just triggered by Covenant's encounter with the ur-vile wedge at the Celebration of Spring, but the ur-viles themselves are one part of a dialectic set up by Donaldson between the evil of the ur-viles and the attempted helpfulness of the Waynhim, who resemble ur-viles in appearance though they are a lighter grey color. The Waynhim maintain and supply the Waymeets for travelers in the Land. A wedge of Waynhim attacks Satansfist's army at the siege of Revelstone. A Waynhim *rhysh* aids Covenant twice in the 2nd "Chronicles." So Donaldson has created beings that are almost mirror images of each other where one group, the ur-viles, are evil, and the other, the Waynhim, are good.

In the 2nd "Chronicles" Donaldson furthers the ambiguity of good and evil surrounding the ur-viles when the dead Foamfollower presents Covenant with his gift of Vain, a being of perfection created by the ur-viles supposedly to atone for their service to Lord Foul. But the mystery of Vain's purpose is not revealed until the end. And when it is, our view of the enemy ur-vile race changes because without their creation, Vain, there would be no new Staff of Law for Linden to use to heal the Land. So ur-viles and Waynhim are the evil and good sides of the same coin, and ur-viles themselves can be both enemies and allies. In fact, ur-viles seem to be undergoing a change from evil to good. The dialectic is collapsing in on itself as it must to become the eye of the paradox.

The Cavewights are depicted as large, strong, stupid brutes. The only Cavewight that is named and given a role in the "Chronicles" is Drool Rockworm, who discovers the Staff of Law and from then on is used by Lord Foul to challenge the Lords. Drool's dialogue marks him as unsophisticated in thought and in language. He is obviously not intelligent enough to use the Staff without instruction from Lord Foul. Also, he is easily manipulated into abusing his power to show off by affecting the color of the moon. Drool illustrates the dialectic of power and helplessness as he is deformed and prematurely aged by his use of the Staff and Stone. Cavewights, in general, are fodder in Foul's armies.

Kresh are large and vicious wolf-like creatures who hunger for Ranyhyn flesh. They are especially dangerous because they run in packs. Nevertheless, they are beasts and have no weapons but their teeth and can be subdued by the Ramen using only rope. The Ramen use stealth, concealment in the grass, the *kresh's* own speed, and their ability to rise up quickly from the ground, cast the rope around the neck of the creature, and then pull or twist the rope to break the neck of the beast. However, like wild wolves, the *kresh* are fearful in appearance.

Donaldson does not illustrate many encounters between the peoples of the Land and *griffins*, but the flying, lion-like creatures can be especially dangerous because of their sharp talons and their ability to fly for short distances. On the Quest for the Staff of Law, Irin sacrifices herself to slay a *griffin* while on Korik's first mission to deal with marauders. Another *griffin*, ridden by an ur-vile loremaster, attacks the Company at Soaring Woodhelven. It takes the combined force of Foamfollower grabbing and crushing the bones of the *griffin* and Quaan beheading it to kill the beast, but not before it can claw the Giant's forehead open.

Two other evil creatures use the natural elements of cold and corrosive acid as their weapons. The Arghuleh, or ice-beasts, fight against Covenant and the Search and Hamako and the *rhysh* of the Waynhim. Normally, by their nature they would turn on each other if one were wounded, but because one Arghule has bargained with a *croyel* to unite the Arghuleh, they fight as a unit and aid each other if one is wounded. The Arghuleh are large creatures and as personifications of cold are the opposite of the *skest* of Sarangrave Flats, that are small, green, acid creatures that attack the Search. The multitude of *skest* might have overcome the Search were it not for the *sur-jheherrin*, descendants of the *jheherrin* redeemed by Foamfollower in the 1st "Chronicles," who volunteer to use their clay bodies to absorb the acid of the *skest*. Both the Arghuleh and the *skest* are defeated by their natural opposite: the ice creature

Arghule with the *croyel* by the heat of Hamako's fire; the vitriol of the *skest* by the mud essence of the *sur-jheherrin*. Opposites neutralize each other as they combine.

One final evil creature is not even given a name by Donaldson. During the battle at Dorieth Coriendor when the Raver Fleshharrower sends his Vortex of trepidation against those few of the Wayward and the Lords who have remained behind in the abandoned city, Hile Troy is attacked by bat/eagle-like birds. Even after Troy has killed one of these creatures, it can still harm him as its hot, corrosive blood splashes on his face and takes away his Land-born sight.

In general, Donaldson uses some stereotypical conventions in identifying his evil creatures. The ur-viles fight as a wedge of darkness that seems to absorb light much as Tolkien's Ungoliant can spew out darkness as a light bulb would disperse light. The Cavewights are dumb but strong. Others can use natural elements, like cold or acid, as their weapons. Lord Foul, on the other hand, coincides more with the Christian view of a great evil: one who is beautiful and majestic but corrupt, desiring all others to be miserable. And Foul is the more insidious evil because he attacks his victims' emotions, beliefs, and desires to do good, trying to turn anyone who opposes Despite against himself. But Donaldson also veers away from conventions of good and evil to magnify the fearsomeness and power of his evil creatures, and to reinforce the inevitable juxtaposition of the two in the eye of the paradox.

CHAPTER 6

A Farewell to Armaments

Ernest Hemingway's *A Farewell to Arms* (published in 1929) is just one of many modern novels that depict the horrors of war, the futility of what Donaldson calls the muscle solution to conflicts. As a conscientious objector during the Vietnam War, Donaldson has many reasons for speaking out against the use of power over others. He agrees with every modern writer who has vividly shown that war is hell. At first he seems to follow the Tolkien tradition of advocating that power corrupts. But in the end Donaldson changes the definition of power, from physical power over others to psychological power over ourselves: exercising our own free will, while acknowledging the necessity of the same freedom of choice for everyone else. He joins the debate of the Western canon to say that like the progression from Achilles to Socrates or Moses to Jesus, ultimate power is not over others but over self. However, Donaldson would also like us to say farewell to all weapons and forms of coercion. Throughout the "Chronicles," he reevaluates many kinds and uses of power.

As always, Donaldson presents both sides of the issue of power, how it can be used productively, how it can be used destructively, how the use of it can affect its user, how it can affect others. Probably the most common definition of power is the ability to force others to do something they would not choose to do. In this situation most of us would agree with Mhoram that "power is a dreadful thing."[1] The twentieth century especially became aware of how much power we could wield, and it added to our guilt over our heart of darkness. Just how many weapons of mass destruction do we need to possess in order to feel safe — enough to destroy the entire world ten times? One hundred times? Yet we are also aware that the power to split the atom, which gave us the atom bomb, also gave us the ability to make energy using atomic power. So power itself need not be evil if its use is beneficial to mankind. Or rather, the source of power is not necessarily evil, though its unbridled abuse may be. And the difference between constructive use and abuse is in us, our motivations, our passions for service and not domination. The ambiguities surrounding power are an excellent way for Donaldson to illustrate his eye of the paradox.

Each of the peoples of the Land utilizes power differently. The Bloodguard use no weapons, only physical strength, training, and intelligent fighting techniques honed by centuries of practice. Mostly, their battles are defensive because all their actions must support their Vow to protect the Lords. At one point Korik has to decide whether his primary duty is to ambush and kill some marauders or just escape from them. He is sworn to defend the Lords by his Vow, but the Lords also battle enemies such as these marauders on behalf of the peoples of the Land. So if Korik were to harass the Lords' enemies, even as a preemptive strike, he needs to determine that he has sufficient force to attack and destroy the enemy without wasting his own forces or risking his primary imperative to protect the Lords. If he is not sure of the outcome, he cannot take the risk, but at one point in *Lord Foul's Bane*, Korik does decide that the battle is worth the risk.

At first glance, it might seem that the Bloodguard's use of power is pure, an ideal to be emulated by others in the Land. And evaluated on a purely physical level, this belief is true. As Achilles was a great warrior for his extraordinary prowess in battle, so too are the Bloodguard. In fact, their motives for engaging in any violence or killing are also admirable: not deliberately to hurt or subjugate others, but to protect the Lords. Nevertheless, personal choice is not part of the formula of their service, so Donaldson has not set them up as an ideal. Yes, individually they adhere to the Vow, perhaps for ethical reasons, and perhaps from peer pressure not to embarrass their race. But they act instinctively and abrogate the responsibility of making moral decisions to the Lords. Also their extreme loyalty without question or doubt makes them either/or characters (either the Vow or corruption), which leaves them vulnerable to corruption. The Bloodguard believe that if they are not 100 percent successful and loyal, if they are flawed in any way, it is the same as if they were completely corrupt. They can offer only pure service or none at all. And the Bloodguard have begun to question the Lords' decisions: they feel collective guilt over obeying Kevin when he sent them away because that decision did not allow them the opportunity to fulfill their Vow of defending him and all the other Lords. However, Donaldson, using Covenant, makes the point that *even* flawed creatures can be effective/successful. In fact, Covenant's book *Or I Will Sell My Soul for Guilt* suggests that *only* flawed creatures can use power effectively. Therefore, though the Bloodguard, the *Haruchai*, appear to be ideally heroic, Donaldson believes that they lack important emotional elements — doubt and choice — to be able to find the eye of the paradox. Luckily, through their interactions with Covenant in the 2nd "Chronicles," other *Haruchai* learn the value of imperfection when Cail is able to resist the compulsion of the Clave because he has already been forced to acknowledge his susceptibility to the *merewives,* and he has also learned an important lesson from Brinn's combat with the *ak-Haru Kenaustin Ardenol*: that to win, one must sometimes fall first.

The Ramen are much like the *Haruchai* in that they rely on their own personal skill to protect the Ranyhyn and fight defensively only. They do use a weapon, the rope belt of a cord or headdress of a manethrall (Pietten, the *lillianrill* boy adopted by the Ramen, uses a spear). However, unlike the *Haruchai,* the Ramen make their own choices. They have taken no solemn Vow witnessed by Earthpower to protect the Ranyhyn. Manethrall Lithe is not bound to her role within the Ramen community but can choose to leave the plains of Ra to accompany the Company in seeking the Staff of Law because she has instincts that will help them find the way out of the catacombs of Mount Thunder if they are successful in their quest. Manethrall Rue (originally Gay) travels to Revelstone to warn the Lords when Fleshharrower's army is moving. So they can make choices even if those decisions require them to alter their life-purposes temporarily.

The other peoples of the Land, the *rhadhamaerl* and *lillianrill,* use mostly conventional weapons to protect their homes from attack or to serve the Land as members of the Wayward. When they serve with the Sword, their leaders make choices for their units, but individuals such as Irin can choose to sacrifice themselves or volunteer to be among those who buy more time for the rest of the army by staying behind in Doriendor Corishev. Some members of the communities know additional lore which can help them further serve the Land. For example, Trell knows how to bring the firestones to heat and light and how to reinforce a stone wall against attack because he is a gravelingas of the *rhadhamaerl.* As a hirebrand, Baradakas knows the woodlore of the *lillianrill.* In Revelstone the Lords always have the services of two Hearthralls of Lord's Keep, one a hirebrand and the other a gravelingas. After the Ritual of Desecration, these two different groups preserved and passed down the lore of stone or wood. The special Earthpower of stone or wood is called forth through words or chants of those skilled adepts.

From among the peoples of the *rhadhamaerl* and *lillianrill,* some individuals choose to study at the Loresraat to become Lords or Lorewardens to learn the words and songs of power. Not all those who try to master the lore of Kevin's 1st Ward remain to dedicate themselves to the land as Lords or teachers in the Loresraat. Atiaran attends the Loresraat but eventually chooses to return to Mithil Stonedown. Later, after her quest with Covenant, she decides to return to her studies. So no choice or decision is absolute and unchangeable. Some who study choose to dedicate their lives and understanding of lore to private projects and take the Rites of Unfettering and work in seclusion.

Several Unfettered Ones take a role in Covenant's story: one rescues the Wraiths at the Celebration of Spring; one heals Covenant of his physical wounds and madness after he has eaten the *amanibhavam* grass; another tries to use the *lormilliar* rod Triock brings to him to get a message to the Lords in Revelstone; and one lives above Glimmermere and helps sustain the Earthpower of the lake despite the proximity of the Banefire.

In the 2nd "Chronicles" the Graveler Sunder can still use *orcrest* and the eh-Brand Hollian uses her *lianar* rod, but their power is a corruption of the original *rhadhamaerl* and *lillianrill* lore because the Sunbane, not Earthpower, is the source of their power. They must cut themselves and use their own blood to summon this power. However, their ability to tap into the power of the Sunbane allows Sunder to learn quickly how to use Memla's *ruhk*.

The Lords' use of the lore learned from Kevin's Wards supports the declining world theory, that in a Golden Age of the past, there was more of both knowledge and power, but each has been diminished over time. Eventually, like Northrup Frye who advocates that the epic mode inevitably follows the ironic mode, Donaldson wants to bring about a new Golden Age, based on peace not power. But in the 1st "Chronicles," the Lords bewail the loss of Kevin's lore. The result is that the Lords never feel competent. Prothall offers to step down as High Lord before the Quest for the Staff of Law. Donaldson, however, is making the point that flawed beings are more effective than those who have not yet faced their inadequacies. Then they are making choices based on their passions and are proceeding not with an expectation of winning but because they cannot do otherwise. It isn't prowess that should win battles, but heart, determination, correct choices that are the criteria for success. Mhoram tells Amatin that they cannot take on blame for an undesirable outcome during the siege of Revelstone, only for the determination to do their very best, leaving no effort untried. They know that they don't have all the knowledge of Kevin's Wards, and they perceive that their power is less than that of the Old Lords, but they will still use what wisdom and power they do have to defend the Land. One of the lessons of this crisis of their lordship in *The Power That Preserves* is that each person must rely only on himself, despite his own clear awareness of his weaknesses. Mhoram had counted on Covenant to aid in the fight against Lord Foul, but then the light in the *krill* (which indicated that Covenant was back in the Land) went out and then turned the green of the Illearth Stone. So the ninety-year-old High Lord knows that he must fight the battle against Satansfist himself. But before he rides out to face the Giant Raver, he requires almost impossible tasks from each of the other Lords so that they also can learn to rely on themselves to accomplish heroic tasks without Mhoram, in case he should fall to Satansfist.

The power of the Lords is not limited to their knowledge of lore or control of wood or stone, but can be enhanced or focused through a conduit such as a staff. Each Lord carries a staff to focus his/her Lord's power. The hirebrand Baradakas gives Covenant a staff which functions the same way, despite the fact that Covenant is ignorant about how to call forth his power. The High Lord ordinarily wields the Staff of Law, originally created by Berek. Because it is most apt to the use of the Laws of Nature, it can most effectively call up Earthpower. However, the Staff of Law is lost by Kevin at the Ritual of Desecration and not regained until Prothall takes it away from Drool Rockworm. It passes to Elena, but when she dies at the hands of dead Kevin, whom she had resurrected, and Lord Foul calls her back from death in turn because she has broken the Law of Death when she uses the Power of Command, she must use the Staff for Foul's purposes. In dead Elena's hands, when she is under the compulsion of Foul's will, the Staff of Law can be manipulated to work against natural law and create and prolong an unnatural winter and even threaten the Colossus of the Fall. Lord Mhoram regains the Staff, but it breaks when he strikes Satansfist with it.

Since a Staff of Law is particularly adept for the use of Earthpower, one is necessary to heal the Land in the 2nd "Chronicles." Thus, Covenant asks the Search to take him to the One Tree so he can make a new Staff of Law (though he does not know how to create a new Staff of Law if a limb from the One Tree does not automatically function as one). When this part of his quest fails, he has to choose another goal, and he decides to shut down the Banefire. Through either fate or the choices of Foamfollower in giving Vain to Covenant and of the *Elohim* in assigning Findail as the Appointed to the Search, Linden is eventually able to create a new Staff of Law. She needs to combine the rigidity of Vain with the Earthpower incarnate of the *Elohim*, and to add her own health sense, healing ability, and love of the Land using the wild magic power of Covenant's ring. Once Linden has healed the Land, the First and Pitchwife take the new Staff of Law to Sunder and Hollian in Andelain to be used by new Lords.

Through their study of Kevin's 1st Ward, the Lords have mastered some of the old power. They can create and maintain a Word of Warning; they can also bend one so it does not break and set off an alarm. But when Birinair is caught in the web of a Word, the Lords do not know enough lore or have enough power to free him. Only Covenant's wild magic can break the Word and release the Hearthrall. When Covenant brings the *krill* to life, the Lords are ignorant of how to trigger its power until Mhoram's intuitive understanding of the secret to the Ritual of Desecration. Elena believes that she is making the right choice in using the Power of Command to bring Kevin Landwaster back from death to fight Lord Foul, but her decision is disastrous.

So lore as a source of power has its limitations, especially if one has not completely mastered it all.

Both the ur-viles and the Waynhim utilize a different kind of lore to enhance their individual power by uniting together. In a fighting wedge this unified power can boost the potency of the knife or scimitar wielded by the loremaster at the apex. The Waynhim can volunteer their own blood to augment the endurance and power of the recipient, either Covenant or Hamako. The use of this lore requires certain ritual chants.

The inhabitants of the Land believe that there is power in simple words, songs, chants, and tales. Specific words seem to hold special power. The Unfettered One in Andelain knows many of the Seven potent Words and utters them to release the Wraiths: "*Melenkurion abatha! Binas mill Banas Nimoram khabaal! Melenkurion abatha! Abatha Nimoram!*"[2] The Lords Hyrim and Shetra try to voice words of power near the lake of acid in Sarangrave Flat but cannot make themselves heard above the screaming of the Lurker, so there are limitations to words as power. Other Lords use words like "*Melenkurion Abatha!*" as exclamations. Foamfollower utilizes the song of the Unhomed to propel his boat upstream toward Revelstone. He claims that the story of Bahgoon the Unbearable and Thelma Twofist stopped a war because it took three days to tell. Atiaran sings the song and tells the tale of Berek Halfhand for Mithil Stonedown, and the Lords and inhabitants of the Keep sing a hymn about Kevin's Seven Wards as part of their Vespers ceremony, but the purpose of these songs is to communicate information and reinforce the sense of community, not to call forth power. Yet the result of the telling of tales is often respite for weary soldiers or solace for those who grieve. After the Search escapes *Bhrathairealm*, members of the crew exchange many tales that honor the memory of Hergrom and Ceer, the *Haruchai* who died there. So these words, songs, tales can have a psychological power for good, also.

Beyond the control of beings using just lore, songs, tales, or even the Staff of Law are natural laws such as the Law of Death and the Law of Life. Elena is able to break the Law of Death but only by using Kevin's 7th Ward, the Power of Command. Hile Troy as Caer-Caveral, the Forestal of Andelain, tells Sunder how to break the Law of Life to bring Hollian back to life and also to free Covenant to fulfill his fated purpose. Just as the natural laws of Death and Life can be overridden, in the 2nd "Chronicles" Lord Foul has discovered how to distort the natural cycles of growth, decay, rain, and drought through the Sunbane. Foul tries to break the Arch of Time, but so far the Law of Time has held. So, to Donaldson, even power that follows the laws of nature is not absolute or incorruptible.

On the Macrocosm level, if Donaldson wants to explore the fight against all potential power, even that over which we have no control now (or think we do not) — like life, death, and time — he needs even these extremes. After all, our world knows that human battles (with tanks, aircraft, bombs, and soldiers) and our own corruption and destruction of our world (through pollution, global warming, etc.) are not the only dangers we need to feel competent to overcome if we are to regain our epic vision. We need to predict, prepare for, redirect the danger of (if possible), lessen the intensity of, or destroy the danger from natural phenomena such as drought, hurricanes/tornadoes, tsunamis, volcanoes, earthquakes, fires, floods, land or rock slides. In our modern sense of powerlessness over global problems, we forget that we can already predict the path of storms, and receive early warning of a hurricane, a tsunami, or a volcano. We can build to withstand earthquake or fire damage. We are becoming more powerful over our own environment, not less (the classic Northrup Frye definition of the epic mode). The battles we have yet to focus our attention on are the inner struggles, over our own careless exploitation of our resources, over our apathy, as well as over our own destructive emotions of anger, prejudice, guilt, and despair.

The Lords themselves, unknowingly, have restricted their own abilities to understand the power in Kevin's seven Wards, but in a way Donaldson wants us to restrict our own use of power. After the Ritual of Desecration, to ensure that no one would ever fall victim to the destructive emotions of war, all the people of the Land agree to take the Oath of Peace. It requires that they use the minimum amount of force to keep others from harming those under their protection or the Earth itself. The need to kill is not mandatory if one can merely prevent harm by maiming, wounding, or hurting the enemy.

The either/or stance of the Land's inhabitants about emotional involvement limits their ability to use effectively all power available to them, through lore or prowess. Mhoram finally comprehends the paradox when he realizes that his knowledge of how to call up the Ritual of Desecration also gives him the power to use the *krill* and that he doesn't need to be despairing to access the power, but the pure passions he brings to his battle with Satansfist will save him from the despair that would turn such power to destructive ends. Foamfollower had earlier predicted this moment. He knew Mhoram would never fall prey to despair. Because of his Oath of Peace, Mhoram does not become what he hates nor let the emotions of anger or fear hold sway and cause him to murder. His choice of service to the Land gives him the power to resist. Yet at the end of the siege, Mhoram chooses to discard the *krill* at the bottom of Glimmermere beyond the reach of future Lords, who perhaps would not understand the paradox of power as he had. Mhoram, at the end of *The Power That Preserves*, explains to the people gathered with him before Glimmermere that his interaction with Thomas Covenant taught him not to rely too heavily on the Wards of Lord Kevin. All present know how disastrous Elena's use of the Power of Command was. She had not earned the wisdom of how to choose her commands more astutely since there were still four undiscovered wards of lore that she had not mastered. And Mhoram knows the *krill* can be used without destructive despair to bring it to life, but he cannot guarantee future Lords will also grasp the paradox. So Mhoram chooses the restraint implied in the Oath of Peace over superior power and he discards the *krill* to save future Lords from the temptation of its misuse. Of course, this action effectively prohibits other Lords from testing their own resolve, so Mhoram has not granted to them the freedom of choice. Donaldson does not want us to abandon completely the power we've learned over the ages and go back to the era of swords and bows and arrows because we are too technologically powerful now; instead, he wants us to focus always on how we use our power and whether it enhances or lessens our chances for personal and ultimate peace.

Donaldson makes it clear that Covenant's white gold power is all powerful but also unpredictable. At first Covenant does not know how to call forth the power of his ring, and then in the 2nd "Chronicles" when he wants to use power to aid the Land, the venom in him exacerbates his wild magic power to a point beyond Covenant's control, and any use of wild magic could be increased by the venom enough to bring down the Arch of Time. Findail explains why Lord Foul wants to introduce and continually enhance the venom in Covenant. He is boosting Covenant's power and lessening his control over the wild magic with each new infusion of venom because he wants Covenant to break the Arch of Time. Findail calls this power without control "the helplessness of power,"[3] completing the paradox of power. In Donaldson's eye of the paradox, power in the extreme equals powerlessness. Like a circle which ends where it begins, the juxtaposition of power and its opposite become the same thing. Findail knows that if the venom robs Covenant of his control over the passions that trigger the wild magic power, he is helpless to direct the power and could inadvertently do more harm than good. Power must be linked to conscious moral choice. Uncontrollable power is not beneficial but potentially ruinous. Donaldson is thus making a strong connection between the motivation behind the use of power and its effect. The use of absolute power motivated by despair is catastrophic, as was Kevin's invocation of the Ritual of Desecration. Driven by the right motive, by pure passions of the desire to aid, not the desire to control, power can be good. But used to control others and take away their freedom of choice, power is wrong and does corrupt the user. Therefore, truly and especially because Covenant does not yet have control over his potential for despair, his wild magic could "save or damn the earth."[4] This particular power, the wild magic, is the epitome of Donaldson's eye of the paradox. As Donaldson says, knowledge must be earned, and power must also be controlled by individual will. The motivation for using power will determine if it is productive or destructive. And the one who possesses ultimate power, like Covenant's white gold wild magic ring, has the potential for both, and, therefore, he should not call on that power before he has found the eye of his paradox.

Some power utilized by the peoples of the Land or by Covenant was designed as defensive or protective (a Word of Warning, a Forbidding) or to heal the natural hurts to which the earth is subject (*lillianrill* or *rhadhamaerl* lore). The self-avowed protectors of the Land use combative power and weapons to defend against the aggressive tactics of those who would impose their own will on others. Foul's use of power is designed to subjugate others in body and in spirit. His minions, ur-viles and Cavewights, use lore and weapons in their battles against the Lords. But his Ravers have access to more potent powers.

Of course, the ultimate power of the Ravers is their ability to take possession of the will of another, thus robbing the possessed person of any volition or choice. Donaldson admits that possession is the definitive crime against the necessity of freedom. However, he also paradoxically admits that Linden's use of her health sense to free Covenant from the consummate silence and darkness imposed on him by the *Elohim* and her ability to reach into his mind to persuade him to pull back his wild magic power before he brings down the Arch of Time at the Island of the One Tree are productive uses of possession. So, once again, the eye of the paradox forces us to acknowledge the potential co-existence of good and evil in everything, based on use.

On the other hand, the Illearth Stone is a weapon of evil that no one in the Land has yet demonstrated can be used for good. In this characteristic it resembles Tolkien's One Ring, which can be claimed by a wise ruler and even used for benevolent purposes at first, but will eventually corrupt him or her into becoming another Dark Lord, thus exemplifying that power corrupts. Each Giant Raver is given a small portion of the Stone to accomplish his dark purposes. Using his fragment of the Illearth Stone, Fleshharrower creates a Vortex of Trepidation to use against the Wayward at Doriendor Corishev, and Satansfist prepares another one to send against Revelstone. This powerful weapon does more than just physically destroy Foul's enemies; it is designed to make them afraid and to rob the peoples of the Land of courage, of belief in their own abilities. Some of this fear is generated by the suspense of watching the power grow, not knowing what harm it can do, so it reflects a fear of the unknown. But fear also seems to descend with the wind itself, making the Vortex a psychological weapon as well as a physical one. When one fragment of the Illearth Stone is recovered by the Bloodguard, Korik, Sill, and Doar, their arrogance makes them believe they can turn its power against

Corruption/Lord Foul, but they are themselves defeated and ensnared in the attempt, which leads to the abandonment of the Vow by all the Bloodguard. Donaldson likens the Illearth Stone to the knowledge learned by eating the forbidden fruit from the Tree of Life in the Garden of Eden. Covenant's wild magic power can destroy the Illearth Stone, though the white gold is not sufficient to destroy or even diminish Foul without the laughter of Foamfollower and the dead Lords. So Covenant's wild magic power is effective against other weapons but not against psychological attack; to combat something like despair, one needs free choice.

The ultimate destructive phenomenon, the Ritual of Desecration, can be likened in our world to a nuclear explosion or a chemical or biological weapon that can make of the earth a wasteland for countless years. Kevin believed that a weapon that would destroy the earth would also destroy evil, but this idea shows only that he did not understand the true nature of evil. To Donaldson, a malicious tyrant can be destroyed by a weapon, but evil itself will always come back because it is not a person but the abstract concept of imposing one's will on another and/or stripping others of volition or choice. Thus, definitive power in the "Chronicles" is not a powerful destructive weapon or lore or the ability to harness the power of the Earth itself. Power is tied to the individual ["*You* are the white gold"[5]] and based on his personal choices.

Linden discovers the true nature of power when she is possessed by the Raver — her Power "came from no external source, but only from her own intense self."[6] Covenant has often lectured her on the "necessity of freedom" and how one's own power or self can be voluntarily given up but not taken away. Thus, Lord Foul keeps trying to compel Covenant to hand over his white gold ring of his own free will. Covenant explains to Linden that anyone compelled to do that which he would not choose becomes merely a tool. And a tool is only as skilled or powerful as its user; therefore, Lord Foul could not use Covenant's enforced might to accomplish anything Foul could not do on his own. Lord Foul cannot utilize the wild magic to destroy the Arch of Time unless Covenant chooses to give his ring over to him. Nor can the Raver maintain possession of Linden when she chooses to expel him. She knows that possession is not inevitable. Hollinscrave is able to preserve his essence and still contain the Raver. The *Haruchai* cannot be possessed. But Giants and *Haruchai* are more confident than Linden. They trust their power and autonomy in ways Linden is still learning. And Linden doubts her own ability to make choices since she is still tempted by Covenant's power. So she cannot immediately repel the Raver who takes possession of her, but she believes that she can and learns how to do so. The necessity of freedom protects Linden within herself.

While the importance of finding the eye of the paradox is one of Stephen Donaldson's most important epiphanies in the 1st "Chronicles" and continues to be a truism that he wants us to accept, in the 2nd "Chronicles" Covenant and Linden begin discussing the necessity of freedom from the very start of their sojourn in the Land. Because Covenant voluntarily steps into the fire near Haven's Farm, the question is raised as to whether he is free to make his own choices on this trip through the Land or if he has already become a tool of Lord Foul. Foul, of course, wants Covenant to believe that he loses his power to choose when he voluntarily sacrifices himself for Joan. Lord Foul doesn't acknowledge that no one choice is final; at any time Covenant can make a different decision. So he is not Lord Foul's tool. And therefore he still maintains his freedom of choice.

Through his analysis of the significant issue of the necessity of freedom, Donaldson contributes to the predestination vs. free will debate which has us so conflicted because, as usual, we are looking for an either/or explanation and refusing to accept the both/and eye of the paradox. Donaldson places his Creator outside the Land, unable to affect changes without destroying the Arch of Time that keeps Lord Foul imprisoned, but Donaldson also makes it clear that the Creator would not intervene even given the opportunity. "The Creator doesn't manipulate. He just chooses and then takes his chances."[7] The Creator is not bereft of choice and can decide whom from Covenant's "real" world to place in a position to be summoned to the Land. The Creator, the old beggar in the ocher robe, tests both Covenant and Linden to determine their character strengths and weaknesses (since both will be crucial). But, as he explains to Covenant at the end of *The Power That Preserves* while Covenant is being transported back to his "real" world, he chooses Covenant but cannot help him further because Covenant can only oppose Lord Foul if he is free of all compulsion. That freedom for personal choice is the true hope of the Land.

Covenant later explains the necessity of freedom to Linden. If Foul or one of his Ravers coerces someone to do something against his will, the outcome cannot be greater than Foul is able to accomplish on his own. A tool can only perform what the craftsman is capable of himself. And Lord Foul by himself cannot break the Arch of Time. Therefore, he cannot force Covenant to destroy time. He must allow Covenant the freedom to choose and hope Covenant's choices will accomplish his goals. For that reason Foul is always belittling Covenant, tearing down his confidence and trying to fill him with despair and self-hatred, so he will want to use his power in a destructive way. The same restriction applies to the Creator. He is not able to force his preferred choices on Covenant because the Creator cannot exceed his own limitations. But he is willing to trust in Covenant's basic goodness. Here is the eye of the paradox in the free will vs. predestination dialectic: one can predict the possible choices and wisdom of individuals, but those individuals must make their own personal choices concerning how to act.

The Creator chooses Covenant in part because of his ironic world view. Covenant's leprosy and the way it changes his personality gives him the possibility of uniting the ironic and heroic world views in a way that a purely "good" person could not have done. No one from the Land can because they all embrace the heroic world view and have no need to embrace the paradox. Donaldson is thus acknowledging that far from limiting our potential, our own awareness of our heart of darkness is necessary for our ability to achieve our ultimate power and epic vision. The Creator, in making Covenant his choice, needs someone with a combination of weaknesses, needs, and stubborn determination, but also realizes that making that choice is all he can do; after that, Covenant's personal choices determine the failure or success of his quests. Through the choices Covenant makes with his power, he can regain an epic vision and reevaluate the concept of power. His final choice of self-sacrifice rather than battle is like Foamfollower's decision to endure the excruciating pain of Hotash Slay to help Covenant achieve his mission to confront Foul in the 1st "Chronicles," allowing him to purify himself. At the end of the 2nd "Chronicles" Linden tells Dr. Berenford that Covenant found a way to purify himself the way Foamfollower had in the *caamora* of Hotash Slay. Again his ability to encompass both innocence and experience is an example of the eye of the paradox.

Linden, also, is chosen for her need to heal and to be healed. Her stubborn determination to save the life of the old beggar who seems to have just suffered a heart attack, despite his unresponsiveness, despite the putrid smell of his mouth, despite her own failing strength, proves to him that she "'will not fail, however he may assail you. There is also love in the world.'"[8] Linden is needed for her health sense, her ability to see the Land as all its inhabitants once had, but which also leaves her open to the painful perception of evil in Gibbon Raver. She is needed for her conflicting helplessness, guilt, and anger over the death of her parents as well as her knowledge of and dedication to healing. She needs to resolve the eye of the paradox of her revulsion against possession, her hunger for the power of Covenant's while gold ring, and her ability to possess Covenant completely, which she can't do until she completely understands the necessity of freedom for everyone and lets Covenant make his own decision to hand over his ring to Lord Foul.

The necessity for the respect of allowing each individual the freedom to make his own choices is an essential component of the American mind-set. One person, one vote. The sanctity of the balloting booth and the freedom everyone has to express differing opinions or make vastly different personal choices is a democratic ideal. We may not have achieved it perfectly in our real world which still includes prejudices and attempts to impose our own view of what is crucial on the rest of the world. But more than in any other culture, our melting pot of differences is fostering more tolerance and acceptance of diversity. As important as is the combining of dialectics in the eye of the paradox, acknowledging the necessity of freedom of choice for everyone, to Donaldson, is a vital step in self-actualization or becoming whole. One is an intellectual awareness, an epiphany or insight that resolves conflicts between seeming opposites by accepting both. The other is the assumption of personal responsibility, the acceptance of the consequences of our choices freely made, of respect and compassion enough for others to allow them the same freedom.

Saltheart Foamfollower is the first to respect Covenant's need for choices. When the Giant gives him some *clingor*, Covenant has the choice to hide his talisman of wild magic to avoid being expected to take on responsibility for the Land as Berek had or to reveal his potential power and admit his inability to use it to the Lords. At the time the choice for Covenant is to participate in his "dream" and go mad or not participate and possibly still go mad. Ultimately, modern man faces the same choice with each new crisis in the world; do we get involved, possibly at great cost in money and lives, or do we isolate ourselves from the problems of the rest of the world? Donaldson implies that apathy is a horrible crime but that each individual must make up his own mind for involvement. Covenant faces this decision after the battle of Soaring Woodhelven. He loses the reality of his disease and how it informs his outlook, to the healing of the hurtloam Lena spread on his hands that allows him to feel again. He cannot hide his physical similarity to Berek and has voluntarily admitted his possession of the white gold ring to the Lords. Every time he tries to define his own identity, the Land contrives to challenge him. He does not want to believe in the reality of the Land but actively fights the ur-viles to save the Wraiths at the Celebration of Spring and fights the Cavewights who attack the Lords. He believes that he is participating in the Lords' quest for the Staff of Law to escape the madness with which his newfound health sense threatens him. But he keeps getting drawn into the expectations of the inhabitants of the Land because of his talisman of power. And to believe he is/can be a hero is madness as well (in his modern ironic view). Everything that happens to him pushes him to decide the either/or question of whether the Land is real or not, or to find another way to resolve that paradox.

Donaldson's emphasis on the connection of personal power and the necessity for the freedom of choice is similar to the teachings of Viktor Frankl in his book *Man's Search for Meaning* (first published in English in 1959).

Frankl, a survivor of several Nazi concentration camps, including Auschwitz, advocates that circumstances do not control us but that our own desire for meaning affects how we react to environmental situations.

Donaldson creates for Covenant the same kind of powerlessness over his own suffering or that of others that a prisoner of war would be subject to in order to create an extreme test of Covenant's belief in his ultimate freedom and responsibility to choose his own reactions to horrific circumstances such as those which honed Frankl's ultimate belief: our circumstances may be pre-destined or determined by the will of someone else, but only we ourselves can choose how we will react to those circumstances, what meaning we will find for our own lives through our freedom to choose. Frankl contradicts the early twentieth century belief that stimulus must always produce an instinctive response. "Man is *not* fully conditioned and determined but rather deter-mines himself whether he gives in to conditions or stands up to them. In other words, man is ultimately self-determining. Man does not simply exist but always decides what his existence will be, what he will become in the next moment."[9] Frankl understood Donaldson's eye of the paradox: "Frankl knew well through his experience in the Nazi concentration camps the meaning of unavoidable suffering. He also knew the very darkest of human behavior and the brightest light of human possibility — at the same time. He carried the awareness of both potentialities, and this awareness deepened his humanity and created in him a deep and abiding faith."[10]

From Frankl's awareness of good and evil came his great warning: "Since Auschwitz we know what man is capable of. And since Hiroshima we know what is at stake."[11] In linking Auschwitz and Hiroshima, he is also acknowl-edging that the potential for evil exists everywhere, in anyone, even in the "good guys." The freedom to choose is ours. "'Between stimulus and response, there is a space. In that space lies our freedom and our power to choose our response. In our response lies our growth and our happiness.'"[12] The respon-sibility to choose is also ours. What we become is in our own power, notwith-standing environmental factors or conditions.

> In the concentration camps, for example, in this living laboratory and on this testing ground, we watched and witnessed some of our comrades behave like swine while others behaved like saints. Man has both potentialities within him-self; which one is actualized depends on decisions but not on conditions.[13]

The understanding that choice is still within our power no matter what the circumstances provides the bridge for us to find our way back from our ironic world view (of feeling as if we have no control over our environment, our living conditions) to the epic vision. Covenant eventually accepts his life — all of it, the "real" world and the Land. He is aware of his character traits that make him feel ineffective, powerless, alienated. But he also knows his loves and hopes, his aspirations and dreams to be more heroic. Personal choice is our way out of the collective neurosis we feel within the modern day existential vacuum. The twentieth century is well acquainted with the existential vacuum. Frankl says we become lost to purpose when we lose our trust in our instincts and forget our ability and responsibility to make choices. Furthermore, we no longer allow institutions such as religion or government or even culturally accepted traditions to make our choices for us. Within the necessity for freedom of choice lies Donaldson's answer to the existentialists who argue that predestination cannot exist if there is no Supreme Being to form the overarching plan. If they are right, then there is only choice and man's own personally developed morality. But if they are wrong and there is a plan, it can be achieved only through individual choices. Based on Donaldson's eye-of-the-paradox belief, both predestination and free will must coexist. So choice based on ethical standards still falls on the individual to determine how to fight the evil without and within. "The existential vacuum which is the mass neurosis of the present time can be described as a private and personal form of nihilism; for nihilism can be defined as the contention that being has no meaning."[14] This brick wall of nothingness, the belief in the meaninglessness of individual human lives and the fear that our choices lack meaning, has stopped any forward movement for modern literature.

Donaldson's focus on personal choice supports Frankl's idea that man must create his own meaning and not expect it to be handed to him as a doctrine. Like all great thinkers, Viktor Frankl illuminates truth by turning the spotlight around to ask a creative question: "Ultimately, man should not ask what the meaning of his life is, but rather he must recognize that it is *he* who is asked"[15] How every man accepts the responsibility for his own life, purpose, and happiness defines that man. What kind of world we inherit, what conditions exist today, we may not be responsible for, and yet we have a responsibility to the future to better that world, those conditions. Frankl turns our expectations around and insists that we should not ask what we want or can expect from life but what life wants or expects from us. Again this realization on our part is the bridge from the ironic world view to the heroic, this shift in emphasis from personal desires or needs to responsibilities that affect the whole world.

This attitudinal shift leads not just to self-actualization or understanding of self, but rather to self-transcendence, and thus back to Donaldson's stated purpose in *Epic Fantasy*: "What I want to do is to bring the epic back into contact with the real world. Putting it another way, I want to reclaim the epic vision as part of our sense of who we are, as part of what it means to be human."[16] The responsibility of making ethical choices is part of the epic vision. Frankl claims self-actualization should be our ultimate goal, but it is impossible to achieve by trying to achieve it. It comes only when we serve a cause or purpose greater than ourselves. The people of the Land teach Covenant to forget his self-pity, despair, and anger in the greater goal of saving the Land. This kind of personal and societal transcendence is Donaldson's ultimate goal as well as reintroducing epic vision. Writers of epics almost inevitably illustrate how humans can transcend their limitations as they accomplish seemingly impossible tasks.

Donaldson avows that such personal choices cannot involve limiting the choices of others or the use of the power of coercion. And any means — gun-to-the-head, war, threat of total annihilation (nuclear, chemical, biological) — that does not allow the freedom of choice to others is wrong. Only when we can control ourselves enough to respect the choices of others can we become our Ideal Self, as the Renaissance Christian Humanist would want us to, or transcend our limitations. Stephen R. Covey, author of *Seven Habits for Highly Successful People*, states:

> I have found in my teaching that the single most exhilarating, thrilling, and motivating idea that people have ever really seriously contemplated is the idea of the power of choice — the idea that the best way to predict their future is to create it ... [and that] almost always the purposes and values they come up with are transcendent — that is, they deal with meaning that is larger than their own life, one that truly adds value and contributes to other people's lives.[17]

Viktor Frankl was this kind of person in the Auschwitz ... concentration camp.

In neither of the first two "Chronicles" can Covenant save the Land. His power can make Foul visible and can destroy the Illearth Stone, but he needs Foamfollower and the dead Lords to laugh to diminish Foul. He can absorb the pain of the wild magic Foul hurls at the Arch of Time, but he cannot heal the Land; Linden must use her special skill, her ability to feel, her willingness to accept the pain of the Sunbane, to restore health to the Land. Covenant's choices involve only himself, what he can stand, what he is willing to sacrifice, how he controls his own actions and emotions. And they stem from his moral convictions. He will destroy weapons but not beings, even Lord Foul, the ultimate evil character. So Donaldson is saying that no hero, not even an epic hero, can be held responsible for the fate of the world, only for his own individual choices, thus reinforcing the modern belief that we must all work together to solve the world's problems. Covenant creates his own purpose, his individual weird or wyrd, but it is his imaginative faculty, his ability to accept and welcome fantasy, that makes his choices redemptive. And as the epitome of the modern, ironic, reluctant hero admits to the necessity of imagination, fantasy, and the epic vision, there is hope that the modern age can also transcend the limitations it has taken upon itself, and Donaldson can then claim "to that extent I've succeeded in making epic fantasy relevant to modern literature, to contemporary perceptions of what it means to be human."[18]

Through the first two "Chronicles of Thomas Covenant, the Unbeliever," Stephen R. Donaldson has explored many forms and uses/abuses of power. But in the end, he succeeds in turning our attention away from the question of power to the issue of responsibility. As he explores what it means to be human, he repudiates all forms of coercion and manipulation of the will of others, and he focuses on personal choices and responsibility to determine meaning, as did Viktor Frankl. And he would have us say farewell to all forms of power — all weapons, propaganda, sanctions — to allow each individual to find his own purpose or meaning, his own personal power. In this way we embrace the eye of the paradox of power.

The Time "Machine": Speculations on Time and Space Travel in the "Last Chronicles"

H.G. Wells's *The Time Machine* (published in 1895) analyzes one of science fiction literature's favorite topics — the question of whether or how man can control time. The scientist, called the Time Traveler by Wells, uses his machine to travel into the future to A.D. 802,701, encountering the Eloi and Morlock societies, allowing Wells to discuss his supposedly utopian and dystopian societies. A similar "machine" is used in Robert Zemeckis's film *Back to the Future*: Marty McFly borrows Doc Brown's DeLorean to travel back in time to save Doc Brown from death. The question raised in the film is whether one can change the present by changing the past, and, if so, would the change be for the worse or for the better? In James Cameron's *Terminator* movie, the Terminator deliberately travels to the past in order to prevent John Connor from being born to lead the opposition to the machines in the future, and Kyle Reese follows to prevent any change to history and, in fact, is thereby instrumental in bringing it about.

Stephen R. Donaldson may not have been influenced by any of the science fiction or fantasy works referred to herein, but clearly he is interested in the question of time and is using the "Last Chronicles of Thomas Covenant" to explore time and space travel, and in doing so is uniting the science fiction and fantasy genres.

When Tolkien articulated our innate desires to explore time and space as well as to communicate with the "other" as the two primary desires for fantasy literature, he could have been speaking for science fiction as well. But until Donaldson's "Chronicles" there has been a fairly clear distinction between the way science fiction works and the way fantasy explores such themes. Perhaps Piers Anthony, by deliberately including though separating both genres in his *Split Infinity* series, best contrasts the differences between the kinds of worlds found in science fiction and fantasy. The world of Proton — the science fiction world of robots, futuristic cities, and electronic games — is parallel in almost every way to its alternate universe of Phaze — the fantasy world of unicorns, werewolves, and magic. The protagonist Stile can travel freely between the worlds through a translucent curtain and interacts with both the shapely robot Sheen in Proton and the unicorn who can transform herself into a butterfly as well as into a girl, Neysa, in Phaze. The rich citizens who hold political and financial power in Proton are the same ones who use magic to maintain their power in the castles of Phaze. One world uses technology; the other, magic. One is often set in the future or on a galaxy far away and uses spacecraft and advanced weaponry; the other is typically set in more primitive places and times where swords or bows and arrows are the weapons of choice and horseback is the fastest means of travel. As a result, time travel or unusually rapid movement across distance lends itself to the world of science fiction easier than it does to fantasy literature. However, Donaldson includes both these imaginative methods of travel especially in his "Last Chronicles." Donaldson's eye of the paradox solution blurs the distinction between science fiction and fantasy. Just as he has already integrated the themes of modern literature — the role of the artist, the power of memory, the destructive power of war — in his "Covenant" series, he now addresses one of science fiction's major themes — time and space travel — in his fantasy series. In fact, he has already begun the both/and integration of these themes in earlier "Chronicles."

Donaldson combines the genres of science fiction and fantasy in the kinds of characters he introduces. As science fiction writing explores the question of what it means to be human, it often contrasts man with androids or other mechanical beings or with extraterrestrials. Donaldson has already subtly used the contrast between biologically-born and technologically-made creatures in his "Chronicles" in his entirely new species, the ur-viles and Waynhim, who were manufactured beings created by the Demondim, who in turn had been created by the living Viles. Covenant also interacts with the *jheherrin*, Lord Foul's discarded imperfectly-made creatures, who were eventually able, once Saltheart Foamfollower redeemed them, to produce *sur-jheherrin* by birth. The ur-viles and Waynhim, creatures reliant on lore for their power, also share a common purpose as their weird. Since they operate in concert in a wedge, not individually, they sometimes function like the Borg who act with one mind in many *Star Trek: the Next Generation* episodes ("I Borg," "The Best of Both Worlds," and "Q Who?") and one *Star Trek* movie *First Contact*. Similarly, the Hive/Buggers all take direction from the Hive Queen in Orson Scott Card's *Ender's Game*. These non-individualized, automaton science fiction characters are portrayed negatively. Card, however, provides more ambiguity about the "enemy"; Ender defeats the Buggers, but then he aids in the Hive Queen's search for a new world. In his typical both/and fashion, Donaldson also blurs the moral distinctions between ur-viles, who are seen as evil in the 1st "Chronicles," and the Waynhim, who act in defense of the Land. In later "Chronicles" ur-viles can be helpful, producing Vain in the 2nd "Chronicles" and defending Linden in the "Last Chronicles."

Donaldson also contrasts man with more typical fantasy characters: Giants, griffins, ogre-like Cavewights, and the semi-magical horses — the Ranyhyn. In the fantasy genre, the question of what it means to be human often involves the contrast between man and animal, rather than man and mechanical being or alien species. Donaldson expands the contrast to immortal *Elohim*, dysfunctional Bhrathair, superhuman *Haruchai*, as well as tree- and stone- and horse-loving societies of men. Donaldson always prefers the both/and to the either/or approach.

In addition to his expansion of fantasy characters to include manufactured beings, Donaldson in his "Last Chronicles" is exploring the theme of time using traditional fantasy techniques and also mixing in time travel more easily depicted as a theme in science fiction. As he analyzes many aspects of time, he is, in effect, uniting the science fiction and fantasy genres, which is in keeping with his eye of the paradox solution and the integration of modern literary styles and attitudes within his fantasy plot. Science fiction tries to provide scientific explanations for futuristic capabilities which our present science cannot explain, such as going faster than the speed of light (warp speed), traveling instantaneously across vast space (through worm holes) or traveling back in time (through a time portal). Fantasy doesn't require the scientific explanation that science fiction writers try to provide, so more can be done as long as the "rules" remain logical in the subcreated world. Donaldson explains time travel in more than one way, four so far, as he analyzes the question of whether it is possible to go back in time and how such travel might impact the present and the future. The goal of "good" in Donaldson's stories is to preserve the time line without change as the resulting chaos and the possible breaking of the Arch of Time would eviscerate the universe of the Land. However, since Donaldson has already broken the Law of Death and the Law of Life in the first two "Chronicles," as he explores the Law of Time in the "Last Chronicles," it may prove equally vulnerable. And, in fact, just traveling back in time is already a violation, though not serious enough to destroy the Arch of Time.

To discuss any view of time, it is important first to dispel the most common misconception about time: that time is the 4th dimension. It is not. The best way to refute this concept is by analogy. In Edwin Abbot's book *Flatland*, he portrays the world from the perspective of a 2D man named Mr.

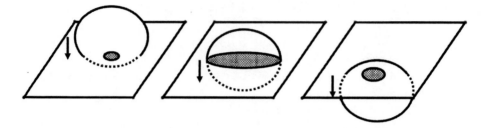

Figure 7. Lord Sphere passing through Flatland through time.

Square from a world in which all people are 2D geometric shapes. The only way Mr. Square can perceive a spherical ball that might pass through the world of Flatland is as a point which grows over time to a small circle, then larger and larger circles until it reaches a circle the size of the circumference of the ball, and then smaller and smaller circles until it is just a dot, and then it disappears from Flatland altogether. Though the size and area of Mr. Square remain constant, the size and shape of the new being, Lord Sphere, can be measured in the 2D world only by adding the areas of each successive circle together over time. Therefore, the whole being of a 3D Lord Sphere can only be measured using time in Flatland. Similarly in a 1D Lineworld, Mr. 2-inch-Square himself cannot be perceived by a Ms. Line, except as a series of 2-inch lines over time, and a Mrs. 2-inch-in-diameter-Circle would be perceived as a point, then lines growing larger until one is 2 inches long and then getting smaller until it is just a point, and then it disappears. The area or mass of Mr. 2-inch-Square or Mrs. 2-inch-Circle would be the sum of all the 1D lines. Ms. Line would perceive the 2nd dimension as time. However, even those in Flatland know that time is not the 2nd dimension. We also know that time is not the 3rd dimension as Mr. Square might suppose because in our 3D world we can perceive "up" and "down" as the physical 3rd dimension, and we can perceive a sphere all at once.

To understand a 4th physical dimension from the perspective of our 3D world, a balloon can illustrate how we can measure the area or mass of a 4D object but only over time. A scientist blows up the balloon and then lets it go. To our perspective it flies around as the air escapes out of it and eventually falls to the ground. Now, if instead of just air, there is some solid material, some mass in the balloon, the scientist could measure the area of this solid material at every point in time from the time he begins to blow up the balloon to the moment it is out of air/matter when it has fallen to the ground. Adding up the 3D areas of the balloon over time could give him what is invisible in our 3D world, the mass of a solid 4D wormlike form that begins small and reaches its biggest spherical shape when he has blown up the balloon and then tapers off in smaller and smaller spheres until the balloon collapses upon itself. We can only imagine a 4D object by using time, as Mr. Square needed the passage of time to understand the 3rd dimension. Therefore, time is not the 4th dimension, but rather time is needed to imagine the next higher physical dimension from that which the senses can perceive.

Time is, therefore, a phenomenon different from the physical dimensions as we know them. Donaldson does not describe time travel in the "Last Chronicles" as the ability to travel along some higher physical dimension called time the way we can navigate our 3D world using our feet or a car or an airplane or any "machine," nor does he suggest we can navigate time the way we can navigate space, by choosing to go right and then left, then up or down, possibly even retracing our own steps. We cannot move sequentially backward on the time line. We cannot run time backward using the Rewind button of a DVR, and though Frank Corasi's film *Click* explored the potential for fast-forwarding or slowing down our lives, this kind of manipulation of time is still impossible in the real world. Nevertheless, Donaldson explores time and the laws of time in several different ways to reveal its properties, noting that as its first rule, time proceeds in regular increments forward. Donaldson reinforces this law in *The Runes of the Earth*: "the Law of Time ... requires that events transpire in sequence."[1] Time, therefore, is in its own continuum entirely separate from space.

Once we see that time is not the 4th physical dimension, we are free to explore this mysterious concept. Time can be perceived differently by mortal men or by other characters in a fantasy who are longer lived or immortal even if these characters all travel on the same time line. Tolkien contrasts the way Ents and elves see the passage of time to the way hobbits, dwarves, and men do. Legolas explains to Frodo as they are leaving Lothlorien that, for the immortal elves, time is both fleeting and yet their sorrow can be long. They live on the same time line but their perception of time's passing is radically different. A similar contrast can be found in Donaldson between the *Elohim* who do not age, and for whom time is not significant, and the mortals of the Search. Infelice interacts with the members of the Search and also shows up millennia later in Andelain with Linden. In addition, the *Elohim* are able to manipulate the perception of time by others, as the *Haruchai* who are first sent away from the *clachan* think no time has passed while all of the *Elohimfest*, the testing, and the conversation with Infelice have taken place for the others.

Joy Chant uses a variable rate of the perception of the passing of time in her *Red Moon and Black Mountain*; the older child Oliver matures into manhood while his two younger siblings, Penelope and Nicholas, remain the same age during the same time period. The Heechee from "The Heechee Saga" by Frederik Pohl experience a gravitational time dilation because they live inside the Schwarzschild radius of a black hole, which means time progresses at a different rate for them than for the universe at large (one year on the periphery of the black hole equals thousands of years outside). The science fiction television show, *Star Trek: the Next Generation* showcases the ability to slow down time for the crew on the Enterprise with Riker at the helm when they enter a time anomaly in "Timescape." Meanwhile Captain Picard, Data, Geordi, and Dr. Crusher can protect themselves from the disruption in time and prevent a potentially fatal explosion from destroying the Enterprise, a Romulan ship, and the unborn young of an alien species because as they move at what seems a normal pace to them, they are actually moving much more quickly in the time of the Enterprise. Donaldson gives this ability to move at a different rate from others in the same physical reality to the Vizard, who can beat up five hundred *Haruchai* while they take three breaths.

We cannot perceive time as one large entity as we can space, though we can watch the seconds tick by on a watch. We can inhabit only one point at any given moment on the timeline; we live always in the now. However, through our imaginations we can visualize time as a 1D line. For us it is like going forward on a walkway moving at a steady pace, yet we are unable to see beyond about a foot ahead or behind, and yet are able to remember or learn what has gone on before, at least in regard to our own personal history or the world's. Throughout the "Chronicles" the Ranyhyn have been exempt from the particular limitation on predictions of the future. Using Earthpower, each has the ability to anticipate the whistle of Covenant or any Lord or *Haruchai* so that it can begin its journey toward the summoner enough ahead of that moment to travel the necessary distance in order to arrive right after the summons. When Mhoram calls Drinny at the height of the battle for Revelstone, though the Ranyhyn had to leave several weeks ahead of time and travel a dangerous road, Drinny still appears almost instantaneously. The Ranyhyn can see as far into the future as necessary for them to respond in a timely fashion. In his typical both/and fashion, Donaldson provides not only an exception for the Ranyhyn but also blurs the distinctions in the question of predestination vs. free will through prophecies that come true or foresight that proves invaluable to the working out of the plot. At first, Lord Mhoram is both seer and oracle and foresees that the Giants are in trouble and that he should pass on the *lillianrill* rod to Triock when he himself no longer needs it. Covenant, on the other hand, redirects the emphasis from the predestination to free will in his insistence on the necessity of freedom of choice. Only the Creator is completely able to resolve this contradiction of oppositions as he chooses Covenant and Linden as his representatives in the Land because of his awareness of what they could accomplish, and then leaves the results to their own personal free will choices.

Time can best be visualized in our 3D world as an arrow moving at a uniform pace in one direction only and separate from our 3D space. However, our imaginations and our understanding of scientific anomalies, which explain how space can tie together two distant places using a wormhole, can help us to speculate about how time might be similarly malleable. First, we can imagine two parallel timelines, one moving forward at 5 units per second and another at 100 units per second. Donaldson uses the idea that time can travel faster or slower depending on which parallel universe Covenant inhabits. Time passes at a different rate in the Land than it does in Covenant's "real" world. Covenant's first quest, to travel to Revelstone and deliver Foul's message to the Lords and then to accompany the Company to recover the Staff of Law, takes about a year in the time period of the Land. However, when Covenant wakes up in the hospital where he has been taken after he falls before the police car, only a day has passed in his "real" world. More telling, the time between the 1st "Chronicles" and the 2nd is ten years in the "real" world, but 3,500 years have passed in the Land. A similar 3,500 Land years go by in the duration of ten years in the "real" world time between the 2nd "Chronicles" and the "Last Chronicles."

We can also imagine a loop in time. If time could form a loop, it would create a phenomenon like the premise of Harold Ramis's movie *Groundhog Day*, in which Phil Connors keeps waking up on February 2 and living through the same day. *Star Trek: the Next Generation* shows the fear of this kind of nightmare situation when the crew of the Enterprise discovers that they are caught in a time loop in "Cause and Effect" and have to figure out how to break out of the loop in order to continue forward toward their future. Sometimes a possible loop in time can create ambiguities and impossibilities. The movie *Somewhere in Time* creates such a paradox because Elise McKenna first meets Richard Collier when she is an old woman to ask him, "Come back to me."[2] Only then does Richard try to find a way to travel back in time and eventually give her the pocket watch that she brings him when she is old. *Star Trek: the Next Generation* again presents an excellent example of this kind of exploration of time. In "Time's Arrow" the crew finds Data's head in a cave in the nineteenth century. Later Data loses his head and the one recovered from the cave is attached to Data's body. But which came first? With the

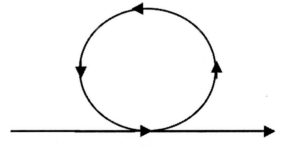

Figure 8. A loop in the timeline.

possibility of a circular continuum of events, an object such as Richard's pocket watch or Data's head can become stuck in the time loop. The most illogical example of contradictory occurrences caused by a time loop is called the Grandfather Paradox. In this paradox, supposedly, a young man travels back in time and accidentally kills his own grandfather before the grandfather has had any children. The young man would then never have been born. Donaldson has not included this variation on the time theme in the "Chronicles" to date. However, clearly anyone who travels to the past must be wary to avoid any kind of disruption to unfolding events.

Another potential manipulation of the time line is the folding of time to allow one to exist at more than one time or to travel from one time to another bypassing all the time in between. Stanley Kubrick in his *2001: A Space*

Odyssey, based on Arthur C. Clarke's science fiction short story "The Sentinel," illustrates the ability of one person, Dave Bowman, to be in the same place but more than one time at once; space-suited Bowman watches his

Figure 9. A fold in the timeline.

older self from a doorway as his older self is eating dinner at a table, and then from the table the older self watches his dying self confined to his bed. Roger Covenant in his disguise as Thomas Covenant tells Linden that he and Jeremiah are able to be in two places at once physically because he has the ability to fold time. However, Roger is not the guardian of the Arch of Time, and the power he gains from Kastenessen's hand seems to involve a repulsing force field and has no control over time, and he is a notorious liar, so we don't know if any actual folding of time takes place.

Though time can be pictured as a 1D line, all the futures possible based on the decisions that are made at any one period of time requires a 2D graphic to explain. Frank Herbert's great science fiction novel *Dune* is an excellent example of how the ability to perceive multiple potential futures can be a blessing and a detriment. In *Dune* Paul Atriedes is prescient and in his waking dreams, he sees snippets of his future. Once he has drunk the Water of Life and neutralized its poison, he becomes the Kwisatz Haderach, and as he becomes addicted to the Spice, he is better able to see possible futures. However, as Paul explains, he can perceive several futures based on his present choices, but a mist or barrier exists that allows him to see some consequences or potential futures but not which choice of his will lead to which possible future. He also admits that there are some futures that he cannot see. He can see a potential time line on which he lies dead, but he cannot see his moment of death or see his murderer. Like Paul Atriedes, in Donaldson's "Chronicles" the *Elohim* and the Insequent are able to perceive several possible futures. Because some of these futures are catastrophic, individual Insequent or *Elohim* may choose to become

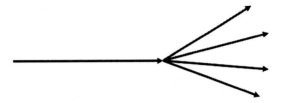

Figure 10. Potential choices at any point on the timeline.

involved in the world's perils to affect the outcome. When the Search visits the *Elohim*, they silence Covenant's mind in an attempt to force Linden to take the wild magic ring. They see too much risk for the Land and especially for the Arch of Time if she does not. However, clearly they did not anticipate the future which ultimately unfolds. Infelice appears in Andelain to dissuade Linden from her purpose of bringing Covenant back to life because she has foreseen the calamitous result: that Linden will rouse the Worm of the World's End.

In keeping with his both/and rather than either/or perspective, Donaldson portrays time as something that can be manipulated through time travel two different ways: at times he describes time like a river, and attempting to ride a *caesure* into the past is likened to swimming against the current since the main principle of time is that it moves only one direction, from the past to the present to the future. In addition, traveling back up a stream implies a sequence from a physical downstream position to an upstream one and the increased difficulty of going against a current or force. Nevertheless, Donaldson also contradicts the idea of movement along a timeline functioning as a movement along the water of a stream (either forward or backward) when he claims the *caesure* which Linden uses to get to the Land's past includes "all moments and none simultaneously."[3] He also defines time as "sequence and causality"[4] which implies first/then sequential moments connected by purpose. The causality part of the equation reinforces Donaldson's theme of the necessity of freedom of choice and action which then produces a new and purposeful outcome. Time, therefore, to Donaldson also adheres to the eye of the paradox law. Time travel in Donaldson's subcreated world does not have to follow a continuum like a river, but the translation from one time to another occurs almost instantaneously, or someone trying to make the translation could become stuck in a no-man's land, lost and frozen. Since the time disruptions of the *caesures* occur in a tornado-like spiral moving across space in the Land, the amount of time Linden uses to get control of her own will and direct her friends toward the correct time can take them across many miles of space. The *caesure* then exists in the spatial world and can be seen to travel across distance while the time within the *caesure* is all time and no time at once.

Within the Land time travel takes place four times in the first two books of "The Last Chronicles of Thomas Covenant." However, typical of Donaldson's imaginative creativity, each trip through time is different. The first two rely on wild magic for the power to traverse time; the last two use other theurgies not totally explained within the texts. Before Linden and her friends attempt to enter a *caesure* or Fall and travel back in time, they understand that the destructive *caesures* are caused by wild magic and involve the disruption of time. Linden experienced the power of the Fall that toppled Kevin's Watch. She was not caught up in the Fall, but needed to use her own wild magic to preserve her life as she fell when Kevin's Watch collapsed. Her new companion, Anele, being a creature of Earthpower, also survived the destruction. Linden figures out that Anele must have been caught in a Fall in his own time and deposited into her present. Though much of what he says seems insane, she understands that he feels guilty because he has lost the new Staff of Law entrusted to him by his parents, Sunder and Hollian, to whom Linden entrusted her newly-made Staff. When Linden determines that she needs that Staff of Law because she cannot master the wild magic of Covenant's ring and is more comfortable with the Earthpower of Law, she decides to hazard entering a *caesure* and even supposes that she will be able to choose a time in the past to exit the *caesure* in order to retrieve her Staff. She hypothesizes that in her current present time, Anele may not be able to find the new Staff of Law in the place he remembers leaving it because she will retrieve/has retrieved it from the past, so it no longer exists in his cave in Linden's present.

Linden, however, does not yet know how to create a *caesure* to use for time travel. Esmer, the conflicted descendent of both Kastenessen's power and the *Haruchai* Cail, is able to find one that had already been created using Joan's wild magic ring, and to redirect its path so that it crosses the Verge of Wandering where Linden and her friends have decided to make the attempt. The actual passage through time is described more like the experience of Dorothy in the tornado when she is on her way to Oz. Within the *caesure* there is danger — of madness, of getting stuck in time. Linden perceives the physical discomfort of the sensation of ants crawling on her skin or the feeling of being stung by many hornets, supposedly caused by being bombarded by many individual moments of time. "She had entered a demesne of flux, inchoate and chaotic; altogether devoid of Time's necessary sequences. Life could not exist outside the stricture of chronology. She remained alive only because she occupied no consecutive moments during which she could have ceased to be."[5] Although it is infinitely cold, Linden perceives the temperature as fire-hot. While in the *caesure,* Linden is reminded that Joan's madness and desire for self-inflicted pain is the source of the *caesure* and that Joan's helplessness and insanity are enhanced by the Raver *turiya* who possesses her. She finally can use the power of Joan's white gold wild magic to turn her own will against the flow of time within the *caesure*.

Deciding when to exit the *caesure* is accomplished by the Ranyhyn who have gained knowledge of what time period to aim for from the ur-viles who learned by sucking the information from Anele's blood. Like a tornado, *caesures* traverse across distance, while occupying all time and no time at each place; Linden and her friends and the ur-viles exit the *caesure* miles away from the Verge of Wandering where they entered it as well as at an earlier time in the Land's history. Apparently, when the Fall arrives at the right place, the power of the theurgy of the ur-viles and the natural Earthpower of the Ranyhyn can resurrect from all the fragments of time that make up the *caesure* the exact time when Anele was last in the past so that they can exit where and when they want to be.

Esmer then appears in the past with them, explaining that his connection to the *Elohim* through his grandfather Kastenessen allows him the same ability as his eldritch ancestor to exist outside of time and manifest himself whenever he chooses. He had similarly "appeared" before Linden at the Verge of Wandering, though he could have used his feet or other more normal means of transport to arrive there. The ur-viles, who were all destroyed in the Land's past, can also appear whenever and wherever Linden is to protect her from Esmer. Obviously, their chants and theurgy give them certain power over time. Therefore, since they understood the need to escape from the time in which Lord Foul was trying to eradicate them, they choose to travel to their future and can move through time to follow Linden. They appear when Esmer does in order to protect Linden from Esmer's ambiguous aid.

Linden is the point of view character of the "Last Chronicles" so far, and Donaldson takes a whole chapter to describe in excruciating detail Linden's passage through time, but he has not explained how others can manipulate time. The reader is limited as Linden is limited in understanding any time travel in which she does not participate or have control. She intuits that Esmer has brought the Demondim to Anele's time to attack her and her friends as part of his personal conflicting desires to both aid and hinder her. However, whether it is Esmer's power or some theurgy of the Demondim themselves that is their source, they have access to the Illearth Stone, which should be impossible because it was destroyed before the end of the 1st "Chronicles" by Thomas Covenant. Linden speculates that they may have found a small remaining piece of the Stone but later learns that they are using a *caesure* or wormhole to the past.

Linden's second experience in time travel, from the past where she recovered her own Staff of Law to the present near Revelstone, is simpler than her first trip because she does not have to fight the current of time from present to past, but it is also more difficult because she herself has to create the *caesure*. Prompted by need and enabled by Esmer's absence since she cannot use wild magic when he is around, Linden finds the door within herself that unlocks the power of Covenant's white gold ring. Though she understands the danger and the evil she encompasses and can anticipate the torment this time, she is able to sever sequential moments from each other using her memory of the *caesure's* pain, thus creating her own Fall. Before she enters it, she directs its path. Then she, her companions, and the remaining few *Waynhim* and urviles who are supporting her, hurry to enter the *caesure*.

Linden does not suffer Joan's madness this time because the power is of her own creating. White wild magic gold is a reassuring force that buoys her because, though it threatens the Arch of Time, it also sustains it. She has no way to determine how long she and her friends remain in the Fall, but it is seemingly less time than in her previous travel to the past before they gallop free, many miles from the South Plains where they entered it.

Because in the Fall she is encased in wild magic herself, she can retain her purpose. Linden is not entirely certain why the Demondim enter the Fall, yet she knows that they don't belong in Anele's time, and she knows that she should not alter history, so probably she calls them into her Fall, or they could get caught up in the *caesure* as Anele once had. Again, Linden invokes the image of a tornado in which the chaos of all and no time exists. Her *caesure* travels across much distance, leaving a path of destruction in its wake. Linden and her friends, with the guidance of the Ranyhyn, choose the time or reconstruct the time in which to leave the Fall but cannot really judge the place or the time at which they have arrived until they have exited.

Because of the destructive power of the *caesure*, Linden must demolish the one she created, but since wild magic would only feed its power or attract its destructive force toward her friends, she retrieves the Staff of Law from Liand and uses Earthpower to reform the time of the world into its proper sequence and causality. When she has safely entered Revelstone and Covenant and Jeremiah have also escaped to or been herded in, Linden realizes that the Demondim, who are laying siege to the Lord's Keep, are using a *caesure* to access the power of the Illearth Stone.

Before Linden agrees to aid Covenant and Jeremiah in their proclaimed purpose of saving the Land, she must prevent the Demondim from using the power of the Illearth Stone against the Masters in Revelstone. Using her health sense, she tries to ascertain the location of the *caesure* they are using to access the Stone. Although she is strengthened by her experiences in Glimmermere, she is also weakened by Kevin's dirt, and is, therefore, not strong enough until the ur-viles and Waynhim add the power of their vitriol and theurgy to enhance her health sense. Then using the Staff of Law, she unmakes the Fall through which the monsters are drawing upon the evil power of the Stone. Though she might have been able to destroy the Stone itself, to do so would have altered history and possibly completely broken the Law of Time, so she refrains.

Covenant explains his presence and Jeremiah's at Revelstone by saying that he has folded time. Since Linden believes that Thomas Covenant is maintaining the Arch of Time, this explanation makes sense to her. Covenant claims that both he and Jeremiah are actually in two places at once to reinforce the notion that, though Linden can see her son, she cannot touch him, and he is still suffering greatly with Foul. Covenant also claims that Linden could counter his ability to fold time if she uses the Staff of Law. Covenant eventually "explains" to Linden the various aspects of her experience in a *caesure*. Part of the experience is her being inside the mind of the Fall's creator, as she is aware of Joan's thoughts and actions during the first passage, and as Liand is aware of her potential for evil during the second. The part that feels like hornets are disconnected moments of time, and the cold, Covenant says, is the bleak future. Linden accepts Covenant's explanations at first. However, Roger Covenant lies, so nothing he says in his guise as Thomas Covenant or as himself can be trusted to explain time travel truthfully, and Linden eventually penetrates Roger's disguise.

Jeremiah reports that his mind was able to be in two places at once, in the "real" world and in the Land, when he finally created the möbius strip with his race car track. He claims that his mind journeyed to the Land whenever his body was put to bed in the "real" world. He says that he feels more real in the Land. Later Linden realizes that the unthinking Jeremiah with a *croyel* on his back provides that explanation.

As Linden and Covenant discuss what do to next, she tells him and Jeremiah of her plan to take her friends and travel to Andelain to seek advice from her Dead as Covenant's Dead had once given him advice, the present of Vain (from Foamfollower), and encouragement. She also hopes to find Loric's *krill*, used by Sunder to break the Law of Life, perhaps to enable her to use both the Staff of Law and Covenant's ring as well as the power of the *krill* itself at one time. Still, she agrees to let Covenant and Jeremiah show her their plan first, not realizing that they intend to take her with them to the past to avoid interference from the *Elohim* in their plan.

When Linden joins Covenant and Jeremiah at Furl Falls on the plateau above Revestone, Covenant asks her to come forward alone and stand between him and Jeremiah as they prepare to do something that will supposedly save the Land. They do not tell her that their plan involves journeying back through time, not via a *caesure* but solely on Covenant's and/or Jeremiah's power. Before they can accomplish their plan, though, ur-viles arrive to prevent them by attacking Covenant and Jeremiah. Then Esmer appears and disrupts the ur-viles' attack so that Covenant and Jeremiah can accomplish their goal. While Covenant and Linden are thus able to travel to the past, Esmer keeps Jeremiah back temporarily.

The power that Covenant and Jeremiah raise over Linden's head instantaneously, like a crack of thunder, causes the place on which she is standing to disappear and a new place and time to appear, throwing her off balance. As she tries to pull herself together, she overhears a conversation Covenant is having with a stranger who fortuitously is also at the same place and time, and she learns that Covenant's plans have been altered and they did not end up where or when he had intended. Thus Covenant's power has some limitation, or someone else has greater power. The stranger he converses with, the cloth-bound Theomach, has been able to interfere. The magical theurgy of the Theomach creates an unsettling sense of slippage to Linden, so that he appears to "shift subtly between different places in time and space."[6] She and Covenant have been translated from spring to winter and 10,000 years into the past, to Berek's present time in the Land. Covenant had apparently aimed for only 9,500 years into the past and a place on the other side of Garroting Deep. He had wanted to appear during the time of High Lord Damelon before Damelon sealed off the entrance to the Blood of the Earth. Covenant now tells Linden his purpose: he wants to use the Power of Command to freeze time around Foul and Kastenessen. Linden cannot explain how this episode of time travel occurred. However, it is painless and instantaneous.

When Linden demands an explanation for how they managed to travel across time, Covenant finally claims that they "slipped between the cracks"[7] in time, which apparently requires even more power than folding time and being in two places at once. Jeremiah did not make the same translation as Linden and Covenant. And the Theomach does not explain from where or when he arrives. Covenant explains that Esmer helped him but tried to keep Jeremiah, but that he and Jeremiah are tied together by the power they use to traverse time, so Jeremiah will be able to join Covenant. When Jeremiah appears at Covenant's side, it is as though he had been disassembled and then reassembled, the way one of the transformers on *Star Trek's* Enterprise might transport someone to the surface of a planet. In fact, the transporter used in the various *Star Trek* series is a good model for the kind of instant travel which defies the laws of space and time that Covenant and Jeremiah apparently can perform.

Linden is not entirely satisfied with Covenant's explanations. Questions arise in her mind about Covenant's power. Can Covenant be in three places at once? He apparently talks to the Manethrall and his cords and Liand through Anele near Glimmermere while he is also conversing with Linden and Jeremiah in his room. If he can be in two places at once, could a third also be possible? Another discordance bothering Linden is the fact that the Covenant who spoke through Anele was gentler than the one supposedly simultaneously demanding of Linden the white gold ring. Also, since Covenant and Jeremiah have the ability to create a small arch of power and travel anywhere or anywhen instantaneously, Linden wonders why they didn't just appear in Revelstone, why they chose to ride in with the Masters apparently barely ahead of the Demondim. Covenant tells Linden that his arrival was a feint to fool Kastenessen and confuse the Demondim so they would not immediately attack Revelstone. Linden, however, begins to doubt.

Once Covenant, Jeremiah, and Linden determine that they are in Berek's present time, before the war against the Old King was won and Berek became the High Lord but after he had called the Fire Lions and made his promise to heal the Land, the Theomach convinces them that they all need to allow Linden's choices to determine how to get to the other side of Garroting Deep or they might disrupt the Land's past. Though they must be careful not to interact significantly with Berek or others of the time period, Linden believes that they can gain some most desperately-needed help if they petition Berek to share supplies with them, so they set out for his camp on foot.

When they arrive, Linden's instincts and knowledge as a healer and her ability to save many of Berek's wounded prompt her to risk changing events in the past. She uses her Staff of Law, her health sense, and her knowledge as a physician to help as many of Berek's wounded as she can. Then she directs Berek to send those in his camp who have begun to experience the greater perception of health sense to find hurtloam. She also advises Berek to wash thoroughly the blood- and scum-encrusted blankets being used on the wounded. Even when attempting to avoid altering the past, Linden still trusts her own motivations and judgments and honors the responsibilities she took on when she swore her Hippocratic Oath. Because of this potential change in the Land's past, the Theomach remains behind to make sure no tales of the healer Linden survive. He also remains to teach Berek about Earthpower, and he tells Berek the meaning of the seven words of power that bound his promise to the Land. The question of whether the past is significantly altered is ambiguous at this point. Obviously, the more Berek understands Earthpower, the more likely he will be to become the Land's first savior and strong servant as High Lord. Therefore, the presence of the Theomach might actually be the means that provides for Berek's enhanced knowledge and skills. Linden also needs to learn the powerful seven words for her eventual confrontation with Covenant and Jeremiah. Is the predestined path of the Land

and Linden's personal future being influenced by choices of the Theomach? Possibly, but Donaldson also insists on the necessity of freedom of choice for Linden as well to complete the eye of the paradox.

The small group with Yellinin, a scout sent along by Berek, travels by horse toward *Melenkurion* Skyweir around the large forest of Garroting Deep. Eventually, Linden sends Yellinin back to Berek's camp. She needs to trust Covenant and Jeremiah to use their power to allow for a faster progress, but they need to be far enough away from Berek that the power will not be noticed. These other elements of rapid travel performed by Covenant and Jeremiah show their control over space in that they can transport themselves and Linden between them under their arch of power to a space three to four leagues distant. This action is a power over time as well as it eliminates the normal time it would take them to walk or ride the distance.

Covenant and Jeremiah with Linden between them travel around Garroting Deep in short increments almost instantaneously. With a noise like a sonic boom, they simply disappear and reappear somewhere else. Apparently, they could be traveling farther with each translation but are trying to avoid drawing attention to what they are doing. Linden is disoriented but otherwise unaffected by the shift except that she perceives that the ground sometimes tilts differently than it had before. After several translations, Linden begins to feel dislocated. It becomes harder for her to regain her sense of balance. Then Linden seems to become caught in a nothingness or parallel reality before the translation can be completed. She is not in the same place where Covenant and Jeremiah reside. She can hear them but not see them.

Linden can also hear the speech of the Viles, though she cannot see them either. She risks conversation with the Viles to try to make peace between them and the Forestal Caerroil Wildwood, though she also believes that if they do not succumb to the seductive hatred of the Ravers, the Land's history might be changed. Of higher importance to her are her role as healer, her need for truth, and her belief in taking responsibility. She, thus, consciously attempts to change the Land's past if her moral imperatives contradict the Land's history. She attempts to counter the lies of the Ravers and might have been successful, but Covenant and Jeremiah intervene to "rescue" her and bring the ire of the Forestal against the Viles. Later she learns that they deliberately put her in a precarious position, vulnerable to the Viles, so that she would relinquish the ring, hoping Covenant would save her. The contrast between her desire to defuse the tension and Covenant's glee at setting the two powers — the Viles and Caerroil Wildwood — against one another is teaching Linden not to trust Covenant. As in Sophocles's *Oedipus Rex* (in which Oedipus's attempts to run away because of the Oracle's prediction that he would murder his father and marry his mother actually lead him into the path of his father where his fate is carried out), the fate of the Land seems to be carried out because of Linden's attempt to divert it and Covenant's interference. The Viles and the Forestal do learn hatred for one another.

Covenant and Jeremiah convey themselves and Linden away from the potential battleground as quickly as possible. In the process, Jeremiah shatters some trees, and at their next stop, he collects the various shards and branches in a pile for a later use. During the next several translations of three to five leagues at a time, the pile of wood is brought along, though it is not physically under the arch they create over Linden.

Finally, Covenant, Jeremiah, and Linden arrive at a plateau near *Melenkurion* Skyweir. No entrances to the mountain are visible on the plateau, and Covenant claims that the Blood of the Earth, which is their ultimate goal, prohibits his kind of power so Jeremiah is going to build a "door." What Jeremiah actually constructs is more like a cage or a small ramshackle hut, but every piece of wood they have brought has its exact place in the deadwood shack. The box-like contraption functions as a door from place to place, like a worm-hole passage from outside the mountain to within. Even more significant to Covenant, once they are inside Jeremiah's construct and he puts the last piece of wood in place, they will simply disappear from the awareness of the *Elohim*. Because Jeremiah's power can baffle the *Elohim*, the Vizard, one of the Insequent, had wanted Jeremiah to create a structure that would lure the *Elohim* in and imprison them. Covenant claims that Jeremiah can make other doors that could connect different times or different realities, though we haven't seen this power so far in the "Last Chronicles."

Jeremiah's "door" also has its precedent in science fiction. The machine that provides the portal on *Stargate* instantly transports one person or a group from one world/reality to another, at first from earth to the planet of the Abydonians. The "time machine" that Miles and Keiko O'Brien's daughter Molly goes through in "Time's Orphan" of *Star Trek: Voyager* transports her to the same place but at a different time, and, of course, the transporter on the Enterprise in *Star Trek* can bypass shuttle travel. All these examples from science fiction involve machines, technology. Jeremiah's skill uses only magic, as would be expected in a fantasy, yet Donaldson is still blurring the distinctions between fantasy and science fiction.

Donaldson creates ambiguity about the time and space travel accomplished by Covenant and Jeremiah's arch over Linden. Did the power to transcend time or space come from Jeremiah, though no constructs have been created or from Kastenessen's hand, now grafted onto Roger Covenant's wrist, or from the *croyel* attached to Jeremiah's back? As an *Elohim*, Kastenessen can transcend time, even as can Esmer, who is only a descendent of Kastenessen's eldritch power. Roger's power is more connected to a force field, which might repel but not move its user. Certainly Covenant's original explanation that he, "Thomas" Covenant, was folding time as an aspect of his power to sustain the Arch of Time cannot be true. Linden, the point of view character, cannot understand nor explain their power.

Linden experiences an altered sense of time twice more in *Fatal Revenant*. When she and the Mahdoubt, another Insequent, are following the Forestal's music through Garrotting Deep toward Gallows Howe, their passage seems to take little time, certainly less time than their return to the Mahdoubt's fire without the buoying influence of Caerroil Wildwood's song. Her transition back to her true present at Revelstone also occurs without Linden's conscious awareness or ability to explain. She is busy gathering the things she needs and sewing her swatch of her shirt to the Mahdoubt's robe and half listening to the Mahdoubt's song. Whether it is the chant or some other power at work, when the song is finished and Linden becomes aware of her surroundings again, she is no longer in front of the Mahdoubt's fire in Garrotting Deep in Berek's time, but on the plateau above Revelstone in her own present time where her friends greet her. This episode of time travel is entirely mysterious. No *caesure* is used, no apparent theurgy. And what role did Linden's gratitude play? The Mahdoubt's control of time comes from superior knowledge, but how it can be used in action remains unexplained. Presumably, she used the same means to go back in time to meet with Linden in the forest, yet we get no report of her previous episode of time travel.

The Mahdoubt uses her ability to manipulate time to extract a promise from the Harrow, another Insequent. After Linden returns and sleeps for a few days, she learns that the Demondim no longer threaten Revelstone because a mysterious man seems to have devoured them. When Linden leaves the confines of Revelstone to confront this man, the Harrow, she is caught by the blackness of his eyes in a spell, and he tries to coerce her into giving over the Staff of Law and Covenant's ring. She feels infinite emptiness and loneliness. The power of eyes to ensorcel is used by Tolkien in *The Silmarillion*. Both Turin and his sister, Nienor/Niniel, are trapped under the gaze of the dragon Glaurung. He is able to rob Turin of his will and Nienor of her memory, even the memory of her own name. Their tragedy is completed when Glaurung restores Nienor's memory so she will realize that she has married her own brother and is carrying his child. Harry Potter uses his spell *"expelliarmus petronas"* to banish the guards of Azkaban who have a similar power to suck out men's souls with their dementors' kiss and leave their victims in utter blackness and nothingness. The original *Star Trek* series included the episode "Dagger of the Mind" in which Captain James Kirk is forced to gaze into a neural neutralizer that threatens to drive him insane with emptiness and actually does kill Dr. Adams when he is left alone, his mind emptied by the neural neutralizer.

Linden is vulnerable to the Harrow's trap, and neither Stave nor the Humbled can save her through sheer might until they concentrate their attacks on his eyes. Once Linden has broken free of the Harrow's gaze, she calls on the Mahdoubt by using the older woman's true name, *Quern Ehstrel*. The Mahdoubt persuades the Harrow to foreswear his coercive practices against Linden by courteously illustrating her ability to translate the Harrow away from the present time to another reality or a different time in which he has no access to Linden. Because the Mahdoubt, an Insequent herself, has interfered with another Insequent, by the laws of their society, she forfeits her sanity. The power of one's true name is also central to Ursula LeGuin's Earthsea trilogy, and friendship is demonstrated by the sharing of this most personal power.

Covenant and Jeremiah's ability to travel instantaneously several leagues at a time is not Donaldson's only exploration of science fiction-like control of space travel in his fantasy series "The Chronicles of Thomas Covenant, the Unbeliever." Covenant and Jeremiah use some sort of spell or theurgy or magic, yet other more scientifically-sound explanations for control of space are possible. A nineteenth century mathematician, Georg Bernhard Riemann, working on higher dimensional geometry postulated what Michio Kaku in *Hyperspace* calls "Riemann's cut." Kaku explains Reimann's theory about the ability to walk from one piece of paper to another through a cut at which they touch. This ability of our minds to imagine being able to go from one 2D world to another separate 2D world through the cut paves the way for the understanding of worm holes which can tie together two 3D worlds or two places on the same 3D world. It is not a large leap to imagine traveling from one place on a 3D world to that same place at a different time in a time worm-hole. Science fiction writers like the concept of the worm hole-like connection between a position in one time period and the same place (or even a new place) at a different time to "explain" time travel. The movie *Star Trek Generations* identifies the Nexus as the doorway to another reality and provides a visual special effect to illustrate the idea of a moving wormhole using the Ribbon, a cloud-like entity moving in space and time, as a way to access the Nexus.

Donaldson uses an ambiguous duration of time and the seemingly magical ability to travel from one reality to a parallel reality in ways similar to those found in popular fantasy novels. Covenant's travel to the Land is not unlike Alice falling down the rabbit hole in *Alice in Wonderland* or Peter, Susan, Edward, and Lucy going through the wardrobe in C.S. Lewis's *The Lion, the Witch, and the Wardrobe*. Terisa, also, in *Mordant's Need* chooses to step through the mirror. Covenant in the 1st "Chronicles," and both Linden and Covenant in the 2nd "Chronicles," and again Linden in the "Last Chronicles" are translated from their "real" world to the Land almost instantaneously as if they are simply moving between alternate universes rather than traveling a long distance through time. They need no machine to make this translation. However, while Alice is aware of what she sees on her fall following the White Rabbit, Covenant and Linden sometimes become unconscious and then "wake up" in the Land. In fact, the translation can include two or three parts. In *Lord Foul's Bane* Covenant, after falling before the police car, first becomes aware of Drool Rockworm and then is moved to a place in which Lord Foul can belittle him and give him the message for the Lords at Revelstone. Finally, Covenant finds himself waking up on top of Kevin's Watch. Though the Land is vast, Covenant shows up where the power that is used to summon him resides. Foul is then apparently able to transport Covenant almost instantaneously across some distance in space to his own demesne and then to Kevin's Watch.

A significant difference between Donaldson's characters and typical fantasy protagonists is that Covenant and Linden do not choose to explore another world. Covenant is summoned to the Land rather than making a conscious decision of his own to step through the mirror or into the wardrobe, which would send him to the Land in the 1st "Chronicles." He is first brought by Drool Rockworm who has found the Staff of Law that was lost by the Lords when Kevin invoked the Ritual of Desecration. Clearly, some sort of Earthpower is needed to make the summons. When Drool is killed by the Fire Lions at the end of *Lord Foul's Bane*, Covenant is released from his summons, translated back, and wakes up in a hospital room in his own "real" time.

In *The Illearth War*, Atiaran tries to summon Covenant using the new lore she has studied but is successful in bringing only Hile Troy, who had probably died in his "real" world. The fire that was consuming him is drawn to the Land as well and immolates Atiaran. Elena later brings Covenant with the Staff of Law which was recovered by Prothall. Again, when she dies, Covenant is translated back to his own world.

The summoning in *The Power That Preserves* is a further refinement by Donaldson in his analysis of travel between the parallel universes of Covenant's "real" world and the Land. Covenant is able to refuse High Lord Mhoram when he is summoned to Revelstone because in his "real" world a young girl, who has been bitten by a snake, needs his help. In the other two books, Covenant seems to faint and "wake up" in the Land. And, although he trips in the hills behind Haven Farm and might have lost consciousness, he recognizes the summoning process and is able to refuse it. Mhoram also allows him to refuse and reverses his incantation. When Foamfollower and Triock summon him again later, though the *lillianrill* tool of Earthpower has less power than the Staff of Law, Covenant believes that they are successful because he is weaker at that time in his "real" world and, also, he does not resist.

In the 2nd "Chronicles" Donaldson establishes ambiguity about whether Covenant's choice to sacrifice himself for his ex-wife Joan and step into the fire means he is voluntarily going down that rabbit hole or wormhole between worlds or if he is again summoned by Lord Foul. Linden, however, has had no experience in the Land and is unaware of where her attempt to save Covenant's life might lead her when she voluntarily plunges into the fire to save Covenant. Lord Foul has many powers and controls the Sunbane through his Raver Gibbon Na-Mhoram, so he doesn't need a Staff of Law to summon Covenant and, seemingly by accident, Linden. Apparently, the actions of the insane members of the cult in constructing their rude altar in Covenant's "real" world also help to open the connection between the worlds. Linden believes that she sees Lord Foul's eyes in the fire before she has been translated to the Land. This image is the first physical incursion of even part of Foul into Covenant's "real" world.

In Linden's translation in *The Runes of the Earth*, she falls into darkness but does not lose consciousness; instead she becomes aware that Joan's madness and possession of her white gold ring are providing the power to draw her into the Land through the will of the Raver *turiya* Herem who possesses Joan. Within this translation Linden is aware of the passage of time, as Alice was, and within the abyss through which she travels to the Land, Linden can make choices, can resist the despair of the Despiser. Also, within this translation Linden is given visions, of herself raising the Worm of the World's End and of a resplendent Land like Andelain threatened by fiery beasts. She considers these visions prophecies as well as warnings for her to restrain the unpredictable power of Covenant's white gold ring which hangs around her neck. Again, as Covenant hears Lord Foul's scorn upon arriving in the Land, so, too, does Linden. The last part of her transition is so chaotic that she appears to lose consciousness and then "wake up" on Kevin's Watch.

An additional aspect of the translation from the Land back to the "real" world for both Covenant and Linden is a period of awareness during the journey. In *The Power That Preserves*, Covenant has time to contemplate his sense of guilt, something that becomes the inspiration for at least one of the books he writes between the time of the 1st and 2nd "Chronicles" in his "real" world. In a discussion with a voice he identifies as the beggar, who he assumes is the Land's Creator, Covenant is reminded of the necessity of freedom and the limitations of a tool, which will become main themes in the 2nd "Chronicles." The Creator wants to give him a gift though he admits that he cannot do what Covenant asks and save Saltheart Foamfollower from death. So he offers Covenant the chance to remain in the Land where he is considered a hero. When Covenant refuses that gift, the Creator says he will counter the negative effects of the antivenin Covenant is allergic to in his "real" world because Covenant has decided that he wants to live, even with his leprosy, showing that he has combated some of his despair after all. Then Covenant is allowed to observe Mhoram throwing the *krill* into Glimmermere and renouncing such power. Many of Covenant's experiences during his translation back to his "real" world powerfully affect his life during the next ten years, and his knowledge of the whereabouts of the *krill* is instrumental for his success during his next sojourn in the Land.

Linden Avery also has a period of reflection and last communion with Covenant while she is undergoing the translation back from the Land to the "real" world in *White Gold Wielder*. Her memory of Pitchwife's song about grief—"My heart has rooms which sigh with dust"[8]—helps her to understand her own parents better than she ever had. Covenant is able to speak with her as she is blown upon the wind of the neverland between the worlds. He has a chance to explain his decision to sacrifice both the white gold ring and his life to defeat Foul, and to reinforce the necessity for embracing the eye of the paradox, Donaldson's main theme from the "Chronicles." Donaldson also has a chance to set up the main dialectic he will explore in the "Last Chronicles": Covenant's integral connection to Foul. When Linden begins to register sensory impressions of her surroundings, she has returned to her "real" world. Her ability to adopt and give Jeremiah so much love comes from her relationship with Covenant in the Land, during which she does, indeed, learn the lesson that the Creator wanted her to: that she has a large capacity for love.

In *The Runes of the Earth* Linden's translation to the Land is much like Covenant's original trips. It is precipitated in the "real" world by her being accidentally shot by Sheriff Lytton's deputies in their gun battle with Roger Covenant, and it is similar to the sacrifice of Covenant from *The Power That Preserves* in the place of the confrontation. Lightning instead of a bonfire reveals Lord Foul's hungry eyes to Linden. And as Covenant died to the "real" world from his confrontation with the insane members of the cult, though he lived on in the Land throughout the 2nd "Chronicles" and supposedly still exists, Linden also believes that she has been shot and finds a bullet wound in her chest, a wound she is able to "heal" for herself during the translation. Since both Roger and Jeremiah are also shot, she does not know if any of the "real" world characters will make it back from the Land.

Two fundamental laws have already been broken in Donaldson's "Chronicles" and a third is under attack. In the 1st "Chronicles" Covenant's daughter High Lord Elena unwisely breaks the Law of Death when she drinks from the Blood of the Earth and calls Kevin Landwaster back from the dead to battle Lord Foul for her. The Land pays a high price when it has to battle Lord Foul's risen dead in the battle for Revelstone. In the 2nd "Chronicles"

Sunder breaks the Law of Life when he kills Caer-Caveral, Hile Troy, the last Forestal, in order to bring his wife Hollian and their unborn child back from the dead. But Covenant is then able to will himself to come back after being killed by Lord Foul to foil Foul's desire to break the Arch of Time. In the "Last Chronicles" Donaldson is exploring the laws of time, how destructive and evil it is to disrupt the natural flow of time, how dangerous it is to travel back in time because of the impact a significant change in history might have on the Land's present and how the result of any such catastrophe could destroy the Arch of Time, the foundation for the Land.

Many questions about time and/or distance travel in the Land are still unexplored or not explained by Donaldson through the first two books of the "Last Chronicles." Clearly, though, the theme of time is central. Lord Foul wants to destroy the Arch of Time; Covenant sacrifices himself to preserve it. However, Covenant himself admits that he is becoming more and more like Foul. To explore fully the characteristics, limitations, and vulnerabilities of time, Donaldson not only uses several techniques from other science fiction and fantasy works, but also adds his own imaginative perceptions and speculations about this most fascinating and mysterious phenomenon. As he incorporates space/time travel possibly borrowed from science fiction sources, he reinforces his own overall theme of the eye of the paradox. Donaldson has united modern literature techniques and themes in his "real" world segments, with the original creativity of his fantasy, and now, with his exploration of time, he also includes the characteristics of time and space travel that science fiction often explores. In an all-encompassing both/and approach he juxtaposes fantasy, science fiction, and modern literature together to help bring the epic back to our literature. He is, therefore, expanding his original eye of the paradox solution to the stagnation of modern literature from a both/and to an all/and juxtaposition.

Chapter Notes

Preface

1. Donaldson, *Epic*, 16.
2. Donaldson, *Epic*, 15.

Introduction

1. Donaldson, *Wounded Land*, 346.
2. Keats, "Ode on a Grecian Urn."
3. Hart, *Smiling*, 121.
4. *Bible*, Standard Revised Edition, John 1:1,14.
5. Tolkien, *Hobbit*, 205.
6. Donaldson, *Power That Preserves*, 104.
7. Shakespeare, *Richard II*, 3.2.59–63.
8. Hart, *Smiling*, 172.
9. Ibid., 175.
10. Ibid., 178.
11. Ibid.
12. Donaldson, *Lord Foul's Bane*, 70.
13. Burns, "My Love is Like a Red, Red, Rose."
14. Donne, "[Batter My Heart, Three-Person God]."
15. Hart, *Smiling*, 178–79.
16. Donaldson, *Lord Foul's Bane*, 267.
17. Donaldson, *Power That Preserves*, 184.
18. Donaldson, *One Tree*, 144.
19. Pope, "An Essay on Man."
20. As cited in Hart, *Smiling*, 208.
21. Arnold, "Dover Beach."
22. Gross and Levitt, *Higher Superstition*, 21.
23. Ibid.
24. Northrup Frye defined the hero of the Epic mode as superior both to other men and to the environment; in the Romantic mode, the hero is superior in degree to other men and superior to his environment; in the High Mimetic mode, the hero is superior in degree to other men and equal to his environment; in the Low Mimetic mode, the hero is equal to other men and equal to his environment; in the ironic mode, the hero is inferior to other men and also inferior to his environment. An easier way to understand this relationship between man and his environment is in picture form:
25. Donaldson, *Epic*, 9.

Epic hero	hero man	hero environment
Romantic	hero man (in degree)	hero environment
High Mimetic	hero man (in degree)	hero = environment
Low Mimetic	hero = man	hero = environment
Ironic	man hero	environment hero

26. Donaldson, *Epic*, 10.
27. Sale, "Tolkien and Frodo Baggins," 251.
28. Donaldson, *Wounded Land*, 15.
29. Yoda says to Luke Skywalker in Irvin Kershner, *The Empire Strikes Back*.
30. Kaku, *Hyperspace*, 112–13.
31. Ibid., 154.

Chapter 1

1. Goddard, *"King Lear,"* 39.
2. Tolkien, *Tolkien Reader*, 38.
3. Tolkien, *Fellowship of the Ring*, 110. Tolkien's seminal poem illustrates his main theme that one has a responsibility to accept and even embrace his fate, but that he can look for unexpected help along the way from others who are fulfilling their own fate by following their paths as those paths join together.
4. Donaldson, *Lord Foul's Bane*, 43.
5. Tolkien, *Tolkien Reader*, 83.
6. Ibid., 41.
7. Attenborough, *Shadowlands*.
8. Donaldson, *Power That Preserves*, 45.
9. Donaldson, *Lord Foul's Bane*, 15.

Chapter 2

1. Donaldson, *Power That Preserves*, 45.
2. W. A. Senior, *Stephen R. Donaldson*, 20.
3. Donaldson, *Lord Foul's Bane*, 5.
4. Donaldson, *Wounded Land*, 23.
5. Donaldson, *Lord Foul's Bane*, 15.
6. Ibid., 7.
7. Ibid., 4.
8. Donaldson, *Lord Foul's Bane*, 7–8.
9. Yeats, "Sailing to Byzantium."
10. Donaldson, *Lord Foul's Bane*, 15.
11. Ibid., 7.
12. James Baldwin, "Sonny's Blues."
13. Donaldson, *Wounded Land*, 9.
14. Donaldson, *Lord Foul's Bane*, 45.
15. Ibid.
16. Ibid., 139.
17. Donaldson, *Wounded Land*, 18.
18. Donaldson, *One Tree*, 389.
19. Donaldson, *Power That Preserves*, 361.
20. Donaldson, *One Tree*, 395.
21. The entire story is available in *Lord Foul's Bane* on pages 141–42.
22. Donaldson, *Lord Foul's Bane*, 142.
23. The entire story can be found in *Lord Foul's Bane* on pages 223–24.
24. Donaldson, *Lord Foul's Bane*, 139.
25. Ibid.
26. Ibid., 224.

27. This story can be found in Donaldson, *One Tree*, pages 52–53.
28. J. R. R. Tolkien, *Silmarillion*, 15.
29. This story can be found in Donaldson, *One Tree*, pages 113–14.
30. This story can be found in Donaldson, *Wounded Land*, pages 114–15.

Chapter 3

1. Donaldson, *White Gold Wielder*, 472.
2. Donaldson, *Lord Foul's Bane*, 45.
3. Donaldson, *Wounded Land*, 15.
4. Donaldson, *Illearth War*, 82.
5. Ibid., 206.

Chapter 4

1. Donaldson, *White Gold Wielder*, 475.
2. Donaldson, *Lord Foul's Bane*, 61.
3. Donaldson, *Power That Preserves*, 103.
4. Ibid., 290.
5. Donaldson, *Lord Foul's Bane*, 213–14.
6. Ibid., 307.
7. Ibid., 252.
8. Donaldson, *Wounded Land*, 226.
9. Donaldson, *Lord Foul's Bane*, 136.
10. Ibid., 139.
11. Donaldson, *Power That Preserves*, 361.
12. Donaldson, *Lord Foul's Bane*, 139.
13. Ibid., 130.
14. Frost, "The Road Not Taken."
15. Tolkien, *Fellowship of the Ring*, 48.
16. Donaldson, *Fatal Revenant*, 556.

Chapter 5

1. Tolkien, *Return of the King*, 246.
2. Donaldson, *Lord Foul's Bane*, 13.
3. Ibid., 83.
4. Donaldson, *Epic*, 15.
5. Donaldson, *Power That Preserves*, 348.
6. Donaldson, *Lord Foul's Bane*, 139.
7. Donaldson, *Illearth War*, 301.

Chapter 6

1. Donaldson, *Power That Preserves,* 70.
2. Donaldson, *Lord Foul's Bane,* 125.
3. Donaldson, *One Tree,* 457.
4. Donaldson, *Lord Foul's Bane,* 53.
5. Donaldson, *Power That Preserves,* 45.
6. Donaldson, *White Gold Wielder,* 433.
7. Donaldson, *One Tree,* 383.
8. Donaldson, *Wounded Land,* 15.
9. Frankl, *Man's Search,* 154.
10. Pattakos, *Prisoners,* 36.
11. Frankl, *Man's Search,* 179.
12. as cited by Stephen R. Covey, Foreword, Pattakos, *Prisoners,* viii.
13. Frankl, *Man's Search,* 157.
14. Ibid., 152.
15. Ibid., 130.
16. Donaldson, *Epic,* 15.
17. Stephen R. Covey, Foreword, Pattakos, *Prisoners,* xi–xii.
18. Donaldson, *Epic,* 16.

Chapter 7

1. Donaldson, *Runes of the Earth,* 300.
2. Szward, *Somewhere in Time.*
3. Donaldson, *The Runes of the Earth,* 370.
4. Ibid., 303.
5. Ibid., 367.
6. Donaldson, *Fatal Revenant,* 127.
7. Ibid., 126.
8. Donaldson, *White Gold Wielder,* 469.

Bibliography

Arnold, Matthew. "Dover Beach." *The Norton Introduction to Literature*. 893.

Attenborough, Richard, dir. *Shadowlands*. With Anthony Hopkins, Debra Winger. Price Entertainment, 1994.

Baldwin, James. "Sonny's Blues." *Norton Introduction to Literature*. 91–115.

Burns, Robert. "A Red, Red, Rose." *Norton Introduction to Literature*. 945.

Donaldson, Stephen R. *Epic Fantasy in the Modern World: A Few Observations*. Kent, OH: Kent State University Libraries, 1986.

_____. *The Illearth War*. New York: Holt, Rinehart, and Winston, 1977.

_____. *Lord Foul's Bane*. New York: Holt, Rinehart, and Winston, 1977.

_____. *The One Tree*. New York: Ballantine, 1982.

_____. *The Power That Preserves*. New York: Holt, Rinehart, and Winston, 1977.

_____. *White Gold Wielder*. New York: Ballantine, 1983.

_____. *The Wounded Land*. New York: Ballantine, 1980.

Donne, John. "[Batter My Heart, Three-Person God]" *Norton Introduction to Literature*. 950.

Eliot, T.S. "Hollow Men." 15 October 2008 < *http://www.d.umn.edu/cla/faculty/tbacig/hmcl 1007/1007anth/eliot.html*>.

Frankl, Viktor. *Man's Search for Meaning*. New York: Pocket Books, 1959.

Frost, Robert. "The Road Not Taken." *Norton Introduction to Literature*. 1247.

Goddard, Harold C. *King Lear*. *Modern Critical Interpretations*: William Shakespeare's *King Lear*. Edited by Harold Bloom. New York: Chelsea House, 1987. 9–44.

Gross, Paul R., and Norman Levitt. *Higher Superstition*: *The Academic Left and Its Quarrels with Science*. Baltimore: Johns Hopkins University Press, 1998.

Hart, Jeffrey. *Acts of Recovery*: *Essays on Culture and Politics*. Hanover, NH: University Press of New England, 1989.

_____. *Smiling through the Cultural Catastrophe*: *Toward the Revival of Higher Education*. New Haven, CT: Yale University Press, 2001.

Kaku, Michio. *Hyperspace: A Scientific Odyssey Through Parallel Universes, Time Warps, and the 10th Dimension*. New York: Anchor Books, 1995.

Keats, John. "Ode on a Grecian Urn." *Norton Introduction to Literature*. 1099.

Kershner, Irvin, dir. *Star Wars: The Empire Strikes Back*. With Mark Hamill, Harrison Ford, and Carrie Fisher. Lucasfilm, 1980.

The Norton Introduction to Literature. Edited by Alison Booth, J. Paul Hunter, and Kelly J. Mays. New York: W.W. Norton, 2005.

Pattakos, Alex. *Prisoners of Our Thoughts*: *Viktor Frankl's Principles at Work*. San Francisco: Berrett-Koehler, 2004.

Sale, Roger. "Tolkien and Frodo Baggins." *Tolkien and the Critics: Essays on J. R. R. Tolkien's*

The Lord of the Rings. Edited by Neil D. Isaacs and Rose A. Zimbardo. Notre Dame, IN: University of Notre Dame Press, 1968. 247–288.

Senior, W.A. *Stephen R. Donaldson's Chronicles of Thomas Covenant: Variations on the Fantasy Tradition*. Kent, OH: Kent State University Press, 1995.

Shakespeare, William. *Hamlet*. Edited by Barbara A. Mowat and Paul Westine. Washington, D.C.: Folger Shakespeare Library, 2004.

_____. *Macbeth*. Edited by Barbara A. Mowat and Paul Westine. Washington, D.C.: Folger Shakespeare Library, 1992.

_____. *Richard II*. Edited by Louis B. Wright and Virginia A. LaMar. Washington, D.C.: Folger Shakespeare Library, 1970.

Szwarc, Jeannot, dir. *Somewhere in Time*. With Christopher Reeve, Jane Seymore. Universal, 1981.

Tolkien, J.R.R. *The Fellowship of the Ring*. London: George Allen and Unwin, 1964.

_____. *The Return of the King*. London: George Allen and Unwin, 1965.

_____. *The Silmarillion*. London: HarperCollins, 1992.

_____. *The Tolkien Reader*. New York: Ballantine, 1966.

_____. *The Two Towers*. London: George Allen and Unwin, 1966.

Yeats, William Butler. "Sailing to Byzantium." *Norton Introduction to Literature*. 1889.

Index